American Revolution Biographies

American Revolution Biographies

**Linda Schmittroth
and
Mary Kay Rosteck**

Stacy A. McConnell, Editor

U·X·L®

AN IMPRINT OF THE GALE GROUP

DETROIT · SAN FRANCISCO · LONDON
BOSTON · WOODBRIDGE, CT

American Revolution: Biographies

Linda Schmittroth and Mary Kay Rosteck

Staff

Stacy McConnell, *U•X•L Editor*
Judy Galens, *U•X•L Contributing Editor*
Carol DeKane Nagel, *U•X•L Managing Editor*
Thomas L. Romig, *U•X•L Publisher*

Margaret Chamberlain, *Permissions Specialist (Pictures)*

Rita Wimberley, *Senior Buyer*
Evi Seoud, *Assistant Production Manager*
Dorothy Maki, *Manufacturing Manager*

Tracey Rowens, *Senior Art Director*

LM Design, *Typesetting*

Library of Congress Cataloging-in-Publication Data

Schmittroth, Linda
    American Revolution : biographies / Linda Schmittroth and Mary Kay Rosteck ; edited by Stacy McConnell.
        p.   cm.
    Includes bibliographical references and index.
    Summary: Profiles sixty men and women who were key players on the British or American side of the American Revolution.
    ISBN 0-7876-3792-0 (set) — ISBN 0-7876-3793-9 (v. 1). — ISBN 0-7876-3794-7 (v. 2)
    1. United States—History—Revolution, 1775-1783—Biography—Juvenile literature. [1. United States—History—Revolution, 1775-1783—Biography.] I. Rosteck, Mary Kay. II. McConnell, Stacy A. III. Title.
E206 .S36 2000
973.3'092'2—dc21   99-046941
                                                                      CIP

Contents

Volume 1: A-J

Volume 2: K-Z

Advisory Board

Special thanks are due for the invaluable comments and suggestions provided by U•X•L's American Revolution Reference Library advisors:

- Mary Alice Anderson, Media Specialist, Winona Middle School, Winona, Minnesota.

- Jonathan Betz-Zall, Children's Librarian, Sno-Isle Regional Library System, Edmonds, Washington.

- Frances Bryant Bradburn, Section Chief, Information Technology Evaluation Services, Public Schools of North Carolina, Raleigh, North Carolina.

- Sara K. Brooke, Director of Libraries, Ellis School, Pittsburgh, Pennsylvania.

- Peter Butts, Media Specialist, East Middle School, Holland, Michigan.

Reader's Guide

American Revolution: Biographies presents biographies of sixty men and women who took part in, influenced, or were in some way affected by the American Revolution. Among the people profiled in each of the two volumes are American patriots and presidents; colonists who remained loyal to England; Native Americans, royalty, politicians, scoundrels, and military officers from foreign nations who helped or hindered the American fight for freedom; writers, poets, and publishers; and heroic colonial women who wrote, took up arms, acted as spies, or raised funds for American independence.

American Revolution: Biographies not only includes the biographies of such famous patriots as George Washington, Benjamin Franklin, John Adams, Samuel Adams, Thomas Paine, and Thomas Jefferson, it also features the life stories of less celebrated people such as Phillis Wheatley, renowned poet and former slave; Frenchman Pierre Charles L'Enfant, who designed the city of Washington, D.C.; Deborah Sampson, a woman who donned a military uniform and served as an army soldier; and Frederika von Riedesel, a German who chronicled the Revolution while traveling throughout the colonies with her young family as her husband fought for the British.

Other features

American Revolution: Biographies also highlights interesting people with ties to the main biography subjects, and adds details that help round out events of the Revolutionary period. Each entry contains cross-references to other individuals profiled in the two-volume set, and each offers a list of sources—including web sites—for further information about the individual profiled. A timeline and glossary introduce each volume and a cumulative subject index concludes each volume.

American Revolution: Biographies has two companion volumes: *American Revolution: Almanac,* which describes in narrative form the events leading up to the war and the major events of the war; and *American Revolution: Primary Sources,* which contains excerpts from more than thirty Revolutionary-era documents.

Acknowledgments

The authors wish to thank Mary Reilly McCall, who contributed encouragement, enthusiasm, and several biographies to this set.

Comments and suggestions

We welcome your comments on this work as well as your suggestions for topics to be featured in future editions of *American Revolution: Biographies.* Please write: Editors, *American Revolution: Biographies,* U•X•L, 27500 Drake Rd., Farmington Hills, MI 48331-3535; call toll-free: 1-800-877-4253; fax: 248-414-5043; or send e-mail via www.galegroup.com.

Timeline of Events in Revolutionary America

1754   Start of the French and Indian War, pitting the French and their Indian allies against the British for control of North America.

1760   **George III** becomes King of England.

1762   James Otis Jr., brother of **Mercy Otis Warren**, publishes a pamphlet arguing for a limitation on Parliament's right to interfere with colonial affairs.

1763   French and Indian War ends with a British victory. To appease Native Americans, King **George III** forbids colonial settlement west of the Appalachian Mountains.

1765   In March, King **George III** approves the Stamp Act, which taxes the American colonies to pay for the French and Indian War. **Horace Walpole**, British Member of Parliament, opposes the Stamp Act before Parliament and speaks out for the rights of American colonists.

         In July, Boston patriots ("Sons of Liberty") unite in opposition to the Stamp Act. In August, a mob destroys the house of Massachusetts Lieutenant Governor Thomas Hutchinson to protest the act.

In September, **Deborah Read Franklin** defends her property when an angry mob outside her home protests that her husband, **Benjamin Franklin,** has not fought vigorously enough against the Stamp Act.

In October, delegates at a Stamp Act Congress adopt **John Dickinson**'s Declaration of Rights and Grievances, protesting the Stamp Act.

1766   The British government repeals the Stamp Act and replaces it with the Declaratory Act, asserting England's right to make laws that colonists must obey.

British politician **William Pitt** makes a famous speech in Parliament, declaring his opinion that Britain "has no right to lay a tax upon" the American colonies.

1767   In June, British politician **Charles Townshend** pushes through Parliament the Townshend Acts, imposing new taxes on American colonists.

In December, **John Dickinson**'s "Letters from a Farmer in Pennsylvania" appear in colonial newspapers, protesting Parliament's power to tax the colonies.

1768   In February, **Samuel Adams** writes a letter opposing taxation without representation and calls for the colonists to unite against British oppression.

In May, British troops arrive in Boston to enforce the Townshend Acts.

In June, tax collectors seize **John Hancock**'s ship the *Liberty* and sell its cargo.

1769   **George Mason**'s *Virginia Resolves,* which opposes British taxation and other policies, is presented to Virginia lawmakers.

1770   **Benjamin Rush** publishes the first American chemistry textbook.

Hector St. John de Crèvecoeur begins writing the pieces that are later published as *Letters from an American Farmer.*

In March, during the Boston Massacre, five colonists are killed by British soldiers, including a black man named **Crispus Attucks.**

In April, most of the Townshend Acts are repealed by Parliament, except the tax on tea.

In October, **John Adams** and Josiah Quincy successfully defend British soldiers on trial for firing shots during the Boston Massacre.

In November, at the urging of **Samuel Adams**, a committee of correspondence is formed in Boston; it issues a declaration of rights and a list of complaints against British authorities.

1772   **Mercy Otis Warren**'s patriotic play *The Adulateur* is published.

1773   **Phillis Wheatley**'s *Poems on Various Subjects, Religious and Moral* is published in London and sold in Boston.

In May, the Tea Act, a new tea tax, takes effect.

In December, patriots protest the Tea Act by throwing crates of tea into Boston Harbor (the Boston Tea Party).

1774   In March, Parliament passes the Intolerable Acts to punish Boston for the Boston Tea Party.

In May, British General **Thomas Gage** replaces Thomas Hutchinson as Royal Governor of Massachusetts.

In September, the First Continental Congress meets in Philadelphia to discuss the tense situation with Great Britain.

In October, Massachusetts lawmakers, including **John Hancock**, begin war preparations.

1775   In March, British politician **Edmund Burke** gives his speech "On Conciliation" before Parliament, urging the British government to settle differences with colonists. **Patrick Henry** gives a famous speech to Virginia lawmakers explaining why Virginia must arm a citizen army to confront the British.

In April, Massachusetts governor **Thomas Gage** is told to put down the "open rebellion" of the colonists using all necessary force. **Paul Revere** rides to Concord and Lexington to warn the patriots that British soldiers are on the way. The first shots of the Revolutionary War are fired between Minutemen and British soldiers at Concord. The British retreat to Boston. British politician **John Wilkes** presents a petition to King **George III** protesting his treatment of the colonies.

In May, Governor **Thomas Gage** imposes martial law in Massachusetts. The Green Mountain Boys, led by **Benedict Arnold** and **Ethan Allen**, capture Fort Ticonderoga in New York. The Second Continental Congress meets in Philadelphia and appoints **John Hancock** its president. **Mary Katherine Goddard** becomes publisher of *Maryland Journal* and keeps colonists informed about events in the fight for independence.

In June, **George Washington** is appointed commander-in-chief of a new Continental army. Before he arrives in Boston, patriots are defeated by British at the Battle of Bunker Hill.

In July, **George Washington** takes command of Continental army outside Boston. The Continental Congress approves **John Dickinson**'s Olive Branch Petition calling for King **George III** to prevent further hostile actions against the colonists until a reconciliation can be worked out. **Benjamin Franklin** is appointed first American Postmaster General.

In August, King **George III** declares the colonies in open rebellion against Great Britain.

In November, **James Rivington**'s print shop is burned to the ground because patriots are upset that his newspaper publishes articles presenting both sides of the quarrel between England and America.

In December, Continental army soldiers under **Benedict Arnold** fail in an attempt to capture Quebec, Canada.

King **George III** proclaims the closing of American colonies to all trade effective March 1776.

1776   In January, **Thomas Paine**'s *Common Sense* is published, in which he urges independence from England.

In March, British general **William Howe** and his troops abandon Boston for Canada; patriots reclaim Boston. **Abigail Adams** writes her famous "Remember the Ladies" letter to **John Adams**.

In May, the Continental Congress tells each of the thirteen colonies to form a new provincial (local) government.

In June, **George Mason** proposes a plan for a state government to Virginia lawmakers. **Betsy Ross** of Philadelphia is believed to design the first American stars and stripes flag.

In July, Congress adopts the Declaration of Independence. A massive British force lands in New York City to crush colonial rebellion.

In August, General **William Howe** defeats **George Washington** at the Battle of Long Island, New York. In the fighting, **Margaret Cochran Corbin** steps in and takes over firing a cannon when her soldier husband is killed by enemy fire.

In September, **Benjamin Franklin** is one of three men appointed by Congress to go to Paris to seek French assistance in the war. **Nathan Hale** is executed by the British for spying.

In October, the American navy is defeated at Battle of Valcour in Canada, in which **Benedict Arnold** commands a fleet of American ships.

In December, **George Washington**'s troops flee to Pennsylvania; fearing attack, the Continental Congress abandons Philadelphia for Baltimore. The Continental army defeats Great Britain's hired German soldiers in a surprise attack at Trenton, New Jersey.

1777 Loyalist **Flora Macdonald** refuses to take an oath of allegiance to America and loses her plantation.

In June, British general **John Burgoyne**'s troops capture Fort Ticonderoga from the Americans. **George Washington** loses at Brandywine and Germantown near Philadelphia; the British seize Philadelphia.

In July, France's **Marquis de Lafayette** is appointed major general of the Continental army. **Jane McCrea** is killed by Indians scouting for the British. Polish war hero **Casimir Pulaski** arrives to help the American cause.

In August, Mohawk Indian **Mary "Molly" Brant** reports American troop movements to the British, who then beat the Americans at the Battle of Oriskany, New York.

In September, German general Friederich von Riedesel helps the British win the first Battle of Saratoga at Freeman's Farm, New York.

In October, Polish soldier **Thaddeus Kosciuszko** helps Americans defeat General **John Burgoyne** at Saratoga, New York. Baroness **Frederika von Riedesel** and her family are captured by the Americans.

In November, the Continental Congress adopts the Articles of Confederation, America's first constitution.

In December, **George Washington**'s troops set up winter quarters at Valley Forge, Pennsylvania. France's King **Louis XVI** recognizes American independence, paving the way to openly assist the war effort.

1778   In February, France and the United States sign treaties of trade and alliance. German Baron von Steuben joins the Continental army as Inspector General and begins to train troops.

In March, the British fail at an attempt to make peace with the Americans. Frontiersman **Simon Girty** goes over to the British side.

In June, General Sir Henry Clinton (who replaced **William Howe**) abandons Philadelphia and heads for New York. On the way, he is attacked by Americans at the Battle of Monmouth, New Jersey. **Mary McCauley** ("Molly Pitcher") participates in the battle.

In July, France declares war on Great Britain.

1779   Essays and poems by **Jonathan Odell** are printed in newspapers; they encourage the Loyalists and criticize the Continental Congress.

Spain declares war on Great Britain. **Bernardo de Gálvez**, the Spanish governor of Louisiana, begins to openly aid the American cause.

1780   In May, Charleston, South Carolina, falls to British troops.

In June, Massachusetts's constitution asserts that "all men are born free and equal"; this includes black slaves. In *Sentiments of an American Woman*, **Esther De Berdt Reed** calls on colonial women to sacrifice luxuries and instead give money to the American army.

In September, **Benedict Arnold** openly goes over to the British side.

1781   In March, the Articles of Confederation are ratified by all the states.

In August, **Elizabeth Freeman,** a slave living in Massachusetts, sues and wins her freedom under the new Massachusetts constitution.

In October, British general Charles Cornwallis surrenders his troops at Yorktown, Virginia; Great Britain loses all hope of winning the Revolutionary War.

1782   **Benjamin Franklin, John Adams, John Jay,** and Henry Laurens go to France to draw up a peace treaty.

Deborah Sampson, disguised as a man, enlists in the Fourth Massachusetts Regiment and fights against the Tories and Native Americans.

1783   Mohawk Chief **Joseph Brant** and the Iroquois Confederacy begin blocking American westward expansion.

In April, Congress declares the Revolutionary War officially ended; Loyalists and British soldiers pack up their headquarters in New York City and depart for Canada or England.

In May, the Society of Cincinnati is formed by former Continental army officers. Among its early members are **George Washington, Alexander Hamilton,** and **Thaddeus Kosciuszko.**

In November, **George Washington** delivers a farewell speech to his army; he resigns his military commission.

1784   In January, the Treaty of Paris is ratified by Congress, bringing the Revolutionary War to an official end.

In March, **Thomas Jefferson**'s plan for dividing the western territories is adopted by Congress.

1785   In January, Congress relocates to New York City.

In February, **John Adams** becomes the first U.S. ambassador to England.

1786 In January, **Thomas Jefferson**'s Virginia Statute for Religious Freedom is passed by the Virginia legislature.

In August, **Daniel Shays** masterminds Shays's Rebellion to protest what he calls unfair taxation.

In September, the Annapolis Convention meets; **Alexander Hamilton** proposes and Congress approves his plan for a 1787 convention to replace the Articles of Confederation with a Constitution.

1787 In May, convention delegates meet in Philadelphia to rewrite the Articles of Confederation.

In July, Congress adopts the Northwest Ordinance (order), based on one written earlier by **Thomas Jefferson**, that prohibits slavery in U.S. territories and provides a method for new states to enter the union.

In October, **Alexander Hamilton**, **James Madison**, and **John Jay** publish the *Federalist* in defense of the new American Constitution.

1788 In February, in Massachusetts, **Samuel Adams** and **John Hancock** agree to support the new Constitution, but only if amendments will be added that guarantee civil liberties.

In June, in Virginia, **James Madison** and his followers succeed in getting ratification of the Constitution despite opposition by **Patrick Henry** and **George Mason**. The U.S. Constitution is adopted by all of the states. Congress is granted land for a new federal capital.

In July, Congress formally announces that the Constitution of the United States has been ratified and is in effect.

In September, New York City is named the temporary seat of the new U.S. government.

1789 **David Ramsay**'s *History of the Revolution* is published.

In April, **George Washington** is sworn in as the first U.S. president.

In July, the French Revolution begins in Paris. King **Louis XVI** will be beheaded in 1792 during this revolution.

In September, the U.S. Army is established by Congress.

1791   The Bill of Rights, written by **James Madison**, is passed by the U.S. Congress.

Pierre Charles L'Enfant is appointed to design the new federal capital, Washington, D.C.

1792   **Judith Sargent Murray** writes an essay stating that women are born equal to men and have the capability to enter all professions if properly educated.

1797   **John Adams** becomes the second U.S. president.

1801   **Thomas Jefferson** becomes the third U.S. president.

1912   The discovery of five skeletons near her property seems to prove true the legend that **Nancy Morgan Hart** killed five Tory soldiers during the American Revolution.

Words to Know

A

Abolitionism: The belief that measures should be taken to end slavery.

Absolutism: Also known as absolute power; a system in which one person—usually a king or queen—rules without any kind of restrictions on his or her actions.

Agent: A person who conducts business on another's behalf.

Allegiance: Loyalty to king, country, or a cause.

Articles of Confederation: An agreement among the thirteen original states, approved in 1781, that provided a loose form of government before the present Constitution went into effect in 1789.

Artillery: The science of using guns; a group of gunners in an army; or the weapons themselves, especially cannons that throw bombs across a battlefield.

Assemblies: One of the names used by the colonies for their lawmaking bodies.

B

Boston Massacre: An encounter between British troops and townspeople in Boston in 1770, before the Revolutionary War. The British fired into a crowd and five Americans were killed.

Boston Tea Party: An incident on December 16, 1773, in which Boston patriots dumped 342 chests of English tea into Boston Harbor to protest British taxes.

Boycott: A refusal to buy, sell, or use certain products from a particular company or country, usually for a political reason.

Brigadier general: A military position just below major general.

Bunker Hill, Battle of: The first great battle of the Revolutionary War, fought near Boston in June 1775. The British drove the Americans out of their fort at nearby Breed's Hill to Bunker Hill; the Americans gave up only when they ran out of ammunition, proving they were willing to take on trained British soldiers.

Burgesses: An old term for members of the British Parliament; the lawmaking body of colonial Virginia called itself the House of Burgesses.

C

Coercive Acts: The British name for the Intolerable Acts.

Colonel: A military rank below brigadier general.

Colonial: Relating to the period before the United States declared independence.

Colonial agents: Men appointed by lawmaking bodies in the colonies to live in London, England, circulate among important people, and report back on what was happening in the British Parliament. Benjamin Franklin served as an agent for several colonies.

Colonies: Territories that are settled by emigrants from a distant land and remain subject to or closely connected with the parent country.

Committees of Correspondence: Colonial groups that shared information, coordinated the activities of colonial agitators, and organized public opinion against the British government.

Committees of Safety: One of many colonial committees that had the authority to call up militias (groups of volunteer soldiers) when they were needed.

Common Sense: A pamphlet written by Thomas Paine in 1776 in which he urged the colonies to declare independence immediately.

Confederacy: A union of states.

Confederation: A group of states united for a common purpose.

Conservatives: People who wish to preserve society's existing institutions.

Continental army: An army of American colonists formed during the American Revolution.

Continental Congress: An assembly of delegates from the American colonies (later states). The delegates governed before and during the Revolutionary War and under the Articles of Confederation. The Continental Congress first met in 1774.

The Crisis: Also known as *The American Crisis,* a series of pamphlets written by Thomas Paine in which he discussed issues of the American Revolution.

D

Declaration of Independence: The document establishing the United States as a nation, adopted by the Continental Congress on July 4, 1776.

Delegates: Representatives.

Democracy: A system of government in which power belongs to the people, who rule either directly or through freely elected representatives. See also **Republic.**

"Don't fire until you see the whites of their eyes": A famous command said to have been given by either William Prescott or Israel Putnam, American officers at the Battle of Bunker Hill. In order for colonial weapons to be effective, the shooter had to be close to his victim.

Duties: Taxes on imported or exported goods.

E

Essays: Short pieces of writing that deal with a single subject.

F

Federalist: One who supports a strong central government instead of a loose organization of states.

Founding Fathers: A general name for male American patriots during the Revolutionary War, especially the signers of the Declaration of Independence and the drafters of the Constitution.

Freedom of the press: The right to circulate opinions in print without government interference.

French and Indian War: A series of military battles between Great Britain and France (and France's Indian allies) that took place on the American frontier and in Canada between 1754 and 1763.

French Revolution: An event lasting from 1789 to 1799 that ended the thousand-year rule of kings in France and established France as a republic. The American Revolution and the American experiment with democracy was an inspiration to many French people, but while the American experiment thrived, the French Revolution ended in chaos.

G

Great Britain: The island off the western coast of Europe made up of England, Scotland, and Wales. Also called "Britain" or "England."

Grievances: Complaints.

H

Hessians: Citizens of Hesse-Cassel, once a part of Germany. German soldiers (mercenaries) were hired by King George III to fight for the British in the American Revolution. Many came from Hesse-Cassel; as a result, all German soldiers were called Hessians.

I

Intolerable Acts: Four laws passed by the British government in 1774 to punish Boston for the Boston Tea Party.

Iroquois Confederacy: A union of the Mohawk, Oneida, Onondaga, Cayuga, Seneca, and Tuscarora tribes. Members were sometimes called "Iroquois" instead of their tribal names.

L

Lexington and Concord, Battle of: The first battle of the Revolutionary War, a minor skirmish fought in Massachusetts on April 19, 1775.

Loyalists: Colonists who remained loyal to England during the American Revolution; also known as Tories.

M

Martial law: Temporary rule by military authorities imposed upon regular citizens in time of war or when civil authority has stopped working. The British-appointed governor of Virginia became so angry at Patrick Henry's "give me liberty or give me death" speech that he declared martial law in Virginia.

Mercenaries: Soldiers for hire; see **Hessians.**

Militia: A military force consisting of citizens rather than professional soldiers.

Minutemen: Armed American citizens (nonmilitary) who promised to be ready to fight alongside regular soldiers at a moment's notice.

Monarchy: Rule by a king or queen.

N

Neutral: Not committed to either side of an issue.

New England: The region in the northeastern United States that includes present-day Connecticut, Maine, Massachusetts, New Hampshire, Rhode Island, and Vermont.

The name was probably given by English explorer Captain John Smith, one of the original settlers of Jamestown, Virginia (1607), because the region resembled the coast of England.

"No taxation without representation": A popular phrase of the Revolutionary War era. The colonists were not allowed to choose representatives to Parliament, which passed laws taxing the colonists. This offense against colonial rights is one of the main grievances against Great Britain listed in the Declaration of Independence.

P

Pamphlets: Reading material with paper covers.

Parliament: The British lawmaking body.

Patriot: A person who loves, supports, and defends his country.

Petition: A formal document.

Privateer: A privately owned ship authorized by the government during wartime to attack and capture enemy vessels. Privateer may also refer to the person who commands the ship.

Propaganda: Information and argument designed to influence public opinion about political matters.

Q

Quaker: A member of the religion known as the Society of Friends. Quakers oppose all violence and warfare.

Quota: A share assigned to a group. During the American Revolution, when too few men volunteered to be soldiers in the Continental army, Congress assigned a quota to each colony, representing the number of men the colony was expected to round up and send to serve in the army.

R

Radical: A person who favors revolutionary changes in a nation's political structure.

Rebel: A person who resists or defies ruling authority.

Redcoats: British soldiers who wore red uniforms.

Repealed: Done away with; especially referring to laws.

Republic: A form of government in which people hold the power and exercise it through elected representatives. Today, the words "republic" and "democracy" are used interchangeably, but in the early days of the United States, they differed in meaning. "Republic" was used to mean a system of government in which the will of the people was interpreted by representatives who might be wiser or better educated than the average person. Back then, the elected representatives had to own property.

Resolution: A formal statement of a decision or expression of opinion put before or adopted by a lawmaking assembly.

Revenue: Money collected to pay for the expenses of government.

Revolution: A sudden political overthrow; a forcible substitution of rulers.

Revolutionary War: The war for American independence from Great Britain. The fighting began with the Battle of Lexington and Concord in 1775 and lasted through the Battle of Yorktown in 1781.

S

Saratoga, Battle of: A major battle of the Revolutionary War, fought in northern New York state. It is often called the turning point of the war because the American victory there convinced France to send aid.

Satirical writing: Writing that ridicules individuals or groups by pointing out their stupidities or abuses.

Sedition: Acts or language leading to rebellion.

Self-evident: Something requiring no proof or explanation.

Separation of church and state: The principle that government must maintain an attitude of neutrality toward religion. The relationship between church and state has been the subject of argument since the first European settlers arrived in America to escape religious persecution at home.

"Shot heard 'round the world": A phrase from a July 4, 1837, poem by Ralph Waldo Emerson about the Battle of Lexington and Concord. He wrote of the determination of the colonists in standing up for their rights. This led to the establishment of a new kind of democratic nation and encouraged other peoples of the world to move toward democracy.

Skirmish: A minor encounter in war between small bodies of troops.

Stamp Act: A law passed by the British government in 1765 that required the payment of a tax to Great Britain on papers and documents produced in the colonies.

T

Thirteen colonies: The colonies that made up the original United States on the signing of the Declaration of Independence in 1776: Connecticut, Delaware, Georgia, Maryland, Massachusetts, New Hampshire, New Jersey, New York, North Carolina, Pennsylvania, Rhode Island, South Carolina, and Virginia.

Tories: Colonists who remained loyal to England during the American Revolution; also called Loyalists.

Townshend Acts: Laws passed by the British government in 1767. They included a Quartering Act, which ordered the colonies to house British troops, and a Revenue Act, which called for taxes on lead, glass, paint, tea, and other items.

Treason: Betrayal of king and country.

Tyranny: Absolute power, especially power exercised cruelly or unjustly.

U

Unalienable rights: Rights that cannot be given away or taken away.

V

Valley Forge: A valley in eastern Pennsylvania that served as quarters for the Continental army in the winter of 1777–78. General George Washington had been forced to leave the comfort of Philadelphia, and his soldiers suffered from cold and lack of supplies.

W

West Indies: A group of islands between North and South America, curving from southern Florida to Venezuela. Much trade was carried on between colonial America and British-owned islands in the West Indies. The French, Spanish, and other nations owned islands in the West Indies, too. Some Revolutionary War battles were fought there between the French and Spanish navies and the British navy.

Y

Yankee: Once a nickname for people from the New England colonies, the word is now applied to anyone from the United States.

Yorktown, Battle of: The last battle of the Revolutionary War, fought in 1781 near the Virginia coast. General Charles Cornwallis surrendered his army to General George Washington.

Abigail Adams

Born November 22, 1744
Weymouth, Massachusetts
Died October 28, 1818
Quincy, Massachusetts

**Second First Lady of the United States,
women's rights advocate**

A bigail Adams, one of the most well-known women of the eighteenth century, was the wife of one United States president and the mother of another. During her husband's long absences from home, she successfully managed her family's affairs and ran their farm. In a new country based on the principles of equality and independence, this American patriot loved and loyally supported her own country and sowed the seeds for the movement to make women full citizens of the United States.

Abigail Adams was born Abigail Smith on November 22, 1744, to William Smith, a Protestant minister, and Elizabeth Quincy Adams. Both were from wealthy, educated New England families. Adams was a shy but stubborn child who suffered several illnesses during her early years. Her strict mother taught Adams to be charitable, and they often went together to bring food and clothing to the area's needy families.

Adams's father loved learning and gave all of his children full run of his large library. There the young girl learned about poetry, history, drama, religion, and political matters. She educated herself and became one of the best-read women

"I could not have believed if I had not experienced it, how strong the Love of Country is in the humane mind."

Portrait: Abigail Adams.
Reproduced by permission of AP/Wide World Photos.

1

of the time. Her poor spelling and handwriting, however, showed that she was self-taught.

Abigail Adams grew into a tall, slender young woman with a long nose, sharp chin, and piercing eyes. She first met twenty-three-year-old **John Adams** (see entry), a lawyer, when she was fifteen. They began sharing their love for knowledge, and before long he was sending her letters addressed to "Miss Adorable." The couple married on October 25, 1764. For more than fifty years, they remained best friends, and John always relied on his wife's advice.

Family endures constant separations

The couple's first home was a small farm in Quincy (then called Braintree), Massachusetts. Adams stayed at home, overseeing servants and running the household, while John Adams traveled to Boston and other parts of New England building his career as a lawyer and judge. The Adamses had five children, "Nabby" (Abigail), John Quincy, Susanna (who died at the age of thirteen months), Charles, and Thomas.

In 1763 the British began to demand that the American colonists start paying high taxes to help pay off British war debts. The colonists resisted. They believed that to be taxed by the British Parliament—a government body in which they had no representation—was unfair and made them little more than slaves. John Adams was a primary force in the movement toward the Revolutionary War, which finally erupted over this and other issues in 1775.

In 1768 Adams moved his family to Boston, the most active center of revolutionary activity. There Abigail Adams socialized with the city's most important families. Six years later John was elected a delegate to the First Continental Congress, a six-week meeting at which representatives from the colonies discussed what to do about their problems with the British. John's role as a delegate meant even longer separations.

Takes charge at home, writes letters

Although she missed John terribly when he was away on business and political trips, Abigail Adams stood behind his efforts and ambitions. She took on the responsibility of making most of the family decisions herself, including those that pertained to money.

The family's life gradually changed, as the American movement to gain freedom from Great Britain grew stronger. Adams wrote frequent letters to her friends and family in which she frankly expressed her opinions. The letters have been preserved and are honored as some of the best of her time. Their subjects range from politics, manners, and education for women to marriage, health care, and the relationship between religion and morality (what is right versus what is wrong).

Abigail and John Adams often wrote to one another about their feelings and ideas. Quoting William Shakespeare in a letter to her husband, Abigail Adams wrote: "My pen is always freer than my tongue." In later years, Abigail Adams expressed her political opinions in letters to such fellow patriots as **Thomas Jefferson** (see entry), a highly respected lawyer from Virginia who became the third president of the United States. She and Jefferson carried on a long correspondence in which they treated each other as equals. Her letters have been described as newsy, flirtatious, and full of ideas.

Adams's letters gave accounts of the history of the young country and the problems that its people faced on the road to independence. She wrote to John Adams of the conflict between their neighbors who supported Britain and those who supported the revolution. She also wrote about housing colonial soldiers on their way to attack the British, and of her own constant fear of attack by British soldiers.

Hard times for Abigail Adams and America

Women had to undergo many hardships as the Revolutionary War stretched on from 1775 to 1783. Adams's letters told of how she dealt with such difficulties as wartime shortages and the high cost of food and other goods, lack of help to run the family farm, and, especially, loneliness. At one point, her husband served as a diplomat in Europe, representing the United States in its dealings with countries there. In order to make ends meet, Adams was forced to sell or trade the tea, handkerchiefs, and other items her husband sent her from Europe.

Adamses Inoculated for Smallpox

In 1721 an American doctor named Zabdiel Boylston (1679–1766) introduced the process of inoculation for smallpox to Boston. A smallpox epidemic was raging throughout the city and beyond its borders, and inoculations were the best-known way to ward off this serious disease. Smallpox causes fever, vomiting, skin eruptions, and sometimes death and is easily passed to others. Inoculation for smallpox involved injecting a serum with the disease into a person's body in order to cause a minor form of the disease so that the person then could build up protection against getting it.

In 1776, just as America was declaring her independence from Great Britain, another smallpox epidemic broke out in Boston. Many patients were inoculated and then quarantined in hospitals and other sites to keep them away from others who did not have the disease. Most patients recovered after the three- or four-week isolation period and were protected from getting the disease again.

During the outbreak, people who wanted to leave Boston were required to undergo a "smoking." It was thought that exposing them to a room filled with dense smoke for a period of time would clear them of the smallpox germs. People with the disease who remained in the city were permitted to wander freely, attending

She once told John that, because of the loss of his companionship for half of their marriage and his reduced time for moneymaking, she believed she had struggled and sacrificed more on behalf of the American cause than most women in the country.

Impressions of France

Throughout her life Abigail Adams furthered her education and developed her mind. For example, in 1784 she went with her husband to Paris, France, where for eight months he represented the U.S. government in its dealings with France. While there, Abigail Adams paid close attention to French manners and morals and observed French culture.

From an early age, Adams's family had taught her to be careful with money. She was amazed by the number of ser-

church and visiting friends and family. In fact, patients were instructed to get as much fresh air as possible, as this was wrongly thought to be a way to help cure the disease.

In July 1776 Abigail Adams and her children went to the home of a relative and were inoculated. She brought with her straw beds, sheets, bedspreads, money for medical fees, and a cow to supply fresh milk. After the inoculations, Adams and her family suffered from sore eyes, weakness, fever, nausea, and headaches. It took some of them up to six weeks to recover from being inoculated. Two of the children tolerated the ordeal quite well, but two had to be inoculated a second time when the first shot failed to produce results. Adams's daughter Nabby got much sicker than anyone else, and her son Charley had to be inoculated a third time. When he finally did get the disease, he was extremely ill. Fortunately, the boy recovered. The whole process lasted two months and proved very difficult for everyone. Finally protected against the disease, Abigail Adams was able to travel about Boston freely, gathering the latest information and gossip, which she sent to her husband, John, who was in Philadelphia, Pennsylvania, on the new nation's business.

vants that upper-class Europeans needed to maintain a large house and the time and money they spent on looking fashionable. She disapproved of the behavior of the wealthy French people, telling her friends that they mainly pursued luxury and pleasure, and she disliked Paris, calling it "the dirtiest place I ever saw."

Life in London society

In 1785 Abigail Adams accompanied John Adams to England, where he served as the first U.S. minister to the court of **George III** (see entry), king of Great Britain. As an official representative of her country, Adams carried out her duties—mostly entertaining—with intelligence and dignity. Among the people the Adamses encountered in England were former colonists who had fled America to escape revolutionary activities. These Loyalists (people who were loyal to England) felt deeply resentful toward representatives of the new American government. They wrote critical newspaper articles about John and Abigail Adams and made them feel unwelcome, although officials of the British government and members of royalty generally treated them with courtesy. In London, her son, the brilliant John Quincy Adams, later an American president, served as his father's secretary.

Champions women's need for education

Abigail Adams believed strongly that education was as important for women as for men. She thought it was necessary if they were to do a proper job in raising children, running their homes, and being good mates. Indeed, during her stay in London she took the opportunity to study science, an area about which most women were taught little. Adams frequently wrote in her letters about the need for women to be educated.

At the same time, Adams understood the limited role that women of her time were allowed to play in American society. For example, a woman was expected to marry, and after marriage all her belongings became the possessions of her husband. She had no rights even to her children. Only after the death of her husband could she make decisions for herself.

Abigail Adams apparently accepted her role as a woman but not without voicing certain criticisms. She believed that women, like men, had the right to independence. She objected to the legal codes that prevented married women from owning property.

As early as 1776, Adams had made a very strong appeal for women's rights in a letter she wrote to her husband, who was then involved with drafting the Declaration of Independence. She begged him in doing so to "remember the ladies ... and be more generous and favorable to them than your ancestors."

Life in Washington, D.C.

In 1788 Abigail and John Adams returned to a fine new house in Quincy, Massachusetts, that served as their main residence for the rest of their lives, except when John held national political office. Abigail Adams continued to support her husband who, in 1789, became vice president of the

United States under **George Washington** (see entry). She developed a friendship with First Lady Martha Washington, using the experience she had gained visiting the European royal courts to help with official entertaining.

In 1791 health problems forced Abigail Adams to return home to Quincy. But she temporarily returned to the nation's capital, Washington, D.C., in 1797 when her husband defeated Thomas Jefferson and became the second president of the United States. As First Lady, Abigail Adams resumed formal entertaining. Conditions in Washington were then quite primitive: the city was located in a wilderness, and the White House was still under construction. She shared her complaints with her immediate family but conducted her duties at dinners and receptions with dignity.

Adamses return home after loss of election

President John Adams frequently consulted with his wife about important matters, both personal and governmental. Many of the political ideas held by Abigail Adams were rather conservative. She wanted to preserve existing traditions and tended to resist changes. John and Abigail Adams's conservative attitudes were unpopular among many American citizens, who believed that America should welcome foreigners and encourage freedom of the press. Their attitudes may have contributed to John Adams's defeat by Thomas Jefferson in the presidential election of 1800.

Following John Adams's defeat in the election, he and Abigail Adams returned to their home in Quincy, where they lived together for eighteen years, without the strain of politics. Still, there were hardships. The Adamses suffered the loss of their daughter, Nabby, to cancer, and Abigail Adams had to bear her own long-term illnesses.

On October 28, 1818, seventy-three-year-old Abigail Adams died at home of typhoid fever, a highly infectious disease usually transmitted by impure food or water. Her husband remained heartbroken for the next eight years, but had the satisfaction of seeing their son, John Quincy Adams (1767–1848), become the sixth U.S. president in 1824. After John Adams died in 1826, he was buried next to Abigail Adams in Quincy's United First Parish Church.

Renewed interest in Abigail Adams was sparked in 1875 when her grandson, Charles Francis Adams, published *The Familiar Letters of John Adams and His Wife Abigail During the Revolution*. Today readers still enjoy learning about the customs, habits, and manners of their daily life as well as the details about the American Revolution the letters reveal.

For More Information

Adams, Charles Francis. *The Familiar Letters of John Adams and His Wife Abigail During the Revolution*. New York: Houghton-Mifflin, 1875.

Akers, Charles W. *Abigail Adams: An American Woman*. Boston: Little, Brown, 1980.

Beller, Susan Provost. *Woman of Independence: The Life of Abigail Adams*. White Hall, VA: Shoe Tree Press, 1992.

Bober, Natalie S. *Abigail Adams: Witness to a Revolution*. New York: Atheneum Books, 1995.

Butterfield, L. H., March Friedlaender, and Mary-Jo Klein, eds. *The Book of Abigail and John: Selected Letters of the Adams Family, 1762–1784*. Cambridge, MA: Harvard University Press, 1975.

Gelles, Edith B. *Portia: The World of Abigail Adams*. Bloomington: Indiana University Press, 1992.

Levin, Phyllis Lee. *Abigail Adams: A Biography*. New York: St. Martin's Press, 1987.

Meeker, Clare Hodgson. *Partner in Revolution: Abigail Adams*. New York: Benchmark Books, 1998.

Withey, Lynne. *Dearest Friend: A Life of Abigail Adams*. New York: The Free Press, 1981.

John Adams

**Born October 1735
Braintree, Massachusetts
Died July 4, 1826
Quincy, Massachusetts**

**President and vice president of the
United States, diplomat, lawyer, writer**

John Adams was an enemy of British oppression who worked tirelessly for American independence. A man with a great mind, he wrote vivid diaries, letters, and essays; gave patriotic speeches; and negotiated effectively on behalf of his country. Although he could be a vain and stubborn politician, this passionate patriot was one of America's most important founding fathers.

Adams, one of three brothers, was born on his family's farm in Quincy (then known as Braintree), Massachusetts. His father, also named John, was a farmer and a church deacon who directed the affairs of his hometown for more than twenty years. Adams's mother, Susanna Boyleston Adams, came from a respected Brookline, Massachusetts, family. John Adams was very close to his mother. His biographer Page Smith wrote that "she brought a touch of [city worldliness] to the family. She had ... an [unending supply] of [sayings about the right way to behave] which her son took to heart."

As a child, Adams loved spending time in the woods and fields that surrounded his Braintree home. "I spent my time as idle children do in making and sailing boats and ships

"People and nations are forged in the fires of adversity."

Portrait: John Adams.
Reproduced by permission of AP/Wide World Photos.

upon the ponds and brooks, in making and flying kites, in driving hoops, playing marbles, playing quoits, wrestling, swimming, skating and above all in shooting, to which diversion I was addicted to a degree of Ardor which I know not that I ever felt for any other Business, Study, or Amusement," he would later write in his autobiography. This love for the outdoors once prompted a young Adams to tell his father of his plans to become a farmer. However, his parents had different ideas for the future of their son. The Adamses were firm believers in education, and decided that their son should attend Harvard and become a clergyman.

Graduates from Harvard, studies law, marries

After finishing his elementary studies, Adams attended what is now Harvard University in Cambridge, Massachusetts, just outside Boston, where he received excellent grades and graduated in 1755. After graduation, the nineteen-year-old young man moved to Worcester, Massachusetts, and began teaching grammar school, deciding against entering into the ministry. Once settled in his new position, Adams started to study law. In 1758 Adams completed his law studies, returned to his parents' home, and was admitted to the Boston bar. Over the next several years, Adams built up his law practice and more significantly began to involve himself in Revolutionary politics.

In 1764 Adams married bright, strong-willed **Abigail Adams** (see entry), the daughter of a noted clergyman. In the first decade of their marriage, the couple had five children—Abigail (called "Nabby"), John Quincy, Susanna (who died at the age of thirteen months), Charles, and Thomas.

While Adams traveled around New England establishing his reputation as a lawyer, Abigail kept him posted about events at home. Through his wife's family he came to know many of the area's wealthiest and most powerful people. In an age when many men considered women of lesser value than men, Adams considered the well-informed Abigail his intellectual equal, and he listened to her informed views on public affairs.

Gains fame for defending liberty

In the 1760s American colonists became angry with England. The British governing body, called Parliament, in an effort to raise money to pay off war debts, passed laws that required the colonists to pay high taxes and had adopted other measures the colonists thought unfair. Americans especially disliked the Stamp Act of 1765, which required them to buy a stamp to place on every printed document and other paper items they used. They protested by tearing down the house of the British-appointed governor in Boston, Thomas Hutchinson, setting fire to the tax office, and refusing to buy any British-made goods.

Joining the protest against the Stamp Act of 1765, Adams wrote several articles for the *Boston Gazette* that were also published in England. The colonists had never had any representatives in the British Parliament. Adams argued that it was wrong for Parliament to tax the colonies without the colonists having any say in the matter. "No taxation without representation" became the rallying cry. Adams's well-crafted writings made him New England's most popular defender of liberty in the press.

John Adams wrote several articles arguing against the British taxing the colonies without giving the colonists a say in the matter. His articles appeared in the *Boston Gazette* as well as in papers in England. These writings gained Adams his reputation as one of New England's most popular defenders of liberty in the press.
Reproduced by permission of Archive Photos, Inc.

A formal statement that Adams wrote for his own town in protest of the Stamp Act was used as a model by other towns. Adams became a frequent contributor to the newspapers, speaking out against the perceived injustices carried out by the British Parliament. In time the British government gave in and removed all taxes they had placed on the colonists except the one on tea, which they kept to remind the colonists that England was still in charge.

Encourages rebellion but defends fair treatment for all

Representatives of the British government were fearful of angry colonial mobs that protested against proposed new taxes. They demanded that England send troops to Boston to help keep the peace. Their fears proved well founded in the winter of 1770, when the Boston Massacre took place (see **Samuel Adams** entry). In that event British soldiers fired upon a crowd of colonists (who may have provoked the British soldiers with their taunts), killing five colonial citizens who were shouting insults at them.

Despite the cries for revenge that came from many New Englanders, Adams insisted that the "redcoats" (British soldiers wore red uniforms) receive a fair trial. When criticized for defending the British soldiers, Adams responded that in a free country all men deserved the right to be defended against their accusers. Through the efforts of Adams and other colonial lawyers, eight of the soldiers and their commander were set free on the grounds of self-defense. Two were found guilty of manslaughter (killing of a human being without any bad intent). For punishment, they had their thumbs branded with a hot iron.

The Boston Tea Party

Colonial resistance to British policies finally boiled over in an incident known as the Boston Tea Party. On December 16, 1773, angry colonists boarded three British ships anchored in Boston harbor and threw their cargoes of tea into the water to protest the British tax on tea. Adams supported the incident, which many historians consider the event that led the colonists to break away from England and begin their own government. The British responded by closing the port of Boston and passing other measures the colonists called the Intolerable Acts. War came ever closer, and the thirteen colonies realized that to defend themselves effectively, they needed to unite under one central government.

First Continental Congress meets

In 1774 the First Continental Congress was called to discuss and solve the problems of the relations between America and Britain. The citizens of Massachusetts elected John Adams and Samuel Adams as their representatives. In the spring of 1774 delegates met to discuss what to do about the troubles with their mother country. They chose Philadelphia, Pennsylvania, as the site of the meeting because it was far away from where British soldiers were encamped in Boston.

John Adams was deeply committed to the idea of American independence, and devoted himself to the discussion. Adams told the delegates that they had to work together to prepare for a long war ahead. He helped draft a declaration to the king of England and a declaration of the rights of colonists. The members agreed to meet again in May 1775 if by then the king had not addressed their complaints.

Washington chosen to head army

The battle of Lexington and Concord began in April 1775 and, with this battle, the Revolutionary War had begun. The rebels pushed the redcoats back to Boston, trapping them there. Since the king was not responsive to their declaration of rights, the representatives met again in May 1775 in Philadelphia for the Second Continental Congress. During this convention they heard speeches on whether or not the colonies should officially go to war against Great Britain. Like the citizens of the colonies, the congress was deeply divided on the matter of war. New Englanders, who had experienced the worst of the British actions, spoke of the growing threat of the British army. Some southerners spoke in favor of remaining loyal to England. In his autobiography, Adams wrote that the battle at Lexington and Concord "changed the instruments of warfare from Penn to Sword."

In June 1775 the Continental Congress created the Continental army. Headquartered at Cambridge, Massachusetts, the army swelled to more than 16,000 soldiers. At the Second Continental Congress Adams rose and nominated **George Washington** (see entry) to serve as head of the new army. The tall, quiet man had served as a colonel in the Virginia militia, an army made up of citizens rather than professional soldiers. One reason Adams chose Washington was to draw the rich southern plantation owners into the struggle for independence. As a result of Adams's private talks with all the delegates, Washington was the choice of every one of them.

Nurtures move towards liberty

Adams kept a detailed diary of the events of revolutionary times that has proved to be a rich source of information for future generations. The patriotic Adams had respect for the British tradition of laws and freedom, but he believed that a war for American independence from England could not be avoided. Never one to leave anything to chance, he placed his own secretary on the staff of General Washington to keep himself informed of all that went on with the new Continental army.

Throughout 1776 Adams spoke, wrote, and plotted to persuade the Second Continental Congress to declare independence. Still, the delegates hesitated to make a final break from England. Adams became part of a committee chosen to draft a declaration proclaiming independence. His fellow committee members were **Thomas Jefferson,** a lawyer from Virginia who became the third president of the United States; **Benjamin Franklin** (see entries), American politician, scientist, inventor, and writer; Roger Sherman, a politician representing Connecticut; and Robert Livingston, a politician from New York. Adams persuaded Jefferson to be the chief writer, made some small changes in the document when it was finished, and helped to win its approval by the congress. In July 1776 the Declaration of Independence was issued. The Declaration set out in memorable fashion the colonists' grievances and those rights they felt had been trampled by the British Crown.

Suggests national celebration

On July 3, 1776, the eve of what is now celebrated as Independence Day, Adams wrote in a letter to his wife: "The most memorable Epoch [time period] in the History of America has begun.... It ought to be solemnized [celebrated] with pomp and parade, with shows, games, sports, guns, bells, bonfires and illuminations from one end of this continent to the other—from this time forward, for ever more."

With a new, independent United States now established (the name first appeared in the Declaration of Independence), Adams suggested that each state set up its own government. (Four years later he became the main author of the Massachusetts State Constitution.) He also helped organize the American army to make it ready for the coming battle with trained British soldiers, and argued that George Washington must have full authority as commander, answering only to Congress.

Serves his country as ambassador abroad

Adams served the new country in many ways as war broke out. He became the Chairman of the Board of War, a post now called the Secretary of Defense. At various times between 1777 and 1783, as the Revolutionary War raged, he was called upon to visit foreign countries to enlist their aid in the battle against Great Britain. He served as a commissioner to France, where he and Benjamin Franklin, also serving as an American ambassador abroad, convinced the French to fight alongside American soldiers in the war.

Adams served as wartime U.S. Minister to the Netherlands in 1780, where he secured a loan for his country. In 1783 Adams, Franklin, and **John Jay** (see entry) negotiated the Treaty of Paris, which officially ended the Revolutionary War.

In 1785 Adams went to England to serve as the first official representative of the newly independent United States. King **George III** (see entry) wished him well, but Adams's efforts to restore good business relations were blocked by many British officials, who resented the long and bitter conflict. In 1787 and 1788 he responded to foreign critics of his country by writing a three-volume *Defense of the Constitution of the United States.* In the book he argued that "there is danger from all men" who hold power, and that the most dangerous are those who wield the most power.

Becomes vice president

In 1789, after much debate, the U.S. Constitution was adopted, and for the first time in the history of the United States the various states chose electors to meet and select a president. At that time, each elector could cast two votes. They chose George Washington to serve as the first president of the United States. Adams became vice president because he received the second-largest number of votes. (Later the system was changed so that president and vice president were elected by two separate votes.)

Adams called the position of vice president, which he held for eight years, an "insignificant office." He sometimes resented playing second fiddle to Washington, but he supported the president in the belief that the duties of the offices of president and vice president should be carried out with great dignity. However, Adams opposed the attitudes of his Federalist colleagues who believed that the rich and well educated should have more influence than ordinary citizens (see box).

Elected president, has troubles with France

After Washington's second term as president ended, Adams was elected president of the United States in 1796. Thomas Jefferson was Adams's chief rival for the presidency. The election revealed one of the most significant philosophical and political divisions in American history—that between Federalists and Republicans (see box). Federalists believed in a strong central government that exercised financial and commercial powers. On the other hand, Republicans believed that individual states should exercise governmental power. Adams believed in a moderate Federalism, while Jefferson supported the Republican view of government. Adams defeated Jefferson, who became his vice president. The Adamses were the first presidential family to live in the new White House, moving in while the paint was still wet.

During his term as president, Adams helped the new government continue in an orderly manner, but his job was full of difficulties, both at home and abroad. His major challenge involved relations between the United States and France. During Adams's first term, the French, who were at war with Great Britain, grew angry with the United States. They believed the young nation had broken its agreement to serve as a French ally. They ordered that all American ships be captured and that American seamen found on British ships be treated as pirates.

In an incident called the "XYZ Affair" (1797–98), Adams sent three representatives to Paris to try to improve America's troubled relationship with the French. They were met there by three French agents whom the Americans referred to as "X, Y, and Z" in their official messages to Adams. The Americans returned home saying that the French foreign minister refused to deal with them unless they paid him $250,000 and agreed to loan France $10 million.

A threat of war

When Adams reported the French insult, the American people were furious and rallied around him. Congress autho-

Early American Political Parties

With a new constitution and a new national government in place by 1789, it was natural that citizens would organize political parties in order to express their views, and, of course, the parties often disagreed on how the new government should be run.

The Federalists

The group of colonists who had led the movement to create a constitution for the United States formed the Federalist Party. Its membership included people such as John Adams and Alexander Hamilton, a soldier, political leader, economist, and officer in the Continental army. The Federalist Party supported Hamilton's belief in a strong central government and a strong court system and was in favor of a financial system he developed, which was designed to strengthen the federal government and create a national bank.

Hamilton and most other Federalists wanted the country to be run by its wealthiest and best-educated citizens. Adams disagreed with this position of his fellow party members. The Federalists also believed that the United States should not become involved in international affairs—including wars. Adams disagreed. With the election of Republican Thomas Jefferson to the presidency in 1800, the Federalist party lost its popularity and power, never to regain it.

The Republicans

The chief opponents of the Federalist Party were first known as the anti-Federalists and later as the Republican Party. Thomas Jefferson led the Republican Party, whose members called themselves the party of the common man.

By 1820 the Republicans had broken into two separate groups: the National Republican Party, later called the Whig Party, and their opposition, called the Democratic Party. The two parties differed on such issues as the rights of the individual states, taxes on goods that came into and out of the country, and a national treasury system. The National Republicans were made up largely of people from the eastern part of America. The Democratic Party was made up mostly of people from southern and western America.

rized the building of new warships and the raising of an army against the French. At Adams's urging, a series of emergency measures, called the Alien and Sedition Acts, was passed to frighten foreign spies into leaving the country and to silence newspaper editors who opposed the war preparations.

Adams was pressured by members of the Republican Party, led by Jefferson. Republicans said it was wrong for the president to try to silence those who objected to his war policies. Adams also faced troubles from members of his own Federalist Party, who urged him to go forward at once with a war. Even without a formal declaration of war, in 1798 hostilities began at sea between America and France. But things soon cooled on both sides of the Atlantic Ocean, and a peace agreement was finally reached between the two countries.

Retires from public life

Alexander Hamilton (see entry), a member of the Federalist Party like Adams, was furious at the president for sending a peace mission to France. But Adams was fiercely independent and sometimes decided issues on what he thought was good for the country rather than on what his party wanted. The Federalist Party was divided on the French question during the election of 1800, and Adams lost the election to the Republican, Jefferson, by just a few votes.

The defeated Adams, then sixty-six years old, returned to Quincy, Massachusetts, with his wife, Abigail. There he tended his farm, enjoyed his friends and family, and wrote his autobiography. The letters he exchanged with Jefferson during those years provide an excellent portrait of the early nineteenth century. Adams was deeply saddened by the loss of his wife to typhoid fever in 1818. But he took pride in witnessing his son, John Quincy Adams, take the oath of office as the sixth president of the United States in 1824.

On July 4, 1826, the fiftieth anniversary of the Declaration of Independence, ninety-year-old John Adams died at his home. Taking comfort in the idea that the new country was left in good hands, his last words were, "The country is safe. Thomas Jefferson survives." He did not know that the other American hero had died just a few hours earlier.

For More Information

Bowen, Catherine Drinker. *John Adams and the American Revolution.* Boston: Little, Brown, 1950.

Brill, Marlene Targ. *John Adams: Second President of the United States.* Chicago: Children's Press, 1986.

Butterfield, L. H., March Friedlaender, and Mary-Jo Klein, eds. *The Book of Abigail and John: Selected Letters of the Adams Family, 1762–1784.* Cambridge, MA: Harvard University Press, 1975.

Peabody, James Bishop, ed. *John Adams: A Biography in His Own Words.* New York: Newsweek, 1973.

Lukes, Bonnie L. *The Boston Massacre.* San Diego: Lucent Books, 1998.

Sandak, Cass R. *The John Adamses.* New York: Crestwood, 1992.

Smith, Page. *John Adams.* New York: Doubleday, 1962.

Samuel Adams

Born September 27, 1722
Boston, Massachusetts
Died October 2, 1803
Boston, Massachusetts

Political leader, governor of Massachusetts, brewer, publisher

Samuel Adams was a leading organizer of the independence movement in Massachusetts and the other American colonies that culminated in the Revolutionary War and the creation of the United States of America. Though he was an outstanding writer, speaker, and planner, he kept himself so far in the background that historians have found it difficult to determine the total scope of his contributions to the birth of the nation.

Samuel Adams was the son of a generous beer brewer, also named Samuel, and Mary Fifield Adams, his religious wife. Mary Adams passed her Puritan beliefs on to her three children—Samuel, his older sister Mary, and younger brother Joseph. A well-mannered, heavyset boy, Samuel Adams had dark blue-gray eyes, heavy eyebrows, and a large head. At the Boston Latin School, he learned to read, write, and do basic arithmetic. Throughout his life his friends and family called him Samuel; only strangers and people who were making fun of him referred to him as "Sam."

Adams's dislike for the British government began in his childhood, when England ruled the colonies. The Adams's house was the meeting place of a group called the Caucus Club. The members of the Caucus Club sought more political power for the colonists, and young Adams was encouraged to take part in its discussions.

In 1736 Samuel Adams entered what is now Harvard University in Cambridge, Massachusetts. In 1741, when Adams was eighteen, British-appointed governor John Belcher declared illegal the land bank founded by the elder Samuel. The Adams family lost all their money, and Adams had to take a job as a waiter to pay his way through college. Adams did not take kindly to this injustice, and this strengthened his belief that the governor held too much power over the colonists.

Marries, becomes tax collector

Adams earned a Master of Arts degree in 1743, at age twenty-one, and went on to an unsuccessful career in the field of accounting. The friend of his father who had employed young Samuel told the older man that his son seemed to take no interest in the business. Then Samuel's father gave him a large sum of money to start a new business. But the young man lent half of it to a friend, never asking to be repaid, and frittered away the rest. Samuel gained a reputation for being unable to make or hold on to money. He preferred to spend his time discussing how America must become independent of England.

Accounts of the time describe Adams as about five feet six inches tall, with a large head, dark eyes, and a musical voice. Adams had no interest in fashion and wore shabby clothing and shoes. His real interests lay in politics. In 1747 Adams and several friends began the Whipping Post Club, a political organization that published a newspaper, *The Public Advertiser,* written largely by Adams. Its self-proclaimed purpose was to "defend the rights ... of working people." Samuel sharpened his skills as a writer and became well known as a defender of colonial rights.

In 1748 Adams's father died, and he became responsible for taking care of his mother and the family brewing business. Samuel Adams married his first wife, Elizabeth Checkley, in 1749. They had six children, but only young Samuel and Hannah survived to adulthood. Over the years, Adams's neglect of the family's once-successful brewing business led to its decline. The family was happy despite being rather poor.

Adams was appointed Boston commissioner of garbage collection in 1753, and in 1756 was elected one of five tax collectors for the city. Though he did a poor job demanding unpaid taxes, the popular Adams was reelected and held the post of tax collector for the eight years that followed.

Remarries, begins patriotic work

In 1757 Elizabeth Adams died, a few weeks after giving birth to a baby that died at birth. The following year Adams nearly lost the house he had inherited from his father because he was unable to pay the debts he had also inherited.

In 1764 Adams married Elizabeth "Betsy" Wells, the daughter of a family friend. Betsy loved her kind but financially unsuccessful husband. Sometimes she had to accept food and secondhand clothing from concerned neighbors. Though Adams was not financially savvy, he was very knowledgeable when it came to politics. By 1765 Adams had become known as a speaker who stirred up political resistance to England through speeches in taverns and at informal meetings around Boston.

Colonists oppose Stamp Act

During the 1760s money conflicts arose between England and the American colonists. From 1754 to 1763 American colonists had aided England in the French and Indian War, in which France and its Indian allies fought against England over who would control North America. After England won the war in 1763, its flag flew over Canada and a vast area east of the Mississippi River. England was faced with a huge war debt, however, and the British believed that the colonists should help to pay for the war.

In March 1765 the British government passed the Stamp Act, which required colonists to buy stamps and place them on most paper documents and products. The shocked colonists thought that England should be grateful to them for helping win the war. Instead, Americans were being punished with taxes. Later that year Adams was elected to the Massachusetts House of Representatives. To protest the Stamp Act, he began a successful campaign to halt the sale of any British-made goods in Massachusetts. In time the campaign spread to the other colonies. Adams and his supporters hoped that big money losses would turn British merchants against their own government.

Adams works to end the Stamp Act

Adams went around Boston persuading working people to join the Sons of Liberty, an organization he had founded to fight for American rights. The group, which eventually numbered three hundred, sometimes engaged in disruptive activities that the British considered illegal. For that reason, Adams stayed away from the group's public gatherings, although everyone in Boston knew he was its head. Adams preferred to stay in the background, writing articles and organizing demonstrations.

In May 1766 word reached Boston that the Stamp Act had been repealed by the British at the urging of British merchants whose businesses had been suffering. All of Boston celebrated what would prove to be a short-lived victory.

Increases efforts to defy British

In 1767 the British placed new taxes on lead, glass, paint, paper, and tea, items widely used in the colonies. Adams spoke out against "taxation without representation." He said that Parliament, England's law-making body, had no right to tax Americans because the colonists had no representation in Parliament. Massachusetts's law-making body then adopted the Massachusetts Circular Letter, an appeal for the colonies to oppose all new taxes. Copies were sent to all the colonies. A wave of sometimes-violent protests soon broke out throughout the land, especially in Boston.

British officials in America demanded that England send troops to help keep the peace. In the summer of 1768, redcoats (British soldiers, who wore red uniform coats) arrived in Boston. When the citizens of Boston refused to find places to house them, they marched to Boston Common, the popular public park, and set up their tents. By several months later, the number of redcoats had swelled to three thousand, quite a large number in a town of sixteen thousand people. Settled in for the winter, they had very little to do but hang about. Boston residents found their presence increasingly annoying and tensions continued to rise.

In 1768 Adams started a newspaper, the *Journal of Events,* which voiced his opposition to British rule. Throughout his lifetime, Adams wrote letters to newspapers, using a variety of pen names. He wrote stories about redcoats beating up "innocent" citizens and attacking young women. Although most Boston readers knew many of his stories were overstated, they were reprinted throughout the colonies, and many people outside Boston accepted them as truth.

Publicizes Boston Massacre, loses popularity

On March 5, 1770, a violent encounter took place between a group of Boston men and boys and some British soldiers, resulting in the death of five patriots and the wounding of others. Bostonians demanded that the eight redcoats be placed on trial. Adams surprised his supporters by arranging to have his cousin, **John Adams** (see entry), and Josiah Quincy, two well-respected American lawyers, defend the British soldiers in court.

Why did he do this? Some people believe that he thought death sentences for these British soldiers were a certainty, but his gesture would show England that Bostonians could be just and fair-minded people. In the end, none of the British soldiers was found guilty of murder. Six were found not guilty, and two were found guilty of manslaughter (killing of a human being without any bad intent), a charge less than murder, and were punished by being branded on their thumbs. In his diaries, John Adams wrote of his second cousin, Samuel: "He is a Man of stedfast Integrity, exquisite Humanity, genteel [learning], ... engaging manners, reason as well as professed [devotion to religion], and a universal good character."

Adams named the bloody battle between the British soldiers and the patriots the "Boston Massacre" and publicized the story. He and a group of townspeople succeeded in their demands that the British-appointed governor, Thomas Hutchinson, order all British soldiers out of Boston.

On April 12, 1770, the British Parliament did away with all colonial taxes except the tax on tea. Within a few years, even Boston voted to end the boycott of most British goods, except tea. A boycott is a refusal to buy, sell, or use certain products from a particular person, company, or country, usually for a political reason. Adams continued to send letters to newspapers calling for American independence. Some people, who now felt secure from further unfair treatment by the British, began calling him and his ideas "old-fashioned."

Nonetheless, Adams kept working. At his request, the town of Boston appointed a Committee of Correspondence to state the rights of the colonists and publicize them throughout the colonies. In a short time, many such letter-writing networks were set up, and the move toward colonial unity advanced.

Tax rebellion continues

Years went by, and the colonists continued to boycott British tea. In 1773, with a large quantity of unsold tea piling up, the British Parliament passed the Tea Act. It cut the price of British tea for Americans in half, while still keeping a tax on tea. The British believed wrongly that having tea and saving money would prove more important to the colonists than their concerns about taxation without representation. Instead, the Tea Act made the colonists furious. At public protests, Americans pledged not to purchase any English tea. As word spread of England's latest attempt at taxation, Adams became fashionable again, and his letters to newspapers throughout the colonies were widely quoted.

The British went forward with their plan to supply the colonies with tea. In December 1773 three ships loaded with containers of tea entered Boston Harbor. Members of the Sons of Liberty were posted at the dock to make sure that none of the tea came ashore. On December 16, at a Boston town meeting, more than seven thousand citizens decided to make a final request that the ships and their cargo be sent back to England. British officials refused.

The Boston "Tea Party"

A group of forty or fifty men, disguised as Native Americans to protect their identities, went to Boston's dock area. Crying "Boston Harbor a teapot tonight!" they boarded the ships by torchlight and dumped about 340 chests of tea (which would be worth nearly $100,000 today) into Boston Harbor. Adams, who had helped plan the protest, called it "the grandest event which has ever yet happened since the controversy with England opened."

Other such "tea parties" took place throughout the American colonies in 1774. Parliament punished the Americans through a series of measures the colonists called the Intolerable Acts. They barred all ships from entering the harbor until Boston paid for the lost tea. The people of Boston were placed under the command of a military governor, General **Thomas Gage** (see entry), and his soldiers. Citizens were forced to house and feed the soldiers out of their own pockets, and town meetings were outlawed.

Adams worked hard to convince the other colonies that Boston's punishment was a blow to all of them. With Boston Harbor closed, little food could come into the city. Other colonies came to the rescue by sending food over land to Boston. For the first time in colonial history, people seized on the idea of forming a congress made up of representatives of all the colonies.

First Continental Congress

The idea of a congress grew like wildfire. Adams was one of those chosen by the Massachusetts House of Representatives to represent Massachusetts at the congress, which met for the first time on September 5, 1774, in Philadelphia, Pennsylvania. The main order of business was to decide what to do about the conflict with England.

While some, like Adams, wanted to see a complete change in the government, others, such as **George Washington** (see entry) of Virginia, wanted to make only minor and gradual changes. The majority of the representatives sought a middle ground. Some delegates from the southern colonies feared that those from Massachusetts wanted to take over the country. Other delegates thought that only the wealthy and well educated should be in charge of the government. Many delegates feared independence because it might ruin the established system of trade and cause rivalries to break out among the different colonies. Instead of breaking ties with England, they wanted to find a way to restore good relations with the mother country. Realizing it was too soon to talk of independence, Adams said little during most of the First Continental Congress.

The representatives at the Congress approved a series of measures that demanded the repeal of the Tea Act. Although they hoped to avoid war, the congress also urged the colonies to prepare for war, just in case it occurred, by training soldiers and gathering food and supplies. Delegates adopted a Declaration of Rights and Grievances (complaints) and promised to come to the aid of Massachusetts if it were attacked. The First Continental Congress agreed to forbid importation of British goods or the slaves they sought to sell, the use of any already imported British goods, and the export of goods to England. All counties, cities, and towns were to have committees of correspondence to ensure that these policies were carried out. Delegates hoped their united efforts would force England to restore their liberties.

King orders arms seizures

The First Continental Congress ended on October 16, 1774, after the participants agreed to meet again in May of the following year if the British failed to restore the colonists' rights. Adams returned to a Massachusetts now controlled by the Sons of Liberty; only the town of Boston remained under British control. Adams knew that the colony was on the brink of war but urged his men to remain cautious because the time was not yet right for war.

Early in 1775, after he heard the demands of the First Continental Congress, King **George III** of England proclaimed Massachusetts to be in a state of rebellion. He ordered soldiers to seize all firearms and gunpowder that were in the hands of the colonists and to arrest all rebel leaders. Redcoats searched Boston for hidden cannons. Fearing that he and his men might be arrested and hanged, Adams fled with his fellow patriot, **John Hancock** (see entries), to Lexington, Massachusetts.

On April 18, 1775, **Paul Revere** (see entry) made his famous ride through the countryside of Massachusetts. He stopped at the home where the two men were hiding to warn

A statue of Samuel Adams stands before Faneuil Hall in Boston, Adams's hometown and the heart of the American Revolution.
Photo © Dave G. Houser. Reproduced by permission of the Corbis Corporation (Bellevue).

them that the British were on their way to arrest them. Later Adams wrote about the battles of Lexington and Concord and "the shot heard round the world."

Congress meets; Adams does war work

Adams and Hancock made their way to Philadelphia, where the Second Continental Congress met beginning on May 10, 1775. Armed conflict had occurred only weeks before between the British and the colonists at Lexington and Concord. But there was still a great deal of disagreement among the colonists as to whether or not they should declare their independence from England.

The congress formed a committee to write the Articles of Confederation, which would be the blueprint for a new American government. Though he was a member of the committee, Adams spent most of his time trying to persuade other delegates to vote for independence. He also encouraged the formation of a Continental army. After more than a year's efforts, Adams succeeded in getting George Washington named its commander-in-chief. Adams was among the fifty men who signed the Declaration of Independence on July 4, 1776, marking the birth of a new nation.

During the early part of the Revolutionary War, Adams served as chairman of the Committee on the State of the Northern Army, even though he had no military experience. In 1777 he became ill and went home to Massachusetts to recover. Adams returned to Philadelphia in early 1779 to join the Continental Congress. He returned to Boston in mid-1779 to find his family living in poverty because their home had been taken over by British soldiers. Adams, who was earning no money for his efforts on behalf of independence, could not help them.

In 1779 and 1780 Samuel Adams worked with his cousin, John Adams, and others to write the Massachusetts State Constitution, which became law in 1780. Soon after, Adams ran for the new office of First Secretary of Massachusetts, but he lost. He then went to work to help raise money from the various states to support the Continental army, which was seriously short of funds.

In 1781 Adams was elected to the Massachusetts Senate, where he served for several years as president, earning a small salary. He used money he had inherited from his family to purchase the Peacock Tavern and forty acres of land in a town outside Boston. The tavern business provided him an income of $1,000 per year, greatly improving his family's living conditions.

Serves in Massachusetts's government

On September 3, 1783, the United States and England signed the Treaty of Paris, which ended the Revolutionary War with victory for the United States. In 1787 a new U.S. Constitution was written, and in 1788 Adams was among the representatives who passed it. Adams argued for a bill of rights to be attached to the constitution, guaranteeing such basic rights as freedom of religion and freedom of speech. In 1791 the Bill of Rights was added to the U.S. Constitution.

In 1789 Adams was elected lieutenant governor of Massachusetts and served for four years. Upon the death of Massachusetts governor John Hancock in 1793, seventy-two-year-old Adams became the governor. Adams held the post until 1797, putting in long hours each day. When George Washington retired from the U.S. presidency after two terms, Adams ran for the office, capturing the fifth-highest number of votes. He lost to his cousin, John Adams, and **Thomas Jefferson** (see entry), who were elected president and vice president.

Final years

Adams retired from public life in January 1797. For the next several years he relaxed with his family, although people continued to seek him out and ask for his advice. He enjoyed looking back at the time of the revolution. He died on October 2, 1803, in Boston. Although Adams had requested a simple ceremony, he was given an elaborate funeral. Throughout Boston shops were closed, bells were rung, cannons were fired, and flags were flown at half-mast. Adams was buried at Boston's Old Granary Burying Ground. For centuries, visitors have gone there to pay their respects to the founding father whom Thomas Jefferson once called "the Man of the Revolution."

For More Information

Farley, Karin Clafford, and James P. Shenton. *Samuel Adams: Grandfather of His Country*. Austin, TX: Raintree Steck-Vaughn Publishers, 1994.

Fradin, Dennis. *Samuel Adams: The Father of American Independence*. New York: Clarion Books, 1998.

Fritz, Jean. *Why Don't You Get a Horse, Sam Adams?* New York: Coward, McCann & Geoghegan, 1974.

Miller, John C. *Sam Adams: Pioneer in Propaganda*. Boston: Little, Brown, 1936.

Peabody, James Bishop, ed. *John Adams: A Biography in His Own Words*. New York: Newsweek Books, 1973.

Phelan, Mary Kay. *The Story of the Boston Tea Party*. New York: Thomas Y. Crowell, 1973.

Ethan Allen

Born January 21, 1738
Litchfield, Connecticut
Died February 12, 1789
Burlington, Vermont

Military leader, businessman, writer

The fiery Ethan Allen was one of the first heroes of the American Revolution. He is remembered for leading a small group of soldiers against the British at Fort Ticonderoga, New York, in May 1775, and winning the surrender of the fort with no bloodshed. He is honored as the folk-hero of Vermont for strongly promoting its statehood and representing Vermonters' independent spirit.

Little is known about the early life of Ethan Allen. He was born in Connecticut in 1738, one of eight children of Joseph and Mary Baker Allen. His father died when the boy was preparing for college in 1755, cutting short his education and forcing him to take over as head of the large Allen family. In 1757 the young man took part in the French and Indian War (1754–63), which was fought between England and France to determine who would control North America. Allen and his brothers joined a group of soldiers formed to defend nearby Fort William Henry.

"In the name of the Great Jehovah and the Continental Congress!"

Ethan Allen's legendary reply to a British officer asking him by whose authority he had entered the British-held Fort Ticonderoga

Portrait: Ethan Allen.

Colonists in land dispute

Allen saw little military action in the conflict. Upon his return home, he went to work mining iron ore and using it to mold large kettles to sell. In 1762 Allen married Mary Bronson and the couple moved to New Hampshire Grants (as Vermont was then known). Allen and other of his family members purchased land there, both for farming and to sell at a profit. They started a real estate company called the Onion River Land Company. Allen, who loved reading and learning, furthered his education by borrowing books from his neighbor, Thomas Young, a well-educated physician, who enjoyed engaging Allen in conversation.

Not long after settling in New Hampshire Grants, the Allen family became involved in disputes over land ownership. Because of a confusing system of land grants from the British government, both New York and New Hampshire claimed authority over the land where the Allens had settled. In part because of high taxes imposed by New York on settlers in New Hampshire Grants, the Allens supported New Hampshire in the dispute. Ethan Allen and his brothers soon became leaders of a group of like-minded New England settlers in New Hampshire Grants.

The Green Mountain Boys

In 1770, as the land dispute raged, the Allen brothers raised a small force of rough-and-tumble fighters they called the Green Mountain Boys. These citizen soldiers strove to protect their rights and their chances of keeping their land in the area that would later become known as Vermont. Ethan Allen led the Green Mountain Boys in attacks on "Yorkers" (settlers from New York) over the land issue. New York's Governor William Tryon was upset enough to offer a substantial reward for Allen's capture, but the wily Allen managed to avoid being caught.

Jen Fritz, in her book *Traitor: The Case of Benedict Arnold*, describes Allen the soldier as a "tall man with a flashy style, [who] dressed in a green jacket with enormous gold epaulets [ornaments on the shoulder] and carried an oversized sword at his side. He wasn't much on drilling or the fine points of military procedure but he didn't need to be. When he was ready to go, he just said, 'Come on, boys,' and his men, backwoods farmers, came along."

The "Boys" capture "Fort Ti"

When the Revolutionary War (1775–83) broke out and Americans declared their independence from England, Allen turned the Green Mountain Boys into an independent organization of American patriots (a regular American army had not yet been formed). Allen and his men were joined in a historic raid by **Benedict Arnold** (see entry), who later gained attention as America's most famous traitor. At dawn on May 10, 1775, they captured Fort Ticonderoga on Lake George in upper New York from its astonished British commander.

Historian James L. Stokesbury wrote in *A Short History of the American Revolution* that when the Americans rushed the fort on that stormy morning, "opposition was almost nonexistent, and the actual taking of the place consisted largely of shouting and haranguing [arguing] between the American leaders and the two British officers in the post, which was held by a mere 48 men." Allen himself later described the defending troops there as "old, wore out, and unserviceable." They took the fort without a single shot being fired. Ticonderoga was the first British-owned fort to fall to the American colonists.

The fort was important because it was a storehouse of guns and ammunition, which were badly needed by the Americans. Its captured cannon later allowed **George Washington** (see entry) to drive the British troops out of Boston, Massachusetts. After Allen's triumph, he and his men took the lesser post at New York's Crown Point. They also tried to capture St. Johns, Canada, but were unsuccessful.

Capture, confinement, and parole

In the summer of 1775, the Green Mountain Boys were combined with troops from New York and placed under the

Ethan Allen taking Fort Ticonderoga, New York. Allen and his Green Mountain Boys faced little resistance from the British troops stationed there. *Reproduced courtesy of the Library of Congress.*

command of General P. J. Schuyler of the Continental army, newly formed to defend the American colonies from the British. But when it came time to elect a head of the Green Mountain Boys unit, Ethan Allen was not chosen.

Edwin P. Hoyt described what happened during the voting in *The Damndest Yankees: Ethan Allen & His Clan:* "All Ethan's enemies came out of the woods.... He had trod on the toes of the churches [shocking some of their members by his unrestrained behavior]. He had punished several respected citizens for their [sympathy with the Yorkers]. And now these enemies ... saw a chance to strike back at Ethan Allen for his high and mighty ways of the past." Their votes defeated Ethan Allen and placed his cousin, Seth Warner, in charge of the Boys.

Upset by this rejection, Allen gathered up some men and, on his own authority, boldly tried to capture Montreal, Quebec, before the arrival of the main section of the Continental army. He was captured by the British almost at once, put in chains, and shipped to Great Britain, where he was kept prisoner in Pendennis Castle and then sent to Ireland. There he astonished the locals with his enormous size, flowing uncut hair, red stocking cap, and fringed jacket.

Fearing that if they hanged Allen his American followers would take revenge on British captives, the British returned him to America. He was paroled (released from captivity by promising to abide by the conditions set forth by his captors) in New York City in October 1776.

Attains freedom, goes to Vermont

For a while, Allen lived comfortably in New York City on money loaned to him by his brother until the British jailed him for violating his parole. Alexander Graydon, who was a prisoner in New York at the same time as Allen, wrote about his fellow prisoner in his *Memoirs:* "His figure was that of a robust, large-framed man, worn down by confinement ... I have seldom met a man, possessing, in my opinion, a stronger mind, or whose mode of expressions was more [passionate and well-spoken]. His style [combined vulgarity and] phrases [from the Bible], and ... he appeared to me to be a man of generosity and honor."

In early May 1778 the British exchanged Allen for Archibald Campbell, one of their men being held by the Amer-

Ira Allen, Brother of Ethan

Ira Allen was nearly as famous as his older brother Ethan. Born in 1751, he was one of the early Vermont revolutionaries and was appointed to various high positions in its independent government. He served as Vermont's first treasurer and surveyor general.

A partner with Ethan Allen in the Onion River Land Company, Ira developed land for industrial use. He later founded the University of Vermont and designed the Vermont State Seal. Ira Allen played a large role in the discussions of whether to make Vermont a part of Canada.

In 1795, Ira traveled to Europe to purchase guns for the Vermont militia. But he also planned to sell any excess guns he obtained for a healthy profit to pay off his own personal debts. At that time, England and France were at war. In France, Ira purchased thousands of dollars' worth of cannons and shotguns. He then went to London and chartered an American ship, the *Olive Branch,* and loaded it with his cargo of weapons.

Fearing that Allen might be working on behalf of the French, the British seized the ship with all its cargo before it could reach Vermont. As a result, Ira became poor overnight. He left his beloved Vermont in 1803 and spent the years before his death in 1814 living in poverty in Philadelphia, Pennsylvania.

icans. Allen then traveled to Valley Forge, Pennsylvania, where he reported to General George Washington. He was made a colonel in the Continental army "in reward for his fortitude, firmness and zeal in the cause of his country, manifested during his long and cruel captivity, as well as on former occasions." Allen wrote about the experience in his popular book *Narrative of Colonel Ethan Allen's Captivity,* which was published in 1779.

Works for Vermont statehood

In 1779 Ethan Allen returned to the newly formed Republic of Vermont, which had just declared its independence but was not yet recognized by the Continental Congress, America's governing body at the time. By that time, Allen was widely recognized as the most powerful man in Vermont. He and his younger brother, Ira (see box), made efforts to ensure that the new colony stayed independent. Ethan wrote pamphlets, newspaper articles, and letters to Congress arguing the subject.

In 1779 the northeastern area of the United States was still in danger of a British assault from Canada. In addition, New York continued to block Vermont's attempts to be admitted as a state. The British tried to make a deal with the Allens to make Vermont part of Canada, and thus ensure its independent status, but no such deal was finalized.

American troops defeated the British once and for all at Yorktown, New York, in 1781. This brought to an end the negotiations between Allen and the British over the future of Vermont. Later, Allen was accused of betraying his country for engaging in the talks, but in time the charges were dropped. Historians disagree as to whether or not Allen sincerely considered making Vermont part of Canada. Some say he merely pretended to do so to threaten Congress with what could happen if they did not grant Vermont statehood.

Remarriage and a failed book

By the end of the war, the Allen family owned more than 100,000 acres of Vermont land, which they began selling on a large scale. Members of the Allen family were the first explorers of many portions of the state and the first to determine its boundaries. They developed the land by building sawmills and gristmills (where wheat was ground). Although they succeeded in opening up the northern part of Vermont, in the end the land company they started proved to be the financial ruin of many of the Allens.

In 1783 Mary Bronson Allen, mother of Ethan Allen's five children, died. The next year, he quit politics and married Frances Buchanan, a young widow by whom he had three more children. Allen built up an impressive farm on what is now Burlington's Winooski River.

Allen was a believer in the Deist (pronounced DEE-uhst) religion, which worshiped nature as its god. His views on life were published in a witty 1784 book called *Reason, the Only Oracle of Man*, which became known as *Ethan Allen's Bible*.

In his book Allen attacked American clergymen for failing to recognize the dignity of the common man. The book sold few copies but gained a lot of publicity when various churchmen attacked it during their church services. *Reason* became a rare book because many copies were burned in a fire, while many others were destroyed by the book's publisher, who decided the book was anti-God.

Final years

In 1787, when Ethan Allen was fifty-one, his health began to fail. Still, he insisted on working on his farm in Bennington, Vermont, and overseeing the building of a new house in Burlington, which weakened him further. Allen died at his new home on February 12, 1789. Many of his Green Mountain Boys took part in his funeral procession, which was accompanied by muffled drum beats and cannon fire.

At the time of Allen's death in 1789, Vermont was still independent, but had not yet attained statehood. In time, New York dropped its claims on Vermont when it realized that Vermont's vote as a state could help preserve the power of the northern states in Congress. Vermont became the fourteenth state of the United States in 1791, two years after Ethan Allen's death.

For More Information

Boatner, Mark M. "Allen, Ethan" in *Encyclopedia of the American Revolution*. Mechanicsburg, PA, Stackpole Books, 1994, pp. 17-18.

Fritz, Jean. *Traitor: The Case of Benedict Arnold*. New York: G. P. Putnam's Sons, 1981, pp. 29-30.

Graydon, Alexander. *Memoirs of a Life Chiefly Passed in Pennsylvania*. Self-published, Harrisburg, Pennsylvania, 1811.

Holbrook, Stewart. *America's Ethan Allen*. Boston: Houghton Mifflin Co., 1949.

Hoyt, Edwin P. *The Damndest Yankees: Ethan Allen & His Clan*. Brattleboro, VT: The Stephen Greene Press, 1975.

Pell, John. *Ethan Allen*. Boston: Houghton Mifflin Co., 1929.

Stokesbury, James L. *A Short History of the American Revolution*. New York: William Morrow & Co., 1991, pp. 52-53.

Web Sites

"Ethan Allen History." [Online] Available http://www.uvm.edu/~dpayne/eallen/eahistory.html (accessed on 6/22/99).

Benedict Arnold

Born January 14, 1741
Norwich, Connecticut
Died June 14, 1801
London, England

Military leader, traitor

"Having made every sacrifice of fortune and blood, and become a cripple in the service of my country, I little expected to meet the ungrateful returns I have received from my countrymen."

Portrait: Benedict Arnold.
Reproduced by permission of the National Archives and Records Administration.

Benedict Arnold occupies a place in American history as the most famous traitor of Revolutionary times. In the early years of the American Revolution (1775–83), Arnold was known as a brave and skilled military planner who has been credited with the American victory at the Battle of Saratoga in New York. But over the years his contributions have been all but forgotten and his name has come to represent disloyalty to one's country.

Born in 1741, Benedict Arnold V was the son of Benedict Arnold IV, a businessman and landowner, and Hannah Waterman King, a stern and commanding woman. The first Benedict Arnold, who came to America in 1657, once served as the governor of Rhode Island.

When he was eleven years old, Benedict V's prosperous parents sent him away to school in Connecticut, where he studied Latin and mathematics. But his education was cut short when his troubled father lost the family fortune. Young Benedict became the subject of jokes after several incidents found him leading his drunken father home from local taverns. At about this time, the boy decided he must learn to be brave. He started picking on bigger boys to fight with, and began to perform daring feats like leaping over wagons in the roadway.

Early career, marriage

When he was about fourteen, young Arnold left home and went to work for a relative, learning the druggist trade. In his mid-teens, he volunteered to fight in three battles of the French and Indian War (1754–63), a conflict between France and England (won by England) to determine who would control the lands in America. He then deserted to be at his dying mother's bedside. When Arnold's father died in debt in 1761, the young man joined his sister Hannah in New Haven, Connecticut. Arnold's cousin paid the debts left by Benedict IV and set the young man up in a pharmacy business that soon became successful.

In Connecticut Arnold also found success as a sea captain, trading mostly horses and other livestock with Canada and the West Indies (an island chain extending from Florida to South America) and possibly smuggling. An energetic and restless man of average height, Arnold was very strong and muscular. He gained a reputation for getting into fistfights and reportedly twice took part in duels. The dark-haired, gray-eyed businessman married Margaret Mansfield in 1767, and within five years the couple had three children, with two more to follow.

Military exploits

When Arnold became a captain of New Haven's citizen soldiers in 1774, America was about to declare her independence and go to war with Great Britain. In 1775, Arnold marched his men to fight in Boston when he heard that the Revolutionary War had broken out. He took part in the capture of New York's Fort Ticonderoga (pronounced Tie-con-der-OH-guh), and led troops that used captured boats to take over the British fort at St. Johns, New Brunswick, Canada.

Arnold's wife died in 1775. Shortly thereafter, he commanded 1,000 troops on a stressful and finally unsuccessful campaign to capture Quebec, Canada. During the attempt, he received a serious leg wound that required months of recovery. Because of his strong leadership, Arnold was promoted to brigadier (pronounced BRIG-a-deer) general (a position just below major general), and in 1776 he commanded a fleet of ships, battling with British gunboats on Lake Champlain and at Valcour Island in New York. The battles that he helped to win there were of great importance in America's victory in the war.

Historian Carl Van Doren described Arnold's abilities as an officer: "He was original and [bold], quick in forming plans, quick in putting them into vigorous execution. He led his soldiers, not drove them, and held the devotion of the [soldiers under him].... But [when it came to dealing with] officers of rank equal or nearly equal with his, Arnold was [stubborn] and arrogant."

Ups and downs in the military

Arnold's hot temper and impatience earned him many enemies. In the winter of 1776–77, Americans who were his personal enemies accused him of misconduct and incompetence. It took the pleas of General George Washington to keep him from resigning from the army.

Arnold's reputation as a brave warrior grew in 1777 as he led an attack and drove British troops out of Danbury, Connecticut. Although he was then appointed major general, Arnold resented the fact that five of his junior officers had been promoted ahead of him. He protested, and as a result, George Washington changed the date of his promotion so Arnold would appear to have held the post of major general longer than the other five generals.

In 1777, a group of businessmen from Montreal, Canada, accused Arnold of stealing property from them. He was found innocent, but was so angry over the way he had been treated that he resigned from the military. Again Washington stepped in, and Arnold changed his mind and resumed his military duties. Arnold then played a major role in the defeat of British General **John Burgoyne** (see entry) at Saratoga, New York, where he was once again wounded seriously in the leg.

Arnold's leg was slow in healing this time, which prevented him from resuming command of his troops, so in 1778 George Washington made the mistake of appointing Arnold governor of the city of Philadelphia. Arnold soon demonstrated

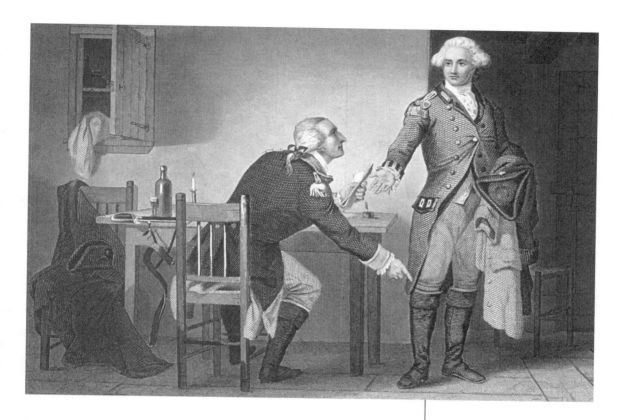

that he lacked the necessary patience and political skills for the job. However, he greatly enjoyed his new appointment, entertained on a grand scale, and used his government position to get involved in business deals that might have been illegal.

Marries again, is accused of corruption, commits treason

In 1779, thirty-eight-year-old Benedict Arnold married the young and beautiful Margaret Shippen, daughter of one of Philadelphia's leading families. The Shippens were suspected of maintaining loyalties to Great Britain. That same year, authorities in Pennsylvania charged Arnold with corruption and taking advantage of his official position for his own personal profit. Biographers suspect he may have needed money to support his new wife in the style she had grown up in. Arnold was sent to Washington to be court-martialed (pronounced COURT-mar-shulled). A court martial is a

Benedict Arnold betrayed Americans by offering military information to the British forces. Arnold passed information to British Major General John André, and suggested that the General conceal the information in his boot.
Reproduced by permission of Archive Photos, Inc.

How Historians See Benedict Arnold

Over the two centuries since Benedict Arnold's death, historians have argued about his true character. Some historians describe him as a monster, who took delight in robbing bird's nests when young and who later became a greedy, self-serving man who was all too eager to sell out his comrades.

But other historians point out that George Washington once called Arnold "the bravest of the brave" in the American Revolution. They observe that he courageously sacrificed his family life, financial security, and health and well being to engage in a conflict that left him physically handicapped and with his reputation smeared by false accusations. They insist his heroic actions must be remembered along with the fact of his treason. Others go so far as to contend that he was forced to become a traitor because he was mistreated and misunderstood by his fellow Americans.

Historian Mark M. Boatner provided an example of these differences of opinion in his *Encyclopedia of the American Revolution.* He wrote "while some writers credit Arnold with winning the two [Revolutionary War] battles of Saratoga almost single-handed, others question whether he was even on the field in the first battle and maintain that the second was won before he charged in to lead a costly, useless attack."

In the mid-twentieth century, new source material was found by historians that has helped them to get a more balanced view of the man, as both hero and traitor. James Kirby Martin, in his 1997 biography *Benedict Arnold, Revolutionary Hero,* wrote: "[Arnold's] treason was shocking because of the magnitude of his contribution to the Revolutionary effort." No doubt historians will continue to unravel the puzzle of this complicated historical figure far into the future.

trial conducted by military personnel for offenses against military law.

Arnold was found guilty of two of the charges against him, but as punishment he merely received a gentle reprimand from George Washington. By this time, though, Arnold was thoroughly angry at the treatment he had received from members of Congress and the military. He blamed them for his soiled reputation. Desperately in need of money, he began to entertain the idea of turning traitor and going to work for Great Britain.

In 1779, Arnold exchanged letters with British General Henry Clinton, and began passing information to the British about American troop movements and other matters in exchange for money. His wife Margaret helped him in his efforts, often acting as a messenger.

Turns traitor, fights former comrades

In 1780, Arnold, whose dealings with the enemy were still unknown to General Washington, talked his way into being appointed head of the fort at West Point on New York's Hudson River. Out of both greed and revenge for how he had been treated by the American military, he offered to hand West Point over to the British in exchange for a large sum of money. But when American soldiers captured British Major General John André later that year, the plan failed. André, who acted as a go-between for Arnold and the British, was court-martialed and hanged for spying.

In September 1780, Arnold escaped from the Americans unpunished and fled to the British. As a reward for assisting them, he was made a brigadier general in the British army. Wearing a British uniform, in 1781 Arnold led troops that burned Richmond, Virginia, and conducted raids against his former American comrades in Connecticut, burning the town of New London.

Life in Britain and in Canada

But Arnold was neither liked nor trusted by his new British comrades, who blamed him for the hanging of the popular Major André. As a general, Arnold was expected to round up British soldiers to serve under him, but he was not very successful at that task. So in December 1781, Arnold and his wife set sail for London, England. There King George III and other

Benedict Arnold's accomplice, British Major General John André, was court-martialed and hanged for spying.
Reproduced courtesy of the Library of Congress.

officials consulted with him on matters concerning America. Still, he felt disliked and neglected, and various business ventures he attempted ended in failure.

By 1785, eager to make money, Arnold moved to St. Johns, New Brunswick, Canada, and got involved in the shipping industry. Around 1786 a son, John Sage, was born to Arnold and a mother whose identity has gone undiscovered by historians.

In 1787, Arnold moved Margaret and their five children from Great Britain to Canada, where they were joined by his widowed sister, Hannah, and the sons from his first marriage. But the local people did not welcome the Arnolds and they never grew to feel part of the community. In 1791, Arnold, Margaret, and their children returned to England, while Hannah and Arnold's older sons returned to America.

Benedict Arnold's remaining years spent in England were unlucky ones. In 1792, Arnold's reputation was tarnished when he fought a duel with the Earl of Lauderdale, who had insulted him in the British House of Lords. Arnold shot but missed the Earl, who finally apologized to him. Arnold's fortunes suffered when he supplied materials for British military boats but lost money on the venture. About this time, he became seriously ill. Arnold suffered from asthma (pronounced AZ-muh, a disease that causes breathing difficulties) as well as swelling of the limbs, among other ailments. His wife said that near the end of his life he grew incapable of even the smallest enjoyment.

Benedict Arnold died on June 14, 1801, in London, leaving his family burdened with debts, lawsuits, and the disgrace of bearing the name of Arnold. Margaret Arnold died soon after in 1804. The couple's four sons went on to serve in the British Army. Benedict Arnold's oldest son by his first wife in America was killed in 1795 in the West Indies, while serving there as a military officer.

For More Information

Allison, Robert J. "Benedict Arnold." In *American Eras: The Revolutionary Era, 1754–1783*. Detroit: Gale, 1998, pp. 288-9.

Boatner, Mark M. "Arnold, Benedict," and "Arnold's Treason," *Encyclopedia of the American Revolution*. Mechanicsburg, Pennsylvania: Stackpole Books, 1994, pp. 25-43.

Brandt, Clare. *The Man in the Mirror: A Life of Benedict Arnold.* New York: Random House, 1994.

Fritz, Jean. *Traitor: The Case of Benedict Arnold.* New York: B. P. Putnam's Sons, 1981.

Martin, James Kirby. *Benedict Arnold, Revolutionary Warrior: An American Warrior Reconsidered.* New York: New York University Press, 1997.

Van Doren, Carl. *Secret History of the American Revolution.* New York: Viking Press, 1941.

Weigley, Russell F. "Arnold, Benedict." *Encyclopedia of American Biography,* second edition. John A. Garraty and Jerome L. Sternstein, eds. New York: HarperCollins, 1995, pp. 41-42.

Black Freedom Fighters

Crispus Attucks
Born 1723
Near Framingham,
Massachusetts
Died March 5, 1770
Boston, Massachusetts

Sailor, leader of the
Boston Massacre

James Forten
Born 1766
Philadelphia,
Pennsylvania
Died 1842
Philadelphia,
Pennsylvania

Sailor, sailmaker,
inventor, businessman,
social activist

Jehu Grant
Former slave

Salem Poor
Born c. 1758
Death date unknown

Soldier

Portrait: Crispus Attucks.
Reproduced courtesy of the
Library of Congress.

In the late eighteenth century, during the time of the American Revolution, black slaves were the second-largest labor force in America, second only to white farmers. The Dutch introduced the first African slaves to North America in 1619, but only about 20,500 had arrived by 1700. When the growing of tobacco, rice, and indigo (a plant that contains a substance used for making blue dye) took off in the 1700s, however, cheap labor was needed, and the importing of Africans began on a large scale. In the fifteen years before the beginning of the war, the slave trade forcibly brought nearly 100,000 Africans to America. Most came on British ships and were destined for Virginia and South Carolina. Newport, Rhode Island, was the major colonial center for importing slaves, but Rhode Islanders would trade rum for slaves, and then sell the slaves in the West Indies. By 1775, when the American Revolution began, the institution of slavery played a major role in the American economy. Although slavery was most widespread in the South, slaves made up roughly 10 percent of the population in New Jersey and New York.

The American Revolution marked a turning point in Americans' way of thinking about slavery. Americans protested against taxes imposed on them by the British to help support the British government and people, calling them unfair and an attack on their rights. As time went on, many colonists came to think it made little sense to be against unfair treatment by the British while at the same time enslaving other human beings themselves. American patriot James Otis posed the question on the minds of many Americans: "Is it right to enslave a man because he is black?" Still, slavery was to continue in America.

It was not until after the Revolutionary War that the men who wrote the Constitution agreed to end the transporting of slaves to North America by 1808. Still, Americans continued to own slaves and their offspring. It took the bloody Civil War (1861–65) to finally bring slavery to an end.

Blacks in the military during the American Revolution

Blacks both enslaved and free played an important role in the American Revolution. Those who sided with the colonists who wanted to break away from British rule fought in many important Revolutionary War battles, including at Ticonderoga in New York and at Lexington, Concord, and Bunker Hill in Massachusetts.

But very early on in the war, southern members of the Continental Congress (the early colonial legislature, with representatives from each of the colonies) began demanding an end to military participation by blacks. They opposed the idea of black men carrying weapons, fearing that slaves might revolt against their owners. Northerners, who might have opposed slavery but wanted a unified country to make war against Great Britain, joined the southerners in ordering General **George Washington** (see entry) to stop recruiting black soldiers. Then the British offered freedom to slaves who joined the British forces against the Americans. During the early part of the American Revolution, nearly one of every sixteen slaves ran away from their masters and joined the British forces.

Americans reacted to these events by reopening enlistment for free blacks, and later slaves, who would support their side. In the end, more than 5,000 black soldiers served on the American side during the war. Many served as foot soldiers, while some were gunners or fighters on horseback. There were quite a number of black seamen as well, and some served as navigators of ships.

Many slaves took advantage of wartime confusion to escape from their masters. Even some of George Washington's slaves fled, including Deborah Squash and her husband Harry, who sailed away on a British ship rather than live as slaves. Following the war, most of the northern states freed black slaves. But many white Americans simply forgot the contributions made by blacks, and not many stories of their bravery were preserved.

Four of the best-known blacks of the revolutionary period were Crispus Attucks, James Forten, Jehu Grant, and Salem Poor. Crispus Attucks participated in early colonial protests against the British and died from British gunfire in 1770 at the Boston Massacre (see **Samuel Adams** entry). James Forten, a sailor, became one of the outstanding leaders of the postwar antislavery movement in the United States. Salem Poor's brave deeds at the Battle of Bunker Hill were recorded for all time. Jehu Grant, a soldier, applied for but was denied payment from the federal government for his war service.

Crispus Attucks

Crispus Attucks was born in 1723, probably on an Indian reservation near Framingham, Massachusetts. He was thought to be of African, Native American, and white ancestry. The details of Attucks's youth are uncertain, but he was probably a Christian and may have once been a slave.

Some stories say Attucks was a crewman on a whaling ship. Sailor James Baily described him as being "a stout fellow, whose very looks were enough to terrify any person." Perhaps the fear he aroused was due to his size and a physical deformity: Mark M. Boatner described him as "gigantic" and "knock-kneed."

As the legend goes, on March 5, 1770, Attucks, about forty-seven years old, was part of a group of men who became annoyed with British soldiers on the streets of Boston, Massachusetts. The soldiers had been stationed there for nearly two years, trying to keep the peace against angry mobs who protested British taxation policies that they referred to as the

Intolerable Acts. Bostonians resented the soldiers' presence in their town.

On this occasion Attucks and the others started throwing snowballs at a British soldier. A British captain, fearing that the situation was becoming dangerous, called for a unit of guards to help the soldier. As the crowd grew more rowdy and began throwing stones, the soldiers fired on them. Eleven colonists were shot, three of whom died on the spot, and two more died later.

Attucks was among the three who died instantly, he of four gunshot wounds to the chest. Attucks and his companions were soon elevated to the status of heroes, but it is the name of Crispus Attucks that has gone down in history as the martyr of the Boston Massacre, the first man to have died in the fight for American independence.

The bodies of the five dead men were brought to Boston's Faneuil (pronounced FAN-yuhl) Hall, and a group of ten to twelve thousand Americans followed the funeral procession to the site where Attucks and three of the four others were buried together.

In the murder trial that followed, **John Adams** (see entry) defended the British soldiers. Though a patriot, he took up the unpopular cause of defending the soldiers because he believed that every man, regardless of his crime, had a right to a lawyer and a fair trial. At the trial witnesses disagreed as to whether or not Attucks had grabbed at the British soldier's weapon, and if the gun went off during the struggle that followed. Testimony also differed as to whether Attucks was fighting at the time, or merely leaning on a stick.

The British officer and his six men on trial for Attucks's murder were found not guilty. After Attucks's death, several black military units were named in his honor. In 1888 a monument to Attucks and the other victims of the massacre was erected at Boston Common, the city's public park.

Monument to Crispus Attucks, one of the first Americans to die in the fight for American independence.
Reproduced by permission of AP/Wide World Photos, Inc.

Portrait: James Forten.
Reproduced by permission of Charles L. Blockson Collection, Afro American Collection, Temple University.

James Forten

James Forten was born a free black in Philadelphia, Pennsylvania, in 1766. He briefly attended a school run by a Quaker (a member of a religious group that opposed slavery) but quit at the age of nine to work at a grocery store to help support his widowed mother. At age fifteen he enlisted in the Continental army, serving on the ship *Royal Louis*. The crew of two hundred included twenty black men.

When an English ship forced the *Royal Louis* to surrender, Forten was fearful. Black prisoners were often sold into slavery in the West Indies rather than being exchanged for white soldiers (the exchange of prisoners was a common practice at the time). Forten befriended the son of the British ship's captain, and the boy persuaded his father to offer Forten a chance to go and live in England. But Forten refused, saying "I am here a prisoner for the liberties of my country; I never, never, shall prove a traitor to her interests!"

Forten was sent to a British prison ship anchored off Long Island, New York. The overcrowded and rotting ship held more than one thousand prisoners. After seven months Forten was released from the prison ship during a general exchange of prisoners. Thousands of other men died on the ship during the course of the war.

Upon his release, Forten made his way to Trenton, New Jersey, where he learned to make sails. He began his own successful sailmaking business and became a wealthy man, returning to Philadelphia in 1798. Forten became a leader of Philadelphia's black community and donated large sums of money to the cause of black civil rights. Forten also donated money to the newspaper *The Liberator,* which spoke out in favor of the abolition of slavery. He supported a movement for American blacks to resettle in Africa and establish their own colony. As president of the American Moral Reform Society, he led a group of men who promoted education of blacks, the abolition of slavery, and ending the drinking of alcohol. Historians consider him one of the most important blacks of his day. Forten died in 1842 and was buried in Philadelphia.

Jehu Grant

Jehu (pronounced YAY-hoo) Grant was a runaway slave from Rhode Island. He served in the Continental army for about nine months during 1777, driving a team of oxen, before his master found him and forced him to return to the farm. In later years, Grant gained his freedom and became a citizen of Milton, Connecticut.

In 1832 the U.S. Congress passed a Pension Act, promising a pension (annual payment) to anyone who could prove he had served in the Revolutionary War. That same year Grant filed a claim for such a pension. For Grant, as for many black soldiers, only their memories of their experiences gave proof that they had served: there were no written records of their service. They were expected to report their experiences to a local court reporter, who then sent the records on to Washington, D.C., for further consideration.

Grant's claim was rejected. The army ruled that he had joined the military by stating falsely that he was free man; therefore, he was not entitled to a pension. Grant was angry at the ruling. With the help of a neighbor, he wrote a letter to the army board defending his right to a pension. He wrote of how he chose to become a soldier as a young man: "I was then grown to manhood, in the full vigor and strength of life ... when I saw liberty poles and the people all engaged for the support of freedom, I could not but like and be pleased with such a thing (God forgive me if I sinned in so feeling)." But the board failed to heed his request, and the old and then-blind Grant died in poverty.

Salem Poor

Salem Poor was born a free man in Massachusetts around 1758. He married while a young man but soon left his wife to enlist in the Massachusetts militia, a military force consisting of citizens rather than professional soldiers. When the

Revolutionary War broke out in 1775, Poor began fighting for the patriot forces in Boston, Massachusetts.

On June 17, 1775, the twenty-eight-year-old Poor fought at the Battle of Bunker Hill, where he helped to turn back the British. Some historians claim that he killed British Colonel James Abercrombie there. Other brave black soldiers who took part in the battle included Pomp Fisk and George Middleton.

That very same month, General George Washington issued an order that black soldiers would no longer be allowed to serve in the military. But he allowed those already fighting, like Poor, to finish their tours of duty. After Washington reversed his ruling at the end of 1775, Poor reenlisted. He fought at the Battle of White Plains in New York and spent the difficult winter of 1776 with Washington's forces at Valley Forge, Pennsylvania.

On December 5, 1775, fourteen Massachusetts army officers signed a petition stating that Poor "behaved like an Experienced Officer, as Well as ... a Brave & gallant soldier." The officers suggested that Poor be paid a reward for his courageous action, but there is no record that he ever received such a payment. Unfortunately, no other information exists regarding the events of Poor's later life.

For More Information

Asante, Molefi K., and Mark T. Mattson. *Historical and Cultural Atlas of African Americans*. New York: Macmillan, 1991, pp. 182–83.

Boatner, Mark M. "Crispus Attucks" in *Encyclopedia of the American Revolution*. Mechanicsburg, PA: Stackpole Books, 1994, p. 49.

Chapelle, Suzanne Greene. "Afro-Americans and the American Revolution," edited by John Mack Faragher. *The Encyclopedia of Colonial and Revolutionary America*. New York: Facts on File, 1990, p. 6.

Curtis, Nancy C. *Black Heritage Sights: African American Odyssey and Finder's Guide*. Chicago: American Library Assn., 1996, pp. 299–300.

Greene, Robert Ewell. *Black Defenders of America, 1775–1973*. Chicago: Johnson Publishing Company, 1974, pp. 3–25.

Kaplan, Sidney, and Emma Nogrady Kaplan. *The Black Presence in the Era of the American Revolution*. Revised edition. Amherst: The University of Massachusetts Press, 1989, pp. 22–23, 50–52, 63–64.

Kranz, Rachel. "Forten, James [Sr.]" in *The Biographical Dictionary of Black Americans*. New York: Facts on File, 1980, p. 57.

Purvis, Thomas L. *Revolutionary America*. New York: Facts on File, 1995, pp. 122, 326.

Robinson, Greg. "Salem Poor" in *Encyclopedia of African-American Culture and History,* Vol. 4, edited by Jack Salzman, David Lionel Smith, and Cornel West. New York: Simon & Schuster, 1996, p. 2185.

Smythe, Mabel M., ed. *The Black American Reference Book.* Englewood Cliffs, New Jersey: Prentice-Hall, 1976, pp. 15–19.

Ward, Harry M. "Crispus Attucks" in *American National Biography,* edited by John A. Garraty and Mark C. Carnes. New York: Oxford University Press, 1999, p. 728.

Winch, Julie. "James Forten" in *American National Biography,* Vol. 8, edited by John A. Garraty and Mark C. Carnes. New York: Oxford University Press, 1999, pp. 276–77.

Web Sites

"Jehu Grant" in *Liberty! Chronicle of the Revolution.* [Online] Available http://www.pbs.orgb/ktca/liberty/chronicle/jehu.html (accessed May 16, 1999).

Joseph Brant

Born c. March 1742
Upper Ohio River (near present-day Akron, Ohio)
Died November 24, 1807
Grand River, Ontario, Canada

Mohawk war chief, politician, missionary

"We are of the same opinion with the people of the United States; you consider yourselves as independent people; we [Indians] ... look upon ourselves as equally independent."

Portrait: Joseph Brant.
Reproduced by permission of the Corbis Corporation (Bellevue).

J oseph Brant was a Mohawk leader who led his people into battle on the side of the British during the Revolutionary War (1775–83). Brant was a skilled politician with the manners of a British gentleman, and he learned to live in both the white and Indian worlds. Brant's loyalty to Great Britain was surpassed only by his loyalty to his people, and he spent his lifetime trying to ensure their land rights and the continuation of their culture.

Joseph Brant was born about 1742 in the forest along the Ohio River near present-day Akron, Ohio, while his parents were on a hunting trip. His father was a Mohawk chief, and his mother may have been part European and part Indian. Brant's name at birth was Thayendanegea (pronounced thay-en-duh-NAY-ghee-uh), meaning "he places two bets."

The Mohawk was one of six tribes that lived peacefully among themselves and belonged to the Iroquois (pronounced IR-uh-kwoy) Confederacy (union). The six tribes were the Mohawk, Oneida (pronounced oh-NEYE-duh), Onondaga, Cayuga (pronounced KEYE-you-guh), Seneca, and Tuscarora. Members of the confederacy were sometimes called "Iroquois" instead of by their tribal name.

After his father's death, Brant's mother married a man named Nicklaus Brant, who was a Mohawk chief and was also part Dutch. Joseph Brant adopted his stepfather's last name and learned both Indian customs and the ways of the whites. He became an accomplished hunter, fisherman, swimmer, trapper, and canoeist.

Brant's older sister, **Mary "Molly" Brant** (see entry), was the wife of Sir William Johnson, the white superintendent of Indian affairs for Great Britain. His job was to make sure American colonists did not trespass on land set aside for the Indians west of the Appalachian Mountains. Johnson was popular with the tribes he dealt with, and Molly Brant was a powerful figure in the Native community.

As a boy Joseph Brant went to live with his sister and brother-in-law at Fort Johnson in upper New York State. There in 1755 young Brant witnessed a battle at Lake George between French soldiers and British soldiers and their Mohawk allies. The battle was part of a larger conflict called the French and Indian War (1754–63), which was fought between England and France over who would control North America. By 1759 Joseph Brant was old enough to fight for the British beside Sir William Johnson in the military campaign at Fort Niagara, New York. The French lost the war in 1763.

About 1760 Brant began attending the white-run Indian Charity School in Lebanon, Connecticut, which later relocated and became Dartmouth College. Brant stayed there for several years, studying Christianity and learning to read and write English.

Battles Pontiac's forces

In 1763 Joseph Brant was called back to Fort Johnson by his sister when trouble broke out in the Ohio Valley. In an incident called Pontiac's Rebellion, Indian troops under Chief Pontiac swept across the western frontier to capture British forts. Pontiac's men were desperately trying to keep American colonists from moving onto their land in great numbers and taking it over.

Brant led Mohawk and Oneida volunteers against the forces of Pontiac. The rebellion was finally put down by a dirty trick on the part of British soldiers, who arranged to have

Family Troubles Cause Heartache

Joseph Brant's eldest son, Isaac Brant, was central to one of the saddest incidents in the life of the Indian leader. From his earliest childhood, Isaac had been a bad-tempered boy who caused many problems for his father. Once Brant paid a large sum of money to a white man after Isaac assaulted the man and killed his horse. Later, in a drunken rage, Isaac broke into the inn where his father, Joseph, was staying and attacked him with a knife. In wrestling the knife away from his son, Brant inflicted a small wound on Isaac's head. The drunken Isaac refused treatment for the wound, which became infected, leading to his death. Although an Indian council found Joseph Brant in no way guilty for his son's death, he had many regrets for his inability to help Isaac live a good life.

smallpox-infected blankets delivered to the Indians. As a result, the awful disease quickly spread, and thousands of Indians were killed, bringing the uprising to an end.

Loses two wives, becomes noted translator

People who knew Brant as a young man described him as tall and muscular, with fairer skin than many other Indians, expressive facial features, and a confident manner. Around 1765 Brant married his first wife, Christine, the daughter of an Oneida tribal chief. They settled in Canajoharie in the Mohawk Valley, on a farm Joseph had inherited. The couple had two children, Isaac and Christina.

After Christine died during the eighth year of their marriage, Brant married her sister, Susannah, who remained childless and died a few years later. Both sisters were victims of tuberculosis, an easily spread lung disease.

While living in Canajoharie, Brant showed his devotion to Christianity by translating a book of the Bible into his native Mohawk language. He also served as secretary to his brother-in-law, Indian agent Sir William Johnson, a position that was considered a great honor. He earned a reputation among the British as an outstanding translator of Mohawk. Brant attended meetings of the Iroquois Grand Council at Onondaga, New York, and provided firsthand information to the British authorities about what the Indians were thinking and doing.

Impresses British, rallies Iroquois

In 1774, after his brother-in-law's death, Brant became secretary to Johnson's nephew, Guy Johnson, who replaced his uncle as Great Britain's Indian superintendent. In November 1775 the two men sailed for England, where Brant impressed members of British society with his excellent command of English, his European-style education, and his translation of the Christian Bible into his native language. Though he often wore knee-high moccasins and a blanket draped over one shoulder, Brant was also comfortable wearing British-style clothing. When in later years Brant took another trip to England, the famous painters George Romney and Benjamin West each painted pictures of Brant in his native costume.

While in England, Brant was given the honor of becoming a British officer. When he returned to America, the colonists were beginning to fight for their independence from England in the Revolutionary War. Captain Brant, as he was now called, led pro-British Indian troops in raids, hoping to stop the American military from importing food and supplies from Europe. He was regarded by the British as a fine soldier and representative of his people.

Beginning in 1776, as the Revolutionary War raged, Brant went from one Indian village to another, trying to rally Iroquois people to the cause of the British. He was afraid that if the American colonists won the war, settlers would take over Indian land. He believed a British promise that land already taken from the Indians would be returned to them if they fought on the side of the British and won.

Gains limited support, fights in bloody battles

Brant hoped that when the Revolutionary War ended, the British would declare an Indian state, possibly headed by himself, west of the Allegheny Mountains. During the early summer of 1777, Brant was part of a council at which he and his sister, Molly Brant, convinced the Mohawk, Seneca, Cayuga, and Onondaga tribes to support the British, with Joseph serving as their war chief. The Oneida and Tuscarora tribes refused to join with the others, and the Iroquois union began to crumble. Also present at the council was a Seneca chief named Red Jacket, who urged the tribes to remain neutral (non-involved) and was then called a coward by Brant.

Brant and the warriors who chose to join him tried to force the American colonists out of the Mohawk Valley by raid-

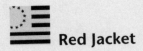

Red Jacket

The Seneca chief Red Jacket (c. 1756–1830), who was born in upper New York State, was another important Indian leader during the late eighteenth and early nineteenth centuries. Named Obetiani at birth, meaning "He Is Prepared," he later took the name Sagoyewatha, meaning "He Causes Them to Be Awake." He received the English name Red Jacket for the red coat presented to him by the British, which he often wore.

Red Jacket served as a representative of the Seneca tribe at meetings of the Iroquois Confederacy and also was a spokesman for the Indians before white groups. He was known more as a speaker than as a warrior, and he urged his tribe to remain neutral during the American Revolution. Unlike Indian leader Joseph Brant, who moved to Canada after the Revolutionary War, Red Jacket stayed in the United States.

Red Jacket supported the United States in the War of 1812 (1812–15), another conflict between the United States and Great Britain. Although he encouraged friendship between Indians and the United States government, he also believed that Indians should keep their own lands and retain their native culture. He represented Indians in court battles regarding land disputes and against Christian missionaries who tried to convert them. Still, some historians accuse him of signing away native lands to stay on good terms with whites.

ing and burning white settlements and driving away their livestock. Pro-British soldiers were also fighting in the area, and they may well have committed some of the violence there. But the Indians were widely blamed for causing all the trouble. To pay them back, Americans launched bloody raids on the Iroquois villages, terrorizing the inhabitants. Brant's warriors went on to fight at the battles of Oriskany (pronounced uh-RIS-kuh-nee), Minisink, and Cherry Valley in New York.

Cherry Valley Massacre makes his reputation

In 1778 Brant's forces joined British soldiers and set out to destroy the town and the fort of Cherry Valley. They launched a surprise attack on more than 250 American soldiers

In an article in the *Encyclopaedia Britannica* of 1889, editors E. C. Stedman and E. M. Hutchinson described an 1805 encounter between Red Jacket and Christian missionary Reverend Cram of the Boston Missionary Society, who wanted to convert the Indians to Christianity. After hearing Cram preach, Red Jacket made a reply that displayed his opinions, his logic, and his speaking skills:

> You say that you are sent to instruct us how to worship the Great Spirit agreeably to His mind, and if we do not take hold [of] the religion which you white people teach, we shall be unhappy hereafter ... How do we know this to be true? If it was intended for us as well as you, why has not the Great Spirit given [it] to us? ... We only know what you tell us about it. How shall we know when to believe, being so often deceived by the white people?...

> You say you have not come to get our land or our wealth but to enlighten our minds ... you have been preaching to the white people in this place. These people are our neighbors. We are acquainted with them. We will wait a little while and see what effect your preaching has upon them. If we find it does them good, makes them honest and less disposed to cheat Indians, we will then consider again of what you have said.

As an old man, Red Jacket suffered from the ill effects of drinking too much alcohol. He lost his position as Iroquois chief in 1827, but the position was restored shortly before his death on January 30, 1830. In a move that certainly would have been against his wishes, missionaries took charge of his body and gave him a Christian burial.

stationed there, killing about 30 men, women, and children, burning houses, and taking more than 70 prisoners. They withdrew the next day upon the arrival of 200 patriot soldiers. This event, called the "Cherry Valley Massacre," established Brant's reputation as a fierce fighter; some whites called him "Monster" Brant.

War ends; efforts to unite tribes fails

By 1781 American general **George Washington** (see entry) and his troops had defeated the British and their Iroquois allies and taken over the Mohawk Valley. At the end of the Revolutionary War, Americans got most of the land in the Mohawk Valley for themselves. With the peace treaty of 1783,

Was Joseph Brant a cold-blooded savage (as some saw him) or a man of courage and vision?
Reproduced by permission of the National Archives and Records Administration.

the border between the United States and Canada was drawn straight through Iroquois lands, and the Indians were never consulted about the matter. Beginning that year, and for more than ten years afterward, Brant tried to bring together the Iroquois and other western Indians to stop American expansion into Indian lands. His efforts were unsuccessful.

Relocates to Canada

In 1779 Brant married for the third and final time, to Catherine Croghan, who was the daughter of a Mohawk woman and George Croghan, an Irish-born Indian agent for the British. Brant and his new wife had seven children.

The British government (which still controlled Canada) gave land in Canada to whites, Mohawks, and other Indians who had been loyal to Great Britain during the war. In 1784 Brant and some of his Mohawks moved to a tract of land along Ontario's Grand River, which became known as the Six Nations Reserve (reservation). The Indians settled in small villages along the river. Brant was provided half his military pay by the British and was given some choice land, where he built a fine English-style home.

Brant believed that Indians would have to learn the white men's methods of farming in order to survive there, and he wanted to lease and sell farmland to whites as a source of income. But a legal disagreement over the control of Indian land emerged, and some of the Indians on the Grand River settlement were unhappy over the way Brant proposed to distribute the money. As a result, the plan was never carried out.

Later life

Joseph Brant revisited England in 1786, where he received funds to build the first Episcopal church in Upper

Canada (the Old Mohawk Church). He spent his later years back in Canada translating the Bible into Mohawk and performing missionary activities. He made constant efforts to secure peace between the United States and the Indian tribes that lived on the frontier.

Although the welfare of his people was Brant's primary concern, his loyalty to the British caused some Indians to become suspicious of him. His power among his own people lessened. As a result, the British felt free to ignore many of the promises they had made to him regarding land and self-rule by the Indians.

Joseph Brant died on November 24, 1807, at the age of sixty-five. He was buried near the church he helped construct at Brantford, Ontario.

Was Joseph Brant a cold-blooded savage (as many Americans saw him) or a man of courage and vision? There are no easy answers. In his vivid account of the American frontier, *A Company of Heroes,* Dale Van Every, like many modern historians, points out Brant's contradictory character traits:

> As a young man [Brant] was the consort [associate] of missionaries and a translator of scriptures [holy writings]. As a mature man he was expelled from this cloistered [protected] atmosphere into a world of tumult [uproar] and crisis in which he was laden with public responsibilities he was to bear to the end of his life. His emotional nature developed a capacity for the deepest friendships and an idyllic [pleasing and simple] marriage.... Such was the respect in which he was held even by his enemies that he could be received by [George] Washington with all the ceremony due a visiting head of state. Yet this man who had acquired so many civilized and cultured instincts was for years the aggressive and dedicated commander of bands of Indian marauders [raiders] whose [activities] were more atrocious than any other in the long and fearful record of frontier warfare.

For More Information

Allen, Robert S. "Brant, Joseph." *The Canadian Encyclopedia.* James Marsh, editor-in-chief. Edmonton, Alberta: Hurtiga Publishers, 1985, pp. 214–15.

Avery, Susan, and Linda Skinner. *Extraordinary American Indians.* Chicago: Children's Press, 1992, pp. 18–22.

Birchfield, D. L., gen. ed. "Red Jacket." *Encyclopedia of North American Indians,* Vol. 3. New York: Marshall Cavendish, 1997, pp. 1119–20.

Bolton, Jonathan. *Joseph Brant*. New York: Chelsea House, 1992.

Johansen, B. E. "Brant, Joseph." *The Encyclopedia of North American Indians*, Vol. 2, edited by D. L. Birchfield. New York: Marshall Cavendish, 1997, pp. 195–96.

Malinowski, Sharon, ed. "Red Jacket." *Notable Native Americans*. Detroit: Gale, 1995, pp. 355–57.

Straub, Deborah Gillian, ed. "Joseph Brant." *Voices of Multicultural America: Notable Speeches Delivered by African, Asian, Hispanic, and Native Americans 1790–1995*. Detroit: Gale, 1996, pp. 71–73.

Van Every, Dale. *A Company of Heroes: The American Frontier 1775–1783*. New York: William Morrow, 1962, pp. 26–27.

Zell, Fran. *A Multicultural Portrait of the American Revolution*. New York: Marshall Cavendish, 1996, p. 56.

Web Sites

Penick, Tom. "The Story of Joseph Brant." *Indigenous Peoples' Literature*. [Online] Available http://www.indians.org/welker/Brant.htm (accessed on 5/19/99).

Mary "Molly" Brant

Born c. 1736
New York
Died April 16, 1796
Kingston, Ontario

Mohawk tribal leader

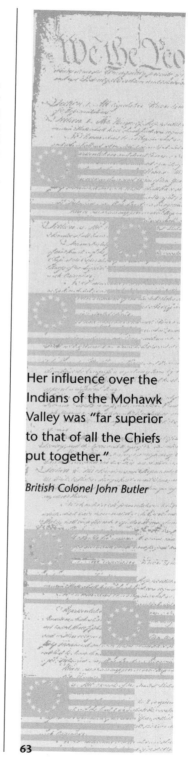

Mary "Molly" Brant, a Mohawk Indian, was one of the most powerful women in the New World in the eighteenth century. She played a major role in helping her British husband maintain good relations with Native Americans in the Mohawk Valley region. After her husband's death, she influenced several tribes to unite around the cause of the British during the Revolutionary War (1775–83).

Her influence over the Indians of the Mohawk Valley was "far superior to that of all the Chiefs put together."

British Colonel John Butler

The time at which Brant lived—the middle of the eighteenth century—was a time of great upheaval for the Mowhawk people, who fiercely resisted European settlement of their land. The Mohawk was one of six tribes (Mohawk, Oneida [pronounced oh-NEYE-duh], Onondaga, Cayuga [pronounced KEYE-you-guh], Seneca, and Tuscarora) that lived peacefully among themselves and belonged to the Iroquois (pronounced IR-uh-kwoy) Confederacy (union). Members were sometimes called "Iroquois" instead of by their tribal name. Many Iroquois, including Molly Brant's parents, were converted to Christianity by missionaries in the seventeenth and eighteenth centuries and were given Christian names.

Mary Brant grew up in the Mohawk Valley, an area with a large Native American and British population.
Reproduced by permission of North Wind Picture Archives.

Brant was named Mary at birth by her father, a Mohawk tribal chief named Peter, and her mother, a native woman named Margaret. Mary was also known by her Indian name, Degonwadonti (pronounced Duh-GONE-wuh-DON-tee). Because she wrote English well, it is thought that as a child she may have attended the British school in Canajoharie, New York, where her family lived.

After the death of her first husband, Brant's mother married a man named Nicklaus Brant, who was part Dutch as well as part Native American. Nicklaus Brant sparked in Mary and her brother, Joseph, an interest in European culture, and gave Mary the English nickname "Molly." She grew up in the house her family owned in the Mohawk Valley, where the Brants were a well-respected family.

Marries British hero and has many children

In the late 1750s, Molly Brant met her stepfather's wealthy friend, Sir William Johnson. Irish by birth and a soldier in the British army, Johnson was the superintendent of Indian affairs for Great Britain. In this position, he was to ensure that American colonists did not trespass on land set aside for the Indians west of the Appalachian Mountains, including the Mohawk Valley region.

Johnson probably first noticed Molly in 1753, when the seventeen-year-old young woman took part in a horse riding competition between some British soldiers and Mohawks. After the death of Johnson's first wife, Molly Brant married the soldier—who was twenty-one years her senior—in a Mohawk ceremony (British law did not recognize their marriage as legal). Molly Brant bore Johnson eight or nine children, and Johnson's wealth provided the children with many advantages. For example, the children had fine clothing and other possessions that other children of the time could not afford. Johnson was also in a position to finance his eldest son Peter's education. Peter Johnson was sent to Montreal, Canada, to study business.

A charming hostess and influential leader

Mohawk women were very involved in tribal decision making and had a much more important role in Mohawk society than did women in white society. The equality between men and women practiced among the Indians caused much conflict in the Brant-Johnson union—Molly was far less submissive than the women Johnson encountered in British society.

Johnson pleased Brant by learning the Mohawk language and taking part in various tribal customs. He became a close friend of her brother, **Joseph Brant** (see entry), perhaps partly because Joseph's friendship could prove useful to the British. Gaining the support of Molly Brant would also have been a benefit to Johnson: Her opinions carried much more weight among the Indians than did those of any white men.

Brant lived with her husband at Fort Johnson, New York, and later at his elegant estate, Johnson Hall, in the Mohawk Valley. Brant managed the household workers, raised the children, and entertained guests, who included both whites and Indians.

Johnson's outstanding military record earned him the title of "Sir" from the British government; Brant, then, was known as "Lady Johnson," though she remained "Miss Molly" to her old friends. She was widely praised by both whites and

Lydia Darragh, Spy for the Continental Army

Like Molly Brant, Lydia Darragh (pronounced DARE-uh) acted as a spy during the Revolutionary War. But unlike Brant, Darragh acted on behalf of the Continental army. Darragh was born in Ireland, where there was a long history of mistreatment of the Irish by the British. She married a Quaker minister named William Darragh, and the couple moved to Philadelphia, Pennsylvania. The couple had five children who grew to adulthood. The family came to love their adopted country.

Lydia Darragh was a midwife (a person who helps women bring their babies into the world). Around 1766 the hardworking woman added to her sources of income by opening a funeral home. When the American Revolution began, her family lived in a fine neighborhood in Philadelphia, across the street from the headquarters of General William Howe, commander-in-chief of the British forces.

The war placed the Darragh family in a painful position. They had to reconcile their religious beliefs with their patriotism (Quakers, members of the Society of Friends, are opposed to war). One of Lydia Darragh's sons, Charles, would quit the Quaker Church in order to become a soldier. Lydia Darragh managed to find a way to help the American cause without giving up her church: she would become a spy.

According to one famous tale, Darragh devised a clever way to pass along information about the British to the Continental army. After she gathered the information, her husband wrote it in code on tiny pieces of paper that were hidden behind the buttons on the coat of their fourteen-year-old son, John. Under the pretense of doing an errand, John then left the city and delivered the message to his brother, Charles, who had become an officer in the Continental army and who was stationed at White Marsh, Pennsylvania.

Another famous tale tells of the time Darragh's house was taken over by the British, who used part of it as a conference area. As the story goes, on the evening of

Indians for her dignity, charm, and hospitality. She was also well respected and held great influence among the people of the Iroquois Confederacy.

Moves to hometown after husband's death

Brant was very generous with her fellow Indians. Using credit extended to her because of her husband's wealth and

December 2, 1777, the Darraghs were ordered to go to bed early, close the doors to their rooms, and stay there until morning. Long after the Darraghs had gone to bed, the British held an important meeting in their house. Lydia Darragh, suspicious, listened to their conversation through the keyhole and learned that General Howe was preparing to leave Philadelphia to launch a surprise attack on the colonial forces of General **George Washington** (see entry). She hurried back to bed, pretending to be asleep when the commanding officer knocked on her door to say that the soldiers were leaving.

Realizing that the situation was critical, the next morning Lydia Darragh asked the British for a pass so that she could leave the city and go to a mill at nearby Frankford to pick up some flour. Stories differ as to whether she passed the information along to another female spy to take to the American military or delivered it herself to her friend, a Continental army officer, who passed it along to General Washington.

The message convinced Washington to move more American troops to the area of White Marsh. When the British marched there, expecting to surprise the Continental soldiers, they met with an American line of defense they could not break through. The British returned in defeat to Philadelphia, where they set up winter quarters. George Washington and his troops then marched on to their famous and difficult winter encampment at Valley Forge, Pennsylvania.

When the British learned that Washington had been tipped off, they brought Lydia Darragh in for questioning. She was released for lack of evidence. Later Darragh was turned away by the Quaker community for taking part in activities of a "war-like" nature. She nonetheless continued with her spying activities and was never caught. Always a good businesswoman, Darragh left behind a sizable estate after her death around the age of sixty in 1789.

good reputation, she purchased blankets, clothing, and other supplies for Iroquois people who were poor and needy. She also distributed cash and provided meals for people. In doing this she was following an old native custom of wealthy tribal members sharing their goods with those less fortunate. Traditionally, the more a person gave to others, the more the person rose in honor and prestige within the group. In performing these charitable acts, she became one of the most influential women among the Mohawk.

Brant's husband, Sir William Johnson, died in July 1774, and her way of life soon changed. She was pressured to give up her home, Johnson Hall, to John Johnson, William's eldest son by his first wife. (It was customary in England and among some families in America that the property of the father should go to the oldest son.) Using some of the money she inherited from her husband, she and her children then moved to a farm near Canajoharie, where they lived comfortably but not in luxury. With some of her inheritance, Brant opened a store, at which she sold rum and other items. A year after her husband's death, the American Revolution began. Because of her ties to the Mohawk tribe, Molly Brant found herself caught up in the war.

Influences Indians to ally with British

At the beginning of the Revolutionary War (1775–83), the tribes of the Iroquois Confederacy decided it was best for them not to take sides in the conflict between Great Britain and the American colonies. As the war continued, the British tried hard to gain the Indians' support. The British wanted the two thousand warriors of the Confederacy to attack the American settlers on the frontier and make the colonists' fight more difficult.

A year after the war began Brant became involved in an effort to rally support for the British among her people. She took the side of Great Britain in part because King **George III** (see entry) had attempted to protect Indian lands from American settlers, who were pushing deeper and deeper into Indian territory. Brant was unable to persuade two of the six Iroquois peoples, the Tuscarora and Oneida, to support the British, but the Seneca, Cayuga, Onondaga, and her own Mohawk people followed her recommendations. Ferocious fighters, they proved a tremendous asset to the British.

Angry patriots drive Brant from hometown

In 1775 Brant's son Peter helped capture the American patriot **Ethan Allen** (see entry) in Montreal, Canada. Her brother, Joseph Brant, led Indian forces in a number of Revolutionary War battles and became the war's most famous Indian warrior.

Early in the war, Brant herself sheltered British soldiers at her home near Canajoharie and provided them with weapons. She occasionally spied on their behalf, informing them of American troop movements in the Mohawk Valley. In time, American colonists and Indians who sided with them took revenge by driving Brant and her family out of their home.

In 1779 a Continental (American) army unit led by General John Sullivan swept through Pennsylvania and northern New York State, burning Indian villages. The unit defeated Brant's Mohawks. In time many of them retreated to Canada along with other native people. Soon the Iroquois Confederacy fell apart.

Spends later years in Canada

When Brant and her children fled from Canajoharie, they lived for a time in the area of Fort Niagara, New York, a British stronghold. Later, Brant moved to Canada's Carleton Island on the St. Lawrence River, where for the duration of the war the British commander-in-chief of Canada provided her with a house and garden, food, and other supplies.

Brant loved the Mohawk people and actively worked for the preservation of their culture. In her later years she was to experience widespread criticism for involving the Iroquois peoples in the Revolutionary War. Her critics claimed that because the Indians had supported the British, the American government took away much of their lands in punishment. But supporters pointed out that Brant had only followed the tribal teaching that Iroquois people should side with their strongest ally.

The British government was grateful to Brant for her help during the war. In 1783 they granted her some land in Kingston, Ontario, along with an English-style house and a pension consisting of the highest rate of annual payments awarded to an Indian at the time. That, along with her inheritance from the Johnson estate, meant that she could live out her remaining years in comfort. She settled among other Loyalists (people who had remained loyal to England) in Kingston, where she resided for the rest of her life.

Several of Brant's daughters married Canadian army officers and became respected members of their community. In her later years, Brant withdrew from tribal affairs and devoted herself to her daughters, who lived nearby. She also joined the local Episcopal Church. Brant died on April 16, 1796, of unknown causes, and is buried in what is now St. Paul's churchyard in Kingston.

For More Information

Allen, Robert S. "Molly Brant" in *American National Biography,* edited by John A. Garraty and Mark C. Carnes. New York: Oxford University Press, 1999, pp. 431–33.

Bataille, Gretchen M., ed. *Native American Women.* New York: Garland Publishing, 1993, pp. 36–37.

Booth, Sally Smith. *The Women of '76.* New York: Hastings House Publishers, 1973, pp. 153–55.

Bourgoin, Suzanne M., and Paula K. Byers, eds. "Mary (Molly) Brant." *Encyclopedia of World Biography.* Detroit: Gale, 1998, pp. 501–03.

Clyne, Patricia Edwards. *Patriots in Petticoats.* New York: Dodd, Mead & Company, 1976, pp. 35–40.

Dockstader, Frederick J. "Molly Brant" in *Great North American Indians: Profiles in Life and Leadership.* New York: Van Nostrand Reinhold, 1977, pp. 45–47.

Hamilton, W. Milton. "Molly Brant" in *Notable American Women,* edited by Edward T. James. Cambridge, MA: Belknap Press, 1971, pp. 229–30.

Malinowski, Sharon, ed. "Molly Brant" in *Notable Native Americans.* Detroit: Gale, 1995, pp. 54–56.

McHenry, Robert, ed. "Mary Brant" in *Liberty's Women.* Springfield, MA: G & C Merriam, 1980, pp. 49–50.

Waldman, Carl, ed. "Molly Brant" in *Who Was Who in Native American History.* New York: Facts on File, 1990, p. 43.

Williams, Selma R. *Demeter's Daughters, The Women Who Founded America, 1587–1787.* New York: Atheneum, 1976, pp. 244–45.

Zeinert, Karen. *Remarkable Women of the American Revolution.* Brookfield, CT: Millbrook Press, 1996, pp. 50–51, 53.

John Burgoyne

Born February 24, 1723
Sutton, England
Died August 4, 1792
London, England

Military leader, politician, playwright

"As long as British soldiers have their bayonets, they have the means to fight their way out."

British general John Burgoyne was best known for leading a failed military campaign against the rebel colonists during the American Revolutionary War (1775–83). Back in England, Burgoyne had to defend himself before the British government for his defeat and was stripped of his military rank and privileges. He spent his later years as a politician, a playwright, and a leader of London society.

Burgoyne was born in 1723 in Sutton, England. His mother, Anna Burenstone Burgoyne, the daughter of a very wealthy man, brought a large sum of money to her marriage. It was soon gambled away by her husband, an army captain named John, who spent a good deal of his life in prison for failing to pay his debts. Anna Burgoyne was rather free with her affections, and it was rumored that young John Burgoyne's real father may not have been Anna's husband, but the child's wealthy godfather, Lord Bingley.

In 1740, after attending the strict Westminster School, young John Burgoyne entered the British army as part of the Thirteenth Dragoons. (Dragoons fought on horseback or on

Portrait: John Burgoyne.
Reproduced courtesy of the Library of Congress.

foot with short guns called muskets.) In 1741 Burgoyne began his rise through the military ranks by becoming a lieutenant.

Marries and moves to France

During the early 1740s Burgoyne lived in London, England. The young soldier became a frequent visitor to the home of the wealthy Earl of Derby, a man who was an important political figure and the father of one of Burgoyne's school friends. In 1743 the twenty-one-year-old Burgoyne, who had very little money, betrayed the trust of his powerful friend by running away with his daughter, Lady Charlotte, and marrying her. This was considered a very serious offense against the manners and morals of the time.

The earl opposed the marriage and gave his daughter only a small amount of money as a wedding gift. He made it clear the couple would have to support themselves financially. Faced with money problems because of Derby's rejection, Burgoyne resigned from the army in 1746 and took his wife to France, where it was cheaper to live. The handsome and elegant Burgoyne and his highborn wife were welcomed into upper-class French society. Once they had settled in France, money never seemed to be a problem. (It is possible that Burgoyne's mother helped the couple financially.)

Rises through military ranks

In those days, a young Englishman like Burgoyne who wanted to get ahead socially and professionally needed a wealthy patron, someone who could use his influence to help the young man. By the mid-1750s, Lord Derby had come to accept his son-in-law, adopted the role of patron, and managed to have Burgoyne accepted back into the army. In late 1754 Lady Charlotte gave birth to a daughter, Charlotte Elizabeth, the couple's only child.

Burgoyne, by then a captain, got his first taste of warfare when he took part in the Seven Years' War (1754–63) in Europe. The conflict was a struggle between England and France for sea power and political control throughout the world. In America the war—which was won in the end by England—was called the French and Indian War.

Burgoyne performed well in combat and demonstrated unusual talents. Using what he had learned about European armies while living in France, he started the British army's first light horse units, groups of soldiers on horseback who could move quickly from place to place. In 1759 he became a commander of one of the first light horse units. This event proved to be a turning point in his military career.

"Gentleman Johnny"

Burgoyne wrote a code of instructions for his officers in which he opposed the use of harsh training methods that were common at the time. He believed his officers could maintain good discipline by treating the soldiers under their command as "thinking beings." He instructed the officers to develop an "insight into the character of each particular man" and declared there was to be no swearing at soldiers or beating them for breaking minor rules. Burgoyne practiced what he preached, and he earned the loyalty of his men to a greater extent than most other commanding officers of his day. Out of respect and affection, Burgoyne's soldiers came to call him "Gentleman Johnny."

Burgoyne had his officers study mathematics, the handling of horses, and especially French, because the best military instruction papers were written in French. The reforms Burgoyne suggested and used were ahead of their time. Similar practices were not widely adopted by the British military until the early nineteenth century.

Gains victory in Spain; is elected to Parliament

By 1761 Burgoyne was eager to increase his military fame. His efforts were helped by Spain's entrance into the Seven Years' War on the side of France. Spain had no wish to attack Great Britain, but she did want French help in seeking revenge against Portugal for an old insult. In 1762 King Joseph I of Portugal asked for assistance from the British against Spain, and Britain sent 7,000 men, including the unit led by John Burgoyne.

In a daring raid in Spain, Burgoyne's soldiers defeated a group of Spanish soldiers, took over a town, and captured many prisoners. When the military campaign ended three months later, Burgoyne received the praise of his superiors and was promoted to colonel of the Sixteenth Light Dragoons. The appointment was one usually held for life and brought with it many financial benefits.

In 1761, while he was away in Spain, Burgoyne had been elected to Parliament, the British lawmaking body. By 1763 his financial situation had greatly improved, because of his military promotion and his wife's recent inheritance. But in 1764 John and Charlotte Burgoyne faced a personal tragedy when their only child died of unknown causes at age ten. From that point on, Lady Charlotte's health began to worsen.

Votes to keep Stamp Act

After the war Burgoyne turned his attention to his duties in Parliament, where he was honored as a military hero. Two years later England was still saddled with huge debts and, as a result, placed a major tax on the American colonists called the Stamp Act of 1765. It required colonists to pay a tax on all paper items they used; only documents with the official British stamp were considered legal.

Most Americans strongly opposed the Stamp Act and protested against it. In time, riots against the Stamp Act broke out in Boston, Massachusetts. American objections to the Stamp Act were so strong that Parliament finally put the measure up for a vote. Forced to take sides, Burgoyne voted to keep the Stamp Act, but his side lost. When the tax was struck down, American tempers cooled for a while, but over time American opposition to "taxation without representation" in Parliament turned into a struggle for American independence from British rule.

Career advances

In 1766 the Burgoynes traveled around Europe so that John could study the organization of European military groups. When the Burgoynes returned to England, John Burgoyne gambled heavily and enjoyed visiting fashionable clubs and acting in plays, often without Charlotte, who stayed home sick. He returned to Parliament in 1768, where he continued to develop his political skills. Burgoyne served in Parliament off and on from 1761 until a few years before his death in

1792. As a member of the Tory Party, he generally favored keeping the American colonies dependent on Great Britain.

During this time, Burgoyne received several profitable military appointments. In 1769 he became Governor of Fort William in Scotland, a job that required little effort and earned him a substantial amount of money every year. In 1772, when he was appointed major-general in the British army, Burgoyne was earning even more.

Fires of freedom burn in America

In 1772 political conflicts between Great Britain and America were on the rise. The citizens of Boston were becoming very rebellious. Years before, at the time the hated Stamp Act had been struck down, the British had passed a bill saying that Parliament had the right to tax the colonies any way they chose. The British imposed new taxes—first the Townshend Acts in 1767, then the Intolerable Acts in 1774. The colonists were furious. They showed their displeasure by refusing to buy British goods and by tarring and feathering customs officials (a painful procedure in which a person is covered with hot tar and sprinkled with feathers). The British government soon decided it needed to strengthen its armed forces in America.

Although the thousands of soldiers sent to the colonies by England were unable to restore order, their number was great enough to cause problems. When available military housing in Boston could not handle the additional troops, the British government insisted that colonists allow the British soldiers to stay in their homes. This demand was very unpopular and made matters worse. Americans continued to resist Parliament's claim that it had a right to tax them. In 1774 Parliament was discussing whether to remove a tax they had placed on tea, an item widely used by rich and poor Americans alike. Again, John Burgoyne opposed lifting the tax.

Leaves Lady Charlotte to fight in America

In February 1775 Parliament and King **George III** declared Massachusetts—where most of the colonial uproar was centered—to be in a state of rebellion. Lieutenant-General **Thomas Gage** was already in Boston, but Parliament did not think he could handle the increasingly dangerous situation there, so, Major-Generals **William Howe** (see entries), Henry Clinton, and Burgoyne were sent to Boston to support Gage. Burgoyne was not eager to make the trip because of his wife's frail health, and because the war was not popular in England.

In the mid-1770s the British Parliament was divided between those who thought the American colonists should be forced back into line under British rule and those who supported the colonists' desire to gain more freedom. The noted British politician **William Pitt** (see entry) the Elder headed the second group. Burgoyne tried to avoid taking sides in the matter so he would not offend important people like Pitt, but it was becoming harder to do because passions were so inflamed.

Burgoyne disappoints Gage

In May 1775 Burgoyne arrived in Boston with Howe and Clinton. Massachusetts was in a condition of extreme disorder, and to Gage's disappointment, Burgoyne proved to be of very little help. Parliament ordered Gage to proclaim martial law, under which military authorities ruled over regular citizens. Before doing as ordered, Gage made one last attempt to bring the colonists back into line. In a move that proved to be a big mistake, he called on Burgoyne to write a manifesto, a public declaration to the Americans describing what the British planned to do and why.

In the manifesto Burgoyne referred to the colonists as an "infatuated multitude" (people who are completely carried away by unreasoning passion) and cautioned them that such a "preposterous parade" as themselves could never hold back the British army. In the document the British offered free pardons to all colonists who would return home peaceably. But Burgoyne's choice of words angered the Americans and failed to persuade the majority of them to part company with their leaders, who were pushing for complete independence from Britain. In fact, his manifesto may have helped to increase the Americans' determination to stand up for their rights.

Meanwhile, life in Boston was proving to be very boring for British soldiers, who were both idle and unwelcome. To lessen his boredom, Burgoyne wrote a humorous play called "The Siege of Boston," which was presented in 1776 at Charlestown, Massachusetts.

Proposes new methods of warfare

Burgoyne noticed that the American fighting style involved moving quickly from one site to another, firing from hiding places behind trees or stone walls. He believed that to beat the Americans, British soldiers would have to abandon the European style of warfare, in which orderly lines of soldiers fired carefully controlled volleys (successions of shots).

Burgoyne proposed that British soldiers use movable cannons; cannon fire would then be followed by swarms of well-trained soldiers on foot. This was a new approach for the British and showed Burgoyne to be an innovative thinker.

Serves under Carleton; wife dies

In March 1776 British soldiers under General Howe were defeated in Boston by troops led by **George Washington** (see entry). Trying to avoid total disaster in America, King George III then appointed General Burgoyne to serve as second in command to General Guy Carleton in Canada. Carleton's troops were defending the city of Quebec from attacks by colonists who wanted to make the area of Quebec part of the United States.

In May Burgoyne arrived in Canada with British soldiers he had rounded up on a 1775 trip home to England. He was joined there by German soldiers hired by King George III after a sufficient number of British volunteers could not be found. Shortly after Burgoyne's arrival in Canada his soldiers drove the weak American forces out of the city of Quebec and nearby areas. In October 1776 Burgoyne helped chase rebels westward to Valcour Island on Lake Champlain in New York.

Burgoyne's military concerns were overshadowed for a time by his own personal loss. On June 5, 1776, Charlotte, his wife of twenty-five years, died. Burgoyne was grief-stricken at her passing.

"Burgoyne's Offensive"

As the Revolutionary War was heating up, Burgoyne suggested a strategy that history refers to as "Burgoyne's Offensive," though some historians claim other men had proposed the same plan as early as 1775. Burgoyne proposed taking control of the Hudson River in northern New York State to prevent the Americans from moving men and supplies across the river to a place where British soldiers were fighting. According to the plan, troops traveling southward from Canada would meet in Albany, New York, with troops coming northward from New York City.

Burgoyne's strategy was approved by George III, but he did not receive the manpower he had requested. In March 1777 Burgoyne was placed in command of an invasion force that was only half the size he said he needed. Further trouble loomed when there was poor coordination between his efforts and those of Generals Clinton and Howe. From June through October 1777 Burgoyne and his men, numbering about 9,000, fought a series of battles called the Saratoga campaign.

Burgoyne captured Fort Ticonderoga in New York on July 6, but soon ran into serious problems brought on by his shortage of troops, overconfidence, the large numbers of the American enemy, and assorted errors. Disaster for the British

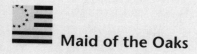

Maid of the Oaks

John Burgoyne's play *Maid of the Oaks* was presented in London in 1774. The project actually began as a masque, written and produced by Burgoyne to celebrate the marriage of his nephew, then Lord Stanley, to Lady Betty Hamilton. (A masque was a type of entertainment popular in England in the sixteenth and seventeenth centuries that featured lavish costumes, music, and dancing.)

Burgoyne spared no expense to ensure the success of the presentation for the young couple. He had a splendid ballroom erected in the garden of a mansion, and all the guests were to come costumed as famous characters from history. According to F. J. Hudleston in his biography *Gentleman Johnny Burgoyne*, there was "an orangerie [a place where orange trees are grown], a concealed band

of music, [young lovers] in fancy dress playing [a bowling game], shepherdesses swinging, with shrieks of apprehension and [swirling] petticoats ... archery, dancing, and [maidens] kicking at a [tambourine] suspended from a tree." John Burgoyne served as the master of ceremonies.

With the help of famed producer David Garrick, Burgoyne revised the plot and the dialogue and the play was presented at London's famous Drury Lane Theatre on November 5, 1774. The plot, in the words of Burgoyne biographer James Lunt, centered on "a woman-about-town outwitting the gentlemen intent on her virtue, but there were one or two good songs, and a [fancy ball] to round off the performance." According to Lunt, the play "was given a respectable reception."

was the result. Outnumbered, surrounded, and short of supplies, Burgoyne finally surrendered to American general Horatio Gates on October 17, 1777. This American victory is widely recognized as the turning point of the Revolutionary War.

Faces punishment; turns to politics and writing

In 1778 Burgoyne returned to England, where he faced harsh criticism for losing at Saratoga. A government committee formed to investigate his failures in America found him guilty of disobedience and neglect of duty, although he defended himself by arguing that he did not have enough supplies and men. King George III punished Burgoyne by taking away some of his military duties. This cut his income in half and ended his rise in the military. While trying to recover from the disappointment, he began courting a young singer named Susan Caulfield. He never married his companion, but she bore him four children. In the years that followed, Burgoyne continued to be active in politics and was known for his efforts to improve the treatment of soldiers.

Burgoyne spent most of his later life both attending and writing plays. In November 1774 his play *Maid of the Oaks* was produced in London and enjoyed moderate success. His humorous 1780 musical play *The Lord of the Manor,* which centered on life in the army, enhanced Burgoyne's writing reputation. His play *The Heiress,* produced in 1786, was witty and proved very popular. He followed this triumph in late 1786 by adapting an opera for the stage about the English king, Richard the Lionhearted (1157–1199), which was not very successful.

On August 4, 1792, shortly after returning home from a play, sixty-nine-year-old Burgoyne died, with Susan Caulfield at his bedside. Examining his career, historians agree that Burgoyne was more successful as an author than he had been as a soldier.

For More Information

Boatner, Mark M. "Burgoyne, John" and "Burgoyne's Offensive" in *Encyclopedia of the American Revolution.* New York: David McKay, 1994, pp. 130–43.

Dorson, Richard M. *America Rebels: Narratives of the Patriots.* New York: Pantheon, 1953.

Hudleston, F. J. *Gentleman Johnny Burgoyne.* Indianapolis: Bobbs-Merrill, 1927.

Lunt, James. *John Burgoyne of Saratoga.* New York: Harcourt, Brace, Jovanovich, 1975.

Tharp, Louise Hall. *The Baroness and the General.* Boston: Little, Brown, 1962.

Edmund Burke

Born January 12, 1729
Dublin, Ireland
Died July 9, 1797
Beaconsfield Estate, Buckinghamshire, England

Politician, political thinker, writer, public speaker

Edmund Burke was the most widely respected British political thinker and speech writer of his time. As a politician and speaker, however, he lacked the ability to lead or bring men together. His ideas continue to find favor today, especially with conservatives who wish to preserve society's existing institutions. He is widely admired for his defense of those who are too weak to defend themselves.

Edmund Burke was born into a middle-class family in Dublin, Ireland, on January 12, 1729. He had a difficult relationship with his father, a Protestant attorney, but was close to his Roman Catholic mother who, he once reported, suffered from "a cruel nervous disorder."

Burke was a sickly child. In 1735, when he was six, his parents sent him away from the big city to live with his mother's brother, Patrick Nagle, in Ballyduff, Ireland. For the sake of his health, he lived there for five years and attended the local school. In 1741, at age twelve, he went to boarding school in County Kildare, Ireland.

Burke entered Dublin's famed Trinity College in 1744. He did well at his studies and founded a debating club there.

"The only thing necessary for the triumph of evil is for good men to do nothing."

Portrait: Edmund Burke.
Reproduced by permission of the Corbis Corporation (Bellevue).

Burke went to England in 1750 to study law. But his heart was not in becoming a lawyer and he made little progress in his legal studies. Not much is known about his activities during the first nine years he spent in England following his graduation from college. It is known that he remained undecided about what to do with his life.

Early books praised

In 1756, when Burke was in his mid-twenties, he published two books on topics in philosophy. In the first, *A Vindication of Natural Society,* he declared that it was a mistake for rationalists to demand a logical justification for why moral and social institutions, such as rule by kings, should exist in society. Rationalists are people who accept reason as the only authority in determining one's opinions or actions. This is as opposed to people who accept other sources as authoritative, for example, the word of God in the Bible. Burke argued that the king and other authorities ruled in a society because it was the will of God.

Burke's second work was *A Philosophical Enquiry into the Origin of Our Ideas of the Sublime and Beautiful.* In this book, Burke wrote about his views on the theory of fine arts and peoples' responses to them.

Historical works

Burke followed in 1757 with a history he wrote with his friend William Burke (no relation) titled *An Account of European Settlement in America.* That same year he thought seriously about moving to America, but his father objected so strongly that Burke dropped the idea.

Parts of *The Early Abridgement of the History of England* also appeared in 1757. The book, though not published until after Burke's death, was his account of the early history of England. In the late 1750s Burke also began writing the first of a series of yearly articles on political events in England for a publication he founded and edited called the *Annual Register.* According to historian Mark M. Boatner III, "Few Englishmen had so profound a knowledge of colonial affairs [in America] as did Burke. His *Annual Register* articles were ... [very] observant, and warmly sympathetic" to America. They were so well respected that many writers on American politics and history borrowed from them shamelessly.

Burke's early works gained him recognition among London's writers and thinkers. He was invited to become a member of "The Club," an organization that included a number of prominent Englishmen of the time and was founded by famed English writer and critic Dr. Samuel Johnson.

Marries, moves to Ireland

Burke, who had not experienced family unity as a boy, made it a vital part of his adult life. In 1757 he married Irish Catholic Jane Nugent, the daughter of his personal physician. He settled into a comfortable family life with his new in-laws, his brother, and his friend William Burke. This core of people provided a sense of family harmony that he had never before experienced. Burke's son, Richard, was born in early 1745. His second son, Christopher, was born in 1758 and died in infancy.

In 1759 Burke became an assistant to William Gerard Hamilton, a well-known Member of Parliament (the British lawmaking body). He went to Ireland as Hamilton's private secretary, serving from 1761 until 1764.

During 1761 Burke worked on a paper about how Catholics in Ireland were discriminated against because of their religion. At that time, they were not fully protected by the laws, as Protestants were, and they could not hold public office. The piece was never completed or printed, but it showed Burke's deep concern with the issue and his determination to do what he could to change matters through his involvement with politics.

Early political career

Burke's political career began in 1765 when he became the private secretary of Charles Watson Wentworth, second Marquis of Rockingham, who was then serving a brief term as Great Britain's prime minister. Burke kept his position with Rockingham until 1782. Burke had inherited little from his family and suffered from financial problems, so he had to find other ways to make money. In December 1765, he entered Parliament as a representative of Buckinghamshire.

Burke was by nature an extremely emotional and sometimes unbalanced man. For the next sixteen years, his political career was bound up with that of Rockingham and his supporters, who served as the opposition party. The opposition is the minority political party in Great Britain. It has fewer numbers than the majority party and serves as a check on the majority party's power. Burke's alliance with Rockingham provided him with stability, independence, and a secure income.

Historians say that if Burke had been willing to abandon Rockingham, he might have had a much more successful political career. But loyalty to Rockingham was an important principle to him. Burke once said, "I believe [that] in any body of men in England I [would] have been in the minority. I have always been in the minority."

In 1770 Burke produced *Thoughts on the Cause of the Present Discontents,* a pamphlet in which he sharply criticized what he saw as corruption within the British government. He also criticized England's King **George III** (see entry) for ignoring his formal government advisers; instead, the king ruled through private advisers and servants.

Discontents was Burke's major discussion of the role of political parties. He defined a political party as "a body of men united in public principle, which could act as a constitutional link between king and parliament, providing consistency and strength in administration, or principled criticism in opposition." His views have influenced how political parties function in Great Britain, the United States, and other countries.

Calls for compromise with colonists

In 1774 Burke became a Member of Parliament from Bristol, a more politically important district than his former district, Wendover. This position was a big step forward in his career and he served in it for six years.

Burke believed that changes in society and government should take place in an orderly manner. In his 1774 paper *On American Taxation,* Burke called on Great Britain to compromise with the American rebels, who were protesting taxes the British had imposed on the colonies to help pay off war debts. According to historian Russell Kirk, Burke believed that the tax on tea, which Americans especially hated, had to be repealed by England for the sake of restoring tolerable relations with the colonists. Burke thought that taxation should only be imposed by force if the colonists refused to contribute money that was needed to defend the British Empire.

Still, Burke believed that it was the right of the British Parliament to retain rule over the colonies. When the disagreements between Great Britain and the colonies came to blows with the outbreak of the Revolutionary War (1775–83), Burke had a difficult time dealing with it. He did not support American independence, but neither did he look forward to the prospect of a British victory. In August 1776 he wrote, "I do not know how to wish success to those whose victory is to separate us from a large and noble part of our empire. Still less do I wish success to injustice, oppression, and absurdity.... No good can come of any event in this war to any virtuous interest."

Burke's qualities

As a politician, Burke's strongest tendency was to engage in argument. But he also displayed persistence, courage, energy, and concentration. Possessing "many of the qualities of leadership, he lacked the sensitivity to gauge and respect the feelings and opinions of others," writers in the *Encyclopedia of World Biography* noted. "Hence his political life was a series of negative crusades—against the [Revolutionary War] ... [and] the French Revolution—and his reputation as a statesman rests on his wisdom in opposition, not on his achievements in office." In other words, it was the intelligence of his ideas and the skillful way he expressed them in Parliament as a member of the minority party, rather than any actions on his part, that gained him great respect.

Though Burke held strong opinions, and he had a vast knowledge of political matters and a great gift for written expression of his thoughts, his delivery of speeches was awkward. Some of them ran longer than eight hours, causing listeners gradually to flee.

Defends Irish Catholics

Burke's homeland of Ireland was part of the British Empire. Although Ireland had its own Protestant parliament, the body had limited powers; its lawmaking activities

required the approval of a British Protestant council. He sympathized with the Roman Catholics, who were being persecuted there by Protestants (the religion of those in power). According to biographer Stanley Ayling, as a result of laws that were passed in the early eighteenth century, "at least three Irishmen in every four had as Catholics been excluded from trades and professions, from public office and from juries, and had been barred from buying freehold land," or land that could be held through life with the right to pass it on through inheritance.

Burke said he regretted that the Irish Catholics were "reduced to beasts of burden" by Irish and English Protestants. He pointed out that all subjects of the king should be able to expect justice. He spoke out for the need for fairness in Britain's policies, specifically with the Irish Catholics. He also pointed out that it would be better for England to deal with the issue of starving people in Ireland than to spend a lot of time debating about the situation.

Though he was a widely respected political thinker and speech writer, as a politician and speaker Edmund Burke lacked the ability to lead or bring men together. *Reproduced by permission of the Corbis Corporation (Bellevue).*

In the spring of 1778, Burke helped to bring about the first measures in Parliament to ease up on criminal penalties against Irish Catholics. But this position was unpopular, as was his support for relaxing restriction on trade between Ireland and Great Britain, and his stand may well have cost him the election to Parliament in 1780.

Opinions on American colonies, India

While serving in Parliament, Burke had written a series of brilliant papers protesting against government efforts to force the American colonists to obey its will, particularly in regard to matters of taxing them. But the British government was determined to show the colonies who was boss, and Burke could not convince it otherwise.

In 1781 Burke became a leading member of the Select Committee on Indian Affairs and a champion for the rights of the people of India (part of the British Empire). In that position, he helped to pass a bill asserting rights for citizens of India. His concerns about the Indian people would continue for many years.

In 1782 Lord Rockingham became Prime Minister of England and he appointed Burke paymaster general, responsible for paying wages to government employees. But Burke's good fortune quickly ended. Rockingham died after being in office for only three months. Burke had already begun to experience mental imbalance, and his condition was aggravated by the loss of his longtime patron.

In the late 1780s Burke gave a series of unpopular speeches that shocked his associates in Parliament. Burke spoke out in favor of punishing corrupt British officials in India who were mistreating the Indian people and using their official positions to enrich themselves. He felt that making an example of them might prevent others from committing similar abuses. In one instance he mounted an extreme attack against Warren Hastings, the governor general of Bengal, India. Burke portrayed Hastings as a monster. But his language was so violent that his comrades were convinced that he had become a political liability and that associating with him would damage their own careers.

Views on revolution

During the last part of the eighteenth century, Burke was one of the first to recognize the significance of the French Revolution (1789–99). A year after the revolution broke out he published *Reflections on the Revolution in France and on the Proceedings of Certain Societies in London,* in which he lamented the end of the French monarchy (the French royal family and people with connections to them were murdered [see **Louis XVI** entry]) and warned of the spread of revolutionary ideas in England. The book was read widely throughout Europe. It caused American patriot **Thomas Paine** (see entry) to write *Rights of Man,* a vigorous defense of the right of people to construct whatever kind of government they choose.

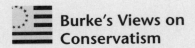

Burke's Views on Conservatism

Many people have the strong desire to keep things the way they are in order to maintain an orderly and stable society. Edmund Burke was one of the first political writers to outline the principles of this way of thinking, which is called conservatism.

The term conservatism was first introduced during the French Revolution (1789-99), which rejected not only rule by royalty but also the very traditions and institutions that had existed throughout Europe for centuries. Widespread violence accompanied this rejection, causing thinkers like Edmund Burke to call for the return of traditional ways and values.

Burke called society "a partnership not only between those who are living, but between those who are living, those who are dead, and those who are to be born." Conservatism represented the continuation of tradition within society. Burke supported keeping the democratic traditions of Great Britain. He claimed this would be accomplished by upholding such British institutions as king, nobility, church, and parliament. Burke argued that within this stable framework, gradual change could take place for the benefit of all citizens.

Achieves distinction in retirement

In 1794 Burke began to represent the district of Malton in Parliament. He planned to retire later in the year and hoped that his son Richard would be named his successor. Burke's plan was not to be. Richard Burke died in 1794 from a lung ailment, leaving his parents grief-stricken.

Edmund Burke enjoyed a unique international status during the last five years of his life. Although he held no official position, European royalty corresponded with him, and Catholics in Ireland honored him as their champion. To recognize his status, King George III offered to make Burke a member of the nobility. But Burke was depressed from the death of his beloved son and said that he much preferred simply to receive money.

Burke spent most of his retirement at his Beaconsfield estate. He tended to his farm, interested himself in the lives of his poor neighbors, and did some writing. His final project was to establish a school for the refugee sons of dead French royalists who had supported the King of France. On the last day of his life, Burke again spoke of his hatred for the revolutionary spirit in France. He believed that for the good of humanity England should declare war against France to put down the French Revolution. Burke died from a stomach ailment on July 9, 1797, with his wife at his side. He was buried at his local parish church.

American patriot Thomas Paine summed up Burke's life by remarking, "As he rose like a rocket, he fell like a stick."

But the famed English poet William Wordsworth called Burke "by far the greatest man of his age."

For More Information

Ayling, Stanley. *Edmund Burke: His Life and Opinions.* New York: St. Martin's Press, 1988.

Bourgoin, Suzanne M., and Paula K. Byers, eds. "Burke, Edmund." *Encyclopedia of World Biography,* 2nd ed. Detroit: Gale, 1998, pp. 138-41.

Kirk, Russell. *Edmund Burke: A Genius Reconsidered.* New Rochelle, NY: Arlington House, 1967.

Web Sites

"Edmund Burke." Bjorn's Guide to Philosophy. [Online] Available http://www.knuten.liu.se/~bjoch509/philosophers/bur.html (accessed on 9/23/99).

"Edmund Burke." *The History Guide: Lectures on Modern European Intellectual History.* [Online] Available http://www.pagesz.net/~stevek/intellect/burke.html (accessed on 9/23/99).

"Edmund Burke." Mallow Famous People. Copyright Aardvark 1997 [Online] Available http://www.mallow.ie/tourist/e-b.html (accessed on 9/23/99).

Smeenge, J.H. "A Biography of Edmund Burke (1729-1797.)" The American Revolution-an .HTML project. [Online] Available http://odur.let.rug.nl/~usa/B/eburke/burke.htm (accessed on 9/23/99).

A tablet in her honor at Corbin Place in New York City praises Margaret Cochran Corbin as the "first woman to take a soldier's part in the war for liberty."

Margaret Cochran Corbin

Born November 12, 1751
Franklin County, Pennsylvania
Died c. 1800
Westchester County, New York

Camp follower, soldier

Margaret Cochran Corbin picked up the gun of her soldier husband and took his place after he was killed by gunfire in a Revolutionary War battle. Wounded herself, she became the first woman in the United States to receive an annual payment from the government as a disabled soldier.

Corbin was born on November 12, 1751, reportedly near Chambersburg, Pennsylvania. She was the daughter of a Scottish-Irish colonist named Robert Cochran, but the name of her mother is unknown. In 1756 Native Americans killed Corbin's father and kidnapped her mother. Five-year-old Margaret and her brother, John Cochran, escaped capture and were raised by their uncle.

Around 1772 Margaret Cochran married John Corbin, a Virginian by birth. Four years later, when her husband joined a unit in Pennsylvania fighting on the American side in the Revolutionary War, Margaret went with him. At that time wives often accompanied their soldier husbands to cook, do washing, and nurse sick soldiers (see box).

On November 16, 1776, British soldiers and their German allies attacked Fort Washington, New York, where John

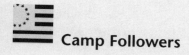

Camp Followers

Camp followers have always been an important part of wartime activities. Camp followers are men, women, and children who accompany soldiers as they travel about during wartime. During the Revolutionary War women often went along with the soldiers to wash and mend clothing, make meals, and nurse the wounded. Commanding officers expected them to register their names and those of their children along with the soldier to whom they were attached.

Camp followers were not from any particular social class. They could be uneducated wives or lady friends, or educated women who were able to provide such services as writing letters for the soldiers, knitting, and managing field hospitals. They could be civilian drivers of wagons, storekeepers who carried items for the soldiers to purchase, or clergymen. During the Revolutionary War, American soldiers had camp followers, as did British and German soldiers (see **Frederika von Riedesel** entry).

Camp followers lived hard lives and were expected to earn their way. They had to keep up with the marching soldiers, and they often carried the unit's pots and pans and the soldiers' personal belongings. They were expected to follow camp rules or suffer punishment. Those who obeyed the rules received a portion of food and drink. Sometimes pregnant women and the wives of officers were permitted to travel in military wagons.

Women and children who stayed in the military camps (while the men went off to fight) often faced danger themselves. When battles became fierce, women such as Margaret Corbin, called half-soldiers, took off for the front to assist their mates. Camp followers could also be a danger to the army. For example, some American camp followers once wandered off to plunder houses that the enemy had abandoned. They brought back smallpox germs in the blankets they stole from the houses, and some soldiers were infected.

Corbin was stationed. Fort Washington was the most important of a chain of forts along the upper end of Manhattan Island (now in New York City). The fighting was fierce, and the gunner whom John was assisting was killed. John took over the cannon, with his strong, tall wife (she was five feet, eight inches tall) at his side. When John was killed by enemy fire, Margaret immediately took her husband's place. She continued to load and fire the cannon by herself until she was wounded by grapeshot—clusters of small iron balls fired by a British cannon. The grapeshot tore into her shoulder and chest, pierced her jaw, and nearly severed her arm.

Original member of Invalid Regiment

The Americans were finally forced to surrender Fort Washington to the British. Corbin was taken to Philadelphia, Pennsylvania, with the other wounded soldiers, and she lived there for a time. It is not known whether or not she received special treatment because she was a woman.

Corbin was enrolled by the military as one of the original members of the Invalid Regiment, a group of disabled soldiers organized by an act of the Continental Congress on June 20, 1777. Its members, who could not engage in battle, performed other light duties at a military post, as each person's health permitted. In 1778 the regiment was stationed at West Point, New York, where it remained until it was finally disbanded in 1783.

Margaret Corbin suffered greatly as a result of her war wounds. She was permanently disabled and did not have the capacity to earn a living on her own. After Corbin returned to Pennsylvania, she faced hard financial times and petitioned the state for assistance.

Board of War grants annual support funds

On June 29, 1779, the Supreme Court of Pennsylvania, moved by her condition, noted Corbin's heroism, and she was granted $30 "to relieve her present necessities." The Pennsylvania government recommended that the Board of War of the Continental Congress look into providing her with a pension (annual payments) for her war service.

In 1780 the Board of War reported that Corbin "still remains in a deplorable situation in consequence of her wound, by which she is deprived of the use of one arm, and in other respects is much disabled and probably will continue a cripple during her life." The board also reported that "as [Corbin] had [courage] enough to supply the place of her husband after his fall in the service of his Country, and in the execution of that task received the dangerous wound under which

Anna Maria Lane and "Mother" Batherick

There are many tales of American women who made valuable contributions during the Revolutionary War. Two such accounts are those of Anna Maria Lane and "Mother" Batherick.

Anna Maria Lane was born in New England, perhaps in New Hampshire, around 1735. She followed her husband, soldier John Lane, as he took part in a number of battles. Anna Maria suffered a wound during warfare in Germantown, Pennsylvania, and recovered at a Philadelphia hospital. According to legend, she was wearing an army uniform and doing battle at the time of her injury.

John Lane was later taken prisoner by the British during the fighting at Savannah, Georgia, in December 1778. He was exchanged for a British prisoner and continued soldiering as part of a Virginia group that fought on horseback. At the same time, Anna Maria Lane served in Richmond, Virginia, as a nurse at the soldier's hospital there.

Years after the war, in 1807, Virginia Governor William H. Cabell asked the state government to pay Anna Maria Lane a pension (payment for her military service). They agreed that she deserved a pension because "with the courage of a soldier [she] performed extraordinary military services and received a severe wound at the Battle of Germantown."

According to historian Patricia Edwards Clyne, Lane's deeds must have been "extraordinary indeed … [since she] was awarded $100 a year, whereas the average soldier's pension was only $40."

Another popular story that has lived on since revolutionary times is that of "Mother" Batherick, who lived in what is now Arlington, Massachusetts. The elderly woman was picking daisies in a field near her house on April 19, 1775, the day war broke out between the American colonists and the British. The town was being guarded by a group of old men, since all the young men had rushed away to join the army. In charge of the elders guarding the town was a retired black soldier. He and his men were hiding behind a stone wall when some British supply wagons came past. The old men yelled at the British soldiers to stop, but the soldiers ignored them. The old men then fired, shooting two British soldiers and four horses. The other British soldiers fled.

Suddenly six of the British soldiers, out of breath from their fast getaway, rode up to Mother Batherick and surrendered. She single-handedly delivered her prisoners to American forces and commented to the British, "If you ever live to get back, you tell King George that an old woman took six of his [soldiers] prisoners."

she now labours, the board can but consider her as entitled to the same grateful return which would be made to a soldier in circumstances equally unfortunate."

The Board of War ordered that Corbin receive a complete suit of clothes or an equal amount of money in cash. In addition, for the rest of her life she was to be given half the monthly pay of a "soldier in the service of these states." Thus, Corbin became the first woman to receive a pension from the U.S. government.

"Captain Molly"

By 1782 Corbin had married a soldier who was also an invalid. Captain Samuel Shaw of West Point wrote in a brief report that "her present husband is a poor ... invalid who is no service to her but rather adds to her trouble." It is not known what happened to her second husband. He may have died or disappeared, since Corbin later lived by herself in various private homes in the area of West Point. In April 1783 she was discharged from the Invalid Regiment.

As Corbin's financial situation became worse, she filed for a rum ration (allowance) that normally was forbidden to women followers of the army. She was granted a full future rum ration as well as money for the period in the past in which the liquor ration had been withheld. She used the money to purchase small necessities to make her life a little better.

In January 1786 William Price, an official at West Point, wrote that Margaret Corbin, by then known as "Captain Molly," "is such an offensive person that people are unwilling to take her in charge." He did not say what made Corbin offensive. According to historian John K. Alexander, in his account of her in *American National Biography,* people who knew her in Highland Falls passed along stories from generation to generation about the "Irish woman who was not [very careful] about her appearance, who could be [sharp-tongued], but who was also respectfully addressed as 'Captain Molly.'"

Death and honors that followed

"Captain Molly" probably lived near West Point from September 1787 to August 1789, and was taken care of by people at the local military supply store. After several difficult and lonely years, she died during her late forties and was buried at a humble gravesite in the village of West Point.

During the nineteenth century, the story of Margaret Corbin was often confused with that of another heroic woman who pitched in to operate cannons during the Battle of Monmouth, New Jersey, and was known as **Molly Pitcher** (see entry). On March 16, 1926, the one-hundred-fiftieth anniversary of her heroic act, Corbin's remains were removed from an unremarkable grave and buried in a place of honor behind the Old Cadet Chapel at West Point.

Other honors to Corbin include a tablet erected in 1909 in Fort Tryon Park in New York City, near the site of the battle in which she fought. In 1926 a patriotic organization erected a monument over her grave at West Point.

For More Information

Alexander, John K. "Margaret Cochran Corbin" in *American National Biography,* edited by John A. Garraty and Mark C. Carnes. New York: Oxford University Press, 1999, pp. 499–501.

Anticaglia, Elizabeth. *Heroines of '76.* New York: Walker and Company, 1975, pp. 1–9.

Blumenthal, Walter Hart. *Women Camp Followers of the American Revolution.* Salem, NH: Ayer Company Publishers, 1984.

Boatner, Mark M. "Margaret Cochran Corbin" in *Encyclopedia of the American Revolution.* Mechanicsburg, PA: Stackpole Books, 1994, p. 284.

Canon, Joel. *Heroines of the American Revolution.* Santa Barbara, CA: Bellerophon Books, 1995.

Claghorn, Charles E. "Anna Maria Lane" in *Women Patriots of the American Revolution.* Metuchen, NJ: The Scarecrow Press, Inc., 1991, p. 120.

Clyne, Patricia Edwards. *Patriots in Petticoats.* New York: Dodd, Mead & Co., 1976, pp. 130–31, 135.

Land, Robert H. "Margaret Cochran Corbin" in *Notable American Women 1607–1950: A Biographical Dictionary,* edited by Edward T. James. Cambridge, MA: Belknap Press, 1971, pp. 385–86.

"Margaret Corbin" in *The National Cyclopaedia of American Biography.* Ann Arbor, MI: University Microfilms, 1967, p. 399.

Meyer, Edith Patterson. *Petticoat Patriots of the American Revolution.* New York: Vanguard Press, 1976, pp. 61–62, 109.

Purcell, Edward L., ed. "Margaret Cochran Corbin" in *Who Was Who in the American Revolution*. New York: Facts on File, 1993.

Weathersfield, Doris. *American Women's History*. New York: Prentice Hall General Reference, 1994.

Whitney, David C. "Margaret Cochran Corbin" in *Colonial Spirit of '76: The People of the Revolution*. Chicago: Encyclopedia Britannica Educational Corp., 1974, p. 158.

Williams, Selma. *Demeter's Daughter: The Women Who Founded America, 1587–1787*. New York: Atheneum, 1976, p. 248.

Hector St. John de Crèvecoeur

**Born January 31, 1735
Caen, France
Died November 12, 1813
Sarcelles, France**

**Map maker, surveyor, farmer,
writer, soldier, government official**

Hector St. John de Crèvecoeur, a Frenchman known in America as Hector St. John, experienced both the American Revolution (1775–83) and the French Revolution (1789–99). He traveled throughout America and Europe as a soldier, writer, and government official. His books describing life in the American colonies during the time of the American Revolution became popular in both France and the United States.

Michel Guillaume Jean de Crèvecoeur (pronounced Mee-SHELL ghee-OHM JHON deh KREV-ker; his original name) was born in 1735 near Caen, France, to a family that was of lower-level noble rank. His father was Guillaume Jean de Crèvecoeur, owner of a large farm, and his mother was Dame Marie-Anne Blouet (pronounced blue-AAY). In French-speaking countries, dame was an honorary title for a noblewoman.

Crèvecoeur was educated in France and England. In France he attended a private school taught by Roman Catholic priests, and most likely studied languages, mathematics, map making, and surveying (determining the boundaries of a tract of land by measuring its lines and angles). Crèvecoeur had nat-

"[In America] individuals of all races are melted into a new race of man, whose labors and [descendants] will one day cause great changes in the world."

Portrait: Hector St. John de Crèvecoeur.
Reproduced by permission of the Corbis Corporation.

ural talent in sketching and painting that also served him well in his map-making jobs later in life.

The events in his life after he left school in France but before he came to North America are uncertain. He went to live for a time in Salisbury, England, where he sharpened his skills in the English language and fell in love with a woman whose death at a young age caused him much sorrow.

In 1754 Crèvecoeur traveled to Canada, where he was a map maker and soldier during the first years of the French and Indian War (1754–63), serving France under commander Marquis (pronounced mar-KEE) de Montclair. The French and Indian War was fought in America by Great Britain and France to decide who would control North America. Crèvecoeur was so skilled at both map making and weaponry that his superiors granted him the rank of lieutenant.

Moves to New York, marries

After the French were defeated by the English in the 1759 battle of Quebec, Canada, Crèvecoeur lost favor with his unit, resigned his position, and moved to the British-controlled American colonies. The reasons for this move are unclear. Historians think it may have been his great love for all things English that motivated Crèvecoeur. The fact that he fought against the English only adds to the mystery.

In 1759 Crèvecoeur moved to the colony of New York, then traveled through the Great Lakes and Ohio Valley regions, on foot, on horseback, and by canoe, working at various surveying jobs and taking notes of his experiences. He became a citizen of New York in 1765, finally settling in that colony's Orange County, where he lived as a farmer from 1769 to 1780.

In their book *St. John de Crèvecoeur: The Life of An American Farmer,* Gay Wilson Allen and Roger Asselinau described Crèvecoeur as having a "fair, full, and round [face], with a prominent nose and large eyes (said to have been brown) and a small, firm mouth. His natural hair was red ... and freckles ... covered his face, arms, and hands.... He was only five feet four inches tall—though that was about average for Frenchmen at the time."

In 1769 Crèvecoeur married Mehetable Tippet (pronounced Muh-HET-uh-bull), the daughter of a landowner from Westchester, New York. The couple named the eldest of their three children (a girl) America-Frances, an indication of their affection for both America and France. For a while the family lived very happily on their farm. But the unfolding of the American Revolution caused problems in their relationships with friends and neighbors, because some stayed loyal to Great Britain while others were supporters of the revolution.

Visits England on his way to France

Crèvecoeur was writing a book during this time, called *Letters from an American Farmer*. He recorded his personal feelings over being forced to take sides in the conflict. He would have preferred to stay neutral (not committed to either side). He said he felt "divided between the respect I felt for the ancient connection [with Great Britain] and the fear of [involving himself on the side of the patriots], with the consequences of which I am not well acquainted." He feared that if society broke down and power was up for grabs, the outcome would be unpredictable and it would be unclear whom he could trust.

Fearing that he might get sucked into the complicated political conflicts of the times and endanger his family, in 1780 Crèvecoeur decided that he must flee to France. Leaving behind his wife and two of his three children at his house in the New York countryside, he went to New York City with his six-year-old son to find a ship heading for France.

In New York, when Crèvecoeur tried to board a ship, English authorities arrested him. Suspected by them of being a spy, he was detained for three months before he was finally cleared. During this time he and his son were near starvation. The deprivation Crèvecoeur experienced caused him various health problems that remained for the rest of his life. Once freed, he and his son continued their journey to Europe without further interference. They stayed in Europe from 1780 to 1783. Before reaching France, Crèvecoeur stopped to visit friends in London, England.

Letters from an American Farmer is published

While staying in England, Crèvecoeur published his most famous book, *Letters from an American Farmer*. He pub-

Excerpt from "What Is an American?" by J. Hector St. John

"He [an "enlightened Englishman" on first seeing America] is arrived on a new continent: a modern society offers itself to his contemplation, different from what he had hitherto seen. It is not composed, as in Europe, of great lords who possess every thing, and of a herd of people who have nothing. Here are no aristocratical families, no courts, no kings, no bishops, no [church rule], no invisible powers giving to a few a very visible one; no great manufacturers employing thousands, no great refinements of luxury. The rich and poor are not so far removed from each other as they are in Europe.

The next wish of this traveller will be to know whence came all these people? They are a mixture of English, Scotch, Irish, French, Dutch, Germans, and Swedes. From this [mixed] breed, that race now called Americans have arisen....

What then is the American, this new man? ... The Americans were once scattered all over Europe; here they are incorporated into one of the finest systems of population which has ever appeared, and which will hereafter become distinct by the power of the different climates they inhabit."

lished it under the name he had adopted in America, James Hector St. John. He may have taken the name in his new land to try to disguise his French origin and appear to be a "typical" American.

In the book Crèvecoeur drew on his experiences in agriculture and his observations on the frontier to produce remarkably detailed sketches of American life. The book was not actually biographical. Rather, it was fiction presented in the form of letters written to a European friend by a farmer who signed the letters simply "James." The letters focused on such topics as manners, customs, education, and plant and animal life found in America.

Crèvecoeur's writings show that he was very moved by the difficulties of the poor independent farmers he encountered in America. They also highlight his strong love of freedom and provide insightful accounts of life in colonial America.

Crèvecoeur's book helped European readers gain insight into American thought and behavior. Doreen Alvarez Saar, in her paper "J. Hector St. Jean de Crèvecoeur," wrote, "The American readers [of Crèvecoeur] were a society of colonials who had just overturned centuries of tradition and were attempting to define themselves as something new, in order to distinguish themselves from those who were exactly like them but born under governments in Europe" that were ruled by kings.

Lives in France, returns to tragedy

In 1780 the profits from sales of his book in England allowed Crèvecoeur to return to his birthplace in the part of France known as Normandy. While Crèvecoeur was there, he introduced the growing of American potatoes to the local farmers. He later claimed to have brought to France the practice of growing such crops as alfalfa and other plants used for animal feed.

In France Crèvecoeur was introduced to and made friends with some of the finest French thinkers of the time. They encouraged him to translate his book into French, a language he had not spoken during his nearly thirty years in America. By the time Crèvecoeur returned to America in 1783 at the end of the American Revolution, after three years' absence, his book had been published in Holland, Germany, and Ireland. He was well known throughout Europe, and especially admired by people with revolutionary ideas.

Back home in the countryside of New York, Crèvecoeur was shocked to find that his house had been burned down, his wife had been killed in an Indian raid, and the two children he had left behind were missing. He was able to find and reclaim his children in Boston, Massachusetts, where a stranger had taken them to safety. The reunited Crèvecoeurs, now a family of four, then moved to New York.

Serves France in America, revisits Europe

Crèvecoeur's book had made him immensely popular in America. He became friends with both **Thomas Jefferson** and **Benjamin Franklin**, and wrote to and received letters from **George Washington** (see entries).

Because he was now well known and respected in France as an expert on America, the French government invited him to become the French consul to New York, Connecticut, and New Jersey. He accepted, moved to New York City, and served in the post from 1783 to 1785 and again from 1789 to 1790. A consul is appointed by the government of a country to look out for the country's citizens and business interests in a foreign country.

While living in New York City, Crèvecoeur helped to found St. Peter's, the city's first Catholic church. He also served as a trustee of the church, helping to manage its affairs. During his time in New York, Crèvecoeur attempted to develop his own business in the form of packet boat service between France and New York. A packet boat travels an established route between various ports, carrying passengers, freight, and mail. But over time, the business failed.

Further writings

Throughout these years, Crèvecoeur wrote a number of articles on medicine and natural history. In 1785, suffering from poor health, he returned to France. There the now famous author worked at improving business relations between France and America and prepared a three-volume version of his *Letters* that was published in France in 1787.

In 1789 Crèvecoeur returned to the United States and to his position as consul. Over the next year, he wrote articles that described life in the farming villages of America. His writing focused on such topics as the raising of potatoes, sheep feeding, and the uses of sunflower oil.

Not all of the articles written by Crèvecoeur were published in his *Letters*. Some, which he wrote under the pen name Agricola (Latin for farmer), were published in London in the eighteenth century but did not appear in the United States until 1925, when they became part of *Sketches of Eighteenth Century America, or More Letters from an American Farmer*. They provided vivid and optimistic discussions about the particular character of people in America.

In his book *American Eras: The Revolutionary Era, 1754–1783*, Robert J. Allison stated that Crèvecoeur presented an idealized view of the American character. He saw Americans as simple people, careful with money and concerned with proper behavior. They demonstrated their character "through the struggle of families to cultivate their land and become self-sufficient [without] the corruption and distractions of civilization." In that way, "Americans would discover the true meaning of independence and realize the universal human rights to property, liberty, and happiness."

Crèvecoeur's descriptions of the productiveness of the land in America inspired hundreds of Frenchmen to sail across the Atlantic. They started a colony of French immigrants in Pennsylvania that flourished for several decades before a group of Indians destroyed it and killed all the inhabitants.

Final years in France

In 1790 Crèvecoeur left American soil for the last time and returned to France. During the years of the French Revolution and the political chaos that surrounded it, Crèvecoeur did his best not to get involved. But on more than one occasion he lost friends and relatives who got caught up in the violence of the times.

After a life full of upheaval, Crèvecoeur attempted to live his final years in France as quietly as possible. He kept in touch with his son, who was a farmer in New York. He enjoyed meetings with the popular artists, scientists, and inventors of the day, and used his spare time to produce his longest work, known in English as *Eighteenth-Century Travels in Pennsylvania and New York*. By then a recognized expert in the field of agriculture, Crèvecoeur wrote well-respected newspaper articles on the subject. During the last year of his life, he spent three months in Munich, Germany, where his son-in-law served as an ambassador. In 1813 he died of a heart attack at Sarcelles, near Paris.

In the centuries since Crèvecoeur's death, his *Letters from an American Farmer* has stood as a testament to the immigrant's appreciation of his new nation. In his review of Crèvecoeur's *Letters,* editor Baron Friedrick-Melchior von Grimm noted: "This book ... perfectly fulfills the object that the author seems to have proposed: that of making the reader love America. There are to be found in it minute details, very common truth and lengthy passages; but it attracts by its simple and true pictures, by its expression of an honest soul."

For More Information

Allen, Gay Wilson, and Roger Asselineau. *St. John de Crèvecoeur: The Life of an American Farmer.* New York: Viking Press, 1987.

Allison, Robert J. *American Eras: The Revolutionary Era, 1754–1783.* Detroit: Gale, 1998, pp. 23, 232.

Bowmen, J.S., ed. "Crèvecoeur, (Michel-Guillaume) Jean de." *Cambridge Dictionary of American Biography.* Cambridge, England: Cambridge University Press, 1995.

Crèvecoeur, Hector St. John de. *Letters from an American Farmer,* Letter III. Reprinted from the original edition with a prefatory note by W. P. Trent and an introduction by Ludwig Lewisohn. New York: Fox, Duffield, 1904.

Emerson, Everett H. "Crèvecoeur." *Encyclopedia of World Biography,* Vol. 4. New York: McGraw-Hill Book Co., 1973, pp. 307-08.

Web Sites

Crèvecoeur, Hector St. John de. *Letters from an American Farmer,* Letter III. reprinted from the original ed. with a prefatory note by W. P. Trent and an introduction by Ludwig Lewisohn. [Online] Available http://xroads.virginia.edu/~HYPER/CREV/letter03.html (accessed on 8/26/99).

Saar, Doreen Alvarez, contributing ed. "J. Hector St. John de Crèvecoeur." [Online] Available http://www.http:www.georgetown.edu/bassr/heath/syllabuild/guide/crevecoe.html (accessed on 8/14/99).

Taaffe, Thomas Gaffney. "Hector St. John de Crèvecoeur." The *Catholic Encyclopedia.* The Encyclopedia Press, Inc., 1913. [Online] Available http://www.knight.org/advent/cathen/04488b.htm (accessed on 8/14/99).

John Dickinson

Born November 8, 1732
Talbot County, Maryland
Died February 14, 1808
Wilmington, North Carolina

Politician, lawyer, writer, soldier

John Dickinson helped guide American public opinion in the years before the American Revolution. He opposed British taxation of the colonies but also opposed the use of force against mother England. He was widely admired for his mastery of legal history and his writing skills, but he lost much of his influence when the Revolution got underway against his urging. Once it had begun, though, he worked to make his new nation stronger. He served in the legislatures of both Delaware and Pennsylvania, also serving as president of each state.

John Dickinson was born in Maryland in 1732 to Samuel Dickinson, a well-respected Quaker judge and farm owner, and his second wife, Mary Cadwalader. Historians disagree on whether or not Dickinson himself was a member of the Society of Friends, the formal name for the religious group whose members are popularly referred to as Quakers. Certainly, his Quaker parents' opposition to violence influenced Dickinson's beliefs as an adult that the American colonists should do everything possible to avoid armed conflict with England.

The Dickinson family owned property in both Delaware and Maryland, and when John Dickinson was a

"To escape from the protection we have in British rule by declaring independence would be like destroying a house before we have another in winter."

Portrait: John Dickinson.
Reproduced courtesy of the Library of Congress.

youngster, the family moved near Dover, Delaware. Dickinson took lessons at home until he turned eighteen. He then began a three-year study of the law under the guidance of attorney John Moland.

In 1753, at age twenty-one, Dickinson went to further his legal education in London, England, where it was common for wealthy young men of his time to study. There he read law books, visited law courts, and debated points of law with his fellow students. He also gained skills in organizing and presenting his views, and developed a fine grasp of the English legal system and English politics. He was disturbed to observe the corruption and incompetence of the members of the British House of Commons, the lower House of Parliament, England's law-making body.

Splits time between Delaware and Pennsylvania

Dickinson became a lawyer in Great Britain in 1757 and soon sailed home to Philadelphia, Pennsylvania. There Dickinson began his own legal practice. After the death of his father in 1760, he split his time between Philadelphia and his second home in Kent County, Delaware. He was elected to the Pennsylvania Assembly in 1762. There he demonstrated his lifelong ability to see both sides of an argument and adopt a middle position.

In his book *John Dickinson, Conservative Revolutionary*, Milton E. Flower described the well-known lawyer as being of average height and slight build, with clear eyes and a prominent nose. Flower wrote, "There was an elegance in [the way he carried himself], a poise and confidence that was particularly notable. His professional approach was [that of a well-spoken person] and so markedly [well educated] that his reputation grew easily."

Condemns Stamp Act

In 1765 the British imposed the Stamp Act on the American colonies to raise money. The colonists were forced to pay taxes on a wide range of documents and other items, including legal papers, newspapers, business documents, and even on playing cards and dice. At first, the colonists bitterly accepted the new form of taxation, but Dickinson foresaw that the Stamp Act's passage would bring on severe problems for the colonies, for one tax could easily lead to another.

Dickinson was a delegate from Pennsylvania to the Stamp Act Congress in New York in 1765. It was called "to consult together on the present circumstances of the colonies." Patriot **Patrick Henry** (see entry) gave a fiery speech against the Stamp Act; the speech helped changed the attitude of Americans from acceptance to open defiance. The Congress adopted Dickinson's Declarations of Rights and Grievances that denounced taxes imposed by England and collected in America.

In this and other writings, Dickinson voiced his fear that England would bleed America dry to pay its own heavy debts, brought on by recent warfare. He opposed the Stamp Act taxes and petitioned England to repeal them. He wrote, "It is inseparably essential to the freedom of a people, and the undoubted right of Englishmen, that no taxes be imposed on them, but with their own consent, given personally, or by their representatives." However, Dickinson also opposed violent resistance to the Act on the part of the colonists.

Responding to American outrage and threats, the British repealed the Stamp Act. But trouble soon began again when Great Britain passed the Townshend Revenue Acts, imposing new taxes on paint, tea, lead, paper, and glass.

Opposes Townshend Acts

In 1767 Dickinson published *Letters from a Farmer in Pennsylvania* to show his opposition to the Townshend Acts. This was his most famous work. In this series of letters that appeared in most of the newspapers in America, he disputed England's right to tax the colonists and suggested that Americans stop importing goods from England. Still, he stopped short of supporting armed resistance or separation from the mother country.

In the letters, Dickinson wrote, "The meaning of [these letters] is, to convince the people of these colonies that they are at this moment exposed to the most [threatening] dangers; and to persuade them immediately, vigorously, and unanimously, to exert themselves in the most firm, but most peaceable manner, for obtaining relief." The letters were well received in the various colonies and discussed at town meetings throughout New England.

Election victory and marriage

In 1770 Dickinson was again elected to the Pennsylvania Assembly. That same year he married Mary Norris of Philadelphia, whom he called "Polly." During their long marriage the couple was to have five children, though only two of them survived beyond infancy. In 1771 Dickinson helped write a petition to King **George III** (see entry) of England, encouraging him to convince the British Parliament to repeal taxes on tea and other items imported by the colonies.

In 1774 Dickinson became a delegate from Pennsylvania to the First Continental Congress, held in Philadelphia. Representatives from the colonies met there to discuss their options regarding their British rulers. According to John C. Miller in his biography *Sam Adams: Pioneer in Propaganda,* John Dickinson believed that "the cause of liberty should be left in the hands of lofty-minded patriots strongly adverse to riots and ... outright rebellion." This was a position opposite to that taken by **Samuel Adams** (see entry), who used his speeches and writings to arouse the anger of the colonists and bring on riots against their English rulers.

At the congress, Dickinson used his writing skills to point out that there were legal limits to the power of the British Parliament over the American colonists, limits that Parliament had exceeded. He also used those skills to protest against Great Britain's unfair trade practices. Dickinson believed that the British government had no right to raise money in the colonies by imposing taxes that Americans hated. However, he also believed Parliament had the power to control colonial trade and pass laws for the colonies.

Opposes war at Second Continental Congress

The Second Continental Congress met in May 1775, shortly after the battles of Lexington and Concord that marked the beginning of the Revolutionary War. Dickinson, along with John Duane of New York, presented a plan in Congress for making up with Britain.

There were strong differences of opinion among those at the Congress about how to handle their disagreements with Great Britain. Dickinson led the group that always supported peace-making efforts, even after fighting had already broken out. His group suggested that the colonists send a petition to the king and try to work out a series of settlements regarding trade and taxes, but prepare for war, just in case.

Adams's criticism of Dickinson's war views

John Adams (see entry), later president of the United States, made fun of Dickinson and accused him and others in Congress who shared his views of trying "to oppose my designs and the Independence of the Country." In his *Autobiography* he referred to Dickinson, as "very moderate, delicate, and timid."

In the document that John Adams called the *Olive Branch Petition,* Dickinson told England that the colonies wanted to negotiate at once and desired "accommodation [settlement] of the unhappy disputes" between England and the colonies and were prepared to "enter into measures" to achieve it. Adams believed that Dickinson sent a mixed message, and described the position as one of "having a sword in one hand and an olive branch [a symbol of peace] in the other." Reportedly, King George III never even read the Olive Branch Petition.

Dickinson and his supporters believed that America was not yet ready for war. In their view, America had everything to gain by putting off the war. They thought that in a few years the colonies would be so powerful that the British would be unable to deny them independence.

Opposition to independence damages popularity

Those who preferred a more aggressive and violent course of action disliked Dickinson's approach to the problems with England. Still, the people of Pennsylvania reelected him to their assembly. But in time, as support for complete independence grew among Americans, his position began to make him unpopular.

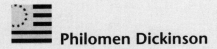

Philomen Dickinson

The older brother of John Dickinson, Philomen Dickinson was born in 1739. He also made a major contribution to the American Revolution and the new American nation. Like his brother John, Philomen could be said to belong to two states, because he lived or served in elective offices in both Delaware and New Jersey. When the Revolutionary War broke out in 1775, he was living on his comfortable Delaware estate. In 1776 he was elected to the New Jersey provincial congress. At that time he was also a general in that state's militia.

That same year, while George Washington and his troops were encamped at Morristown, New Jersey, Philomen Dickinson led a group of soldiers that hampered the British from getting badly needed supplies. He also led a successful surprise attack in Millstone, New Jersey, capturing horses, wagons, and prisoners. In 1777 he was named Major General and Commander-in-Chief of the New Jersey militia, a post he held until the end of the war. He participated in a number of significant battles.

He was three times defeated when he ran for governor of Delaware. In 1785, along with Robert Morris and Philip Schuyler (pronounced SKY-ler), he was appointed to select a site for the capital of the United States. He was defeated by William Paterson to serve Delaware in the U.S. Senate, but completed Paterson's term of office (1790–93) when Paterson succeeded William Livingston as governor. Dickinson died in 1809.

In July 1776 Dickinson voted against the Declaration of Independence that established the United States as a separate nation. He said that his opposition was based on a lack of foreign support for the American colonists' desire for independence, the military unreadiness of the colonists, and their lack of unity. By voting against the Declaration, he was left behind by those who supported independence with patriotic fervor.

Still, Dickinson worked on one congressional committee to prepare for the new nation the Articles of Confederation (a forerunner to the U.S. Constitution). He worked on another committee to obtain treaties with foreign nations to secure their military assistance. And when war finally came, Dickinson was one of only two congressmen who immediately stepped up to fight. In 1776 he served as colonel of the First

Philadelphia Battalion, leading his troops to fight the British in New Jersey.

That same year Dickinson and other like-minded members of the Pennsylvania Assembly opposed the new constitution under which the Assembly was meeting. After his proposals to revise the constitution were rejected by the majority in the body, Dickinson resigned from the Pennsylvania Assembly, resigned his military commission, and relocated his family to their home in Delaware. In time, he fought for the patriot cause in the Delaware Army (not the Continental army under General **George Washington** [see entry]) as a private, a low-ranking soldier.

Holds elected positions, faces criticism

In 1779 Delaware appointed Dickinson to be its delegate to the Continental Congress (it became the U.S. Congress in 1789). In 1781 he became president of Delaware, receiving all the votes except his own. It seems his heart remained in Pennsylvania and he truly did not wish to become president of Delaware, but went along with the wishes of others.

Apparently the anger against him in Pennsylvania cooled down, and in 1782 he was elected to the Supreme Executive Council of Pennsylvania and named president of that state as well. Within two months of the election, he had resigned his position in Delaware and returned to Pennsylvania, where he felt more politically experienced. According to Milton E. Flower, "The Delaware assembly took his desertion with little grace, believing it not only contrary to the spirit of the constitution but 'inconsistent with the dignity, freedom and interest' of their state."

In 1783 one especially vicious critic of Dickinson, signing himself *Valerius,* made bitter personal attacks on Dickinson in a newspaper. He repeated charges that had been leveled at Dickinson even before his election. According to Flower, Valerius charged that Dickinson "had opposed the Declaration of Independence, disapproved of the new state constitution, deserted his battalion when it became a part of the Continental army, and weakened public confidence in Continental currency [money] by advising his brother to refuse acceptance of it." While the other three charges were true, claims that he had deserted his fellow soldiers in battle were false.

Dickinson replied to these attacks in a series of letters that appeared in Philadelphia newspapers. That same year Dickinson helped to found and raise money for western Pennsylvania's new Dickinson College. He presented the school with two farms totaling 500 acres, to provide income for its support, as well as 1,500 books for its library.

Holds various political positions, lives quietly

For several years following his election in Pennsylvania, Dickinson largely involved himself in the financial and political affairs of that state, where he also served as head of the state court. His legal experience and wisdom proved very useful in that post.

In 1787 Dickinson went back to serving in Delaware when he was elected a delegate from that state to several conventions of representatives of all the U.S. states. Because of age and declining health, he did not engage in debates. But he did contribute his writing talents, penning a famous series of letters in support of the U.S. Constitution that he signed *Faubius*.

During the last couple of decades of his life Dickinson rarely appeared in public meetings. However, he did help to draft a new constitution for Delaware in 1792. He became very interested in international affairs during the 1790s. He was a great lover of France, and in 1797 he published fourteen letters encouraging renewal of the friendship between France and the United States, which had cooled following the Revolutionary War. In 1801 he produced two volumes of his writings that were published after his death on February 14, 1808, at Wilmington, Delaware. He was buried in the Friends' (Quaker) burying ground in that town.

Tributes to Dickinson came from a variety of people, including important politicians. Members of the U.S. House and Senate wore black armbands to honor his memory. In 1808 **Thomas Jefferson** (see entry) wrote about Dickinson in a letter to Joseph Bringhurst: "Among the first of the advocates [people who speak out in favor of] the rights of his country when [challenged] by Great Britain, he continued to the last ... [an] advocate of the true principles of our new government."

For More Information

Allison, Robert L. "John Dickinson" in *American Eras: The Revolutionary Era, 1754–1783*. Detroit: Gale, 1998, pp. 218-20.

Boatner, Mark M, III. "Dickinson, John" in *Encyclopedia of the American Revolution*. Mechanicsburg, PA: Stackpole Books, 1994, pp. 330-31.

Boatner, Mark M., III. "Dickinson, Philomen" in *Encyclopedia of the American Revolution*. Mechanicsburg, PA: Stackpole Books, 1994, pp. 331-32.

Bourgoin, Suzanne M., and Paula K. Byers, eds. "John Dickinson" in *Encyclopedia of World Biography*, Vol. 4, 2nd ed. Detroit: Gale, 1998, pp. 543-44.

Faragher, John Mack, gen. ed. "John Dickinson" in *Encyclopedia of Colonial and Revolutionary America*. New York: Facts on File, 1990, pp. 111-12.

Flower, Milton E. *John Dickinson: Conservative Revolutionary*. Charlottesville, VA: University Press of Virginia, 1983.

Ginsberg, Elaine K. "Dickinson, John" in *American National Biography*, Vol. 6, edited by John A. Garraty and Mark C. Carnes. New York: Oxford University Press, 1999, pp. 566-69.

McDonald, Forrest. "Dickinson, John" in *Encyclopedia of American Biography*, edited by John A. Garraty and Jerome L. Sternstein. New York: HarperCollins Publishers, 1995, pp. 288-89.

Miller, John C. *Sam Adams: Pioneer in Propaganda*. Stanford, CA: Stanford University Press, 1936, p. 310.

Peabody, James Bishop, ed. *John Adams: A Biography in His Own Words*. New York: Newsweek Books 1973, p. 156.

Whitney, David C. "John Dickinson" in *The Colonial Spirit of '76: The People of the Revolution*. Chicago, IL: J.G. Ferguson Publishers, 1974, pp. 172-74.

Benjamin Franklin

Born January 17, 1706
Boston, Massachusetts
Died April 17, 1790
Philadelphia, Pennsylvania

Political leader, diplomat, printer, publisher, writer, scientist, inventor

"This is the age of experiments."

Portrait: Benjamin Franklin.
Reproduced courtesy of the Library of Congress.

Benjamin Franklin was a man who combined genius and imagination with humor and common sense; it seemed he could do almost anything. By the time the American Revolution broke out in 1775, Franklin was world-famous as a writer, inventor, and scientist. He then became the world's most famous rebel, although his contributions to the establishment of an independent United States are often overlooked.

Benjamin Franklin was born in Boston, Massachusetts, in 1706. His father, Josiah, was an Englishman who had seven children by his first wife before she died. He moved to New England in 1683 in search of religious freedom, and married Abiah Folger, daughter of an old New England family. She bore him ten more children. Benjamin Franklin was her seventh child and the youngest son.

Not much is known about Benjamin Franklin's mother. In his old age, Franklin told a friend that his mother had taught him common sense and tolerance. In his autobiography (see box), Franklin described his father as healthy and very strong. Josiah Franklin liked to play religious tunes on his violin and sing along at the end of a hard day's work. He was regarded by Boston's leading citizens as a man of some wisdom, and they often asked for his advice in resolving conflicts.

In the Franklin household their Puritan religion was taken very seriously. Puritanism stressed a strict moral code and the value of hard work. Franklin always respected his parents' beliefs, but he later rejected some of the more rigid aspects of Puritanism. As a young adult he gave up going to church altogether and devised a way of worshiping God at home. He put together his own book of prayers; it contained passages from science books and passages from books that discussed right and wrong behavior.

Schooling ends at age ten; goes to work for father

Franklin's older brothers had been sent out at young ages to work for local tradesmen for a certain length of time in exchange for being taught a trade. Franklin was a bright, happy boy who could read the Bible by age five. His father thought he might have a future in the church, so the child was sent to school at age eight. He did well in all his subjects except arithmetic, but looking ahead, his father decided that he would never be able to afford to send the boy to college. So Josiah Franklin took his intelligent youngest son out of school at the age of ten and put him to work in the family business, a candle- and soapmaking shop.

Franklin hated the work. He really wanted to run off to sea. His father forbade it, and for a time the boy satisfied his seagoing urges by learning to swim well and by boating and canoeing whenever he had the chance.

Franklin grew no fonder of his father's trade. Hoping to find something his son liked better, Josiah Franklin often took the boy on walks to watch other tradesmen at work. Franklin found nothing that suited him, but his curiosity was aroused. He began "to construct little Machines for my Experiments." His interest in science would continue throughout his life.

Franklin read everything he could lay his hands on. In his day, that mostly meant books with religious themes. In his old age, he regretted "that at a time when I had such a Thirst for Knowledge, more proper Books had not fallen in my Way."

Becomes printer's apprentice; at last finds satisfying work

Seeing how fond his son was of books, and how much he disliked making soap and candles, Josiah Franklin finally relented when the boy was twelve and permitted him to go as an apprentice to his brother, James, a printer. To young Franklin, the best thing about the printing trade was that "I now had Access to better Books." He especially liked to read about the character and behavior of ancient Greek and Roman leaders. He also read essays that made him want to do good deeds.

In 1721 James Franklin established his own newspaper. Unknown even to James, Benjamin Franklin contributed amusing and popular unsigned articles to the paper. When James learned who had actually written the articles, he was not very happy. The two young men did not get along. Franklin claimed his brother often lost his temper and beat him.

In 1723 the seventeen-year-old Franklin left home forever and moved to Philadelphia, Pennsylvania, the largest city in the colonies. By then he was an expert at printing, a trade that was just opening up in the colonies. He had the whole world in front of him.

At this point in his life, Franklin was a strong, healthy young man, nearly six feet tall. He had abundant dark brown hair, hazel eyes, a large mouth, and a large head in proportion to his body. He soon caught the eye of a young Philadelphia woman named Deborah Read, daughter of a prosperous carpenter (see **Deborah Read Franklin** entry). The couple did not marry until 1730; meanwhile Franklin had several adventures and career advances.

In 1724 Franklin went to England to buy type for a printing press so he could start his own business. His two-year trip to England was the beginning of a lifetime of globetrotting. He got work right away at one of London's most important publishers and made a name for himself by writing on religious matters.

But Franklin grew tired of the frantic pace of London. He thought of touring the continent of Europe and paying for the trip by giving swimming lessons. Instead, feeling guilty over his desertion of Deborah, he returned to Philadelphia in 1726. He worked hard, and by 1730 he was sole owner of *The*

Pennsylvania Gazette. Just before his marriage to Deborah that same year Franklin fathered a child, William. It remains a mystery whether Deborah was William's mother. It is known that William lived in her home but she always treated him poorly.

The Franklins had two other children. Their first, Francis Folger, died in 1736 at age four of smallpox, a contagious disease that causes fever, vomiting, and skin eruptions. Franklin was heartbroken at little Franky's death. His daughter, Sarah, was born in 1743.

Historians still debate the extent of Franklin's feelings for his wife Deborah. She did not share his intellectual and political interests, but she did help Franklin tremendously in the family business. Because of her assistance, Franklin had the luxury of retiring from business early (1748) and devoting himself to a career in public life.

Enters public life, flies kites

During his newspaper days, Franklin did not neglect his social life. He founded a debating club in 1727 that later became the American Philosophical Society. Its members were young men like himself, intellectuals who were interested in doing good works. Members met to discuss religion and how to help their fellow man; they also helped each other rise in the community. By 1740 Franklin's participation in this kind of activity had made him a leader in Philadelphia society.

Franklin's further accomplishments in the years leading up to the American Revolution (1775–83) were many and varied. He fulfilled his childhood desire to do good works by having hospitals built, establishing public libraries at a time when most books were in the hands of private owners, and arranging for the formation of a volunteer fire department. He gained worldwide fame in 1742 for his invention of the Franklin stove, a practical and heat-efficient way of warming houses. His scientific curiosity led to kite experiments in the 1740s and 1750s that helped explain lightning and electricity. These impressive scientific discoveries brought Franklin a great deal of fame throughout Europe.

Franklin next turned his attention to what he thought was lacking in the colony: a school for higher learning where Pennsylvanians could study "the finer arts and sciences." In

1751 he established the Academy, now the University of Pennsylvania. That same year he began his nearly forty-year career as a public official when he was elected to the Pennsylvania Assembly (the colony's lawmaking body).

Writes Albany Plan of Union

In 1753 Franklin was appointed by the governor of Pennsylvania to negotiate treaties of friendship with Native Americans on the Pennsylvania frontier. A war was brewing between France and England, a war that was certain to involve the English colonies and the French and Indians who lived, trapped, and traded on the frontier. If such a war did break out (it did; it was known as the French and Indian War of 1754–63), the Indians were expected to side with the French against the English. English colonists who lived near the Indians would suffer.

Franklin's dealings with the Indians marked the beginning of his diplomatic career. In the time he spent with them, he became fascinated by their way of life, and he had high praise for the union of six native tribes called the Iroquois Confederacy. Their form of government was the inspiration for Franklin's 1754 Albany Plan of Union. Franklin believed that Pennsylvania could not fight the French and Indians by itself and that all the colonies should join together "as one whole and not as different States with separate Interests" to fight this threat. When representatives of all the colonies met in Albany, New York, in 1754, to discuss the war with France, Franklin presented his Plan of Union.

But in 1754 the colonial governments were not yet willing to give up their individual powers and form one united body, and Franklin's plan was rejected.

Begins London phase of his career

In 1757 Franklin went to London as an agent for the Pennsylvania Assembly. Agents were men who were appointed by the colonies to live in London, circulate among important people, and report back on what was happening in Parliament (Great Britain's lawmaking body). The agents made sure Parliament knew what the colonies' needs and wishes were as Parliament prepared to make laws that affected the colonies.

Between 1757 and 1774 Franklin also served at various times as an agent for the colonies of Georgia, New Jersey, and Massachusetts. During those years, he lived almost all of the time in London, and he made friends in high places in government. Franklin believed in the British Empire, and he worked hard to help Great Britain win the French and Indian War. For example, he convinced the Pennsylvania Assembly to help finance the war and provide men to fight for the British.

This time, Franklin enjoyed his time abroad. Now a man of some wealth and fame, he delighted in the comforts and sophistication of the Old World. He toured the European continent, socialized with intellectuals and high-ranking members of society, attended concerts, and accepted honorary university degrees for his scientific work. He was interested in everything and everyone he encountered, and almost everyone he met liked and respected him.

Franklin remained loyal to the British Empire, but along with other Americans, his loyalty was tested after the French and Indian War, and it finally withered and died on the eve of the American Revolution.

Opposes British taxation measures

From 1762 to 1764, Franklin was back in America, serving as deputy postmaster for North America. Over the next twenty years, Franklin would greatly improve America's postal service, and the money he earned was a welcome supplement to his income. He helped support poorer members of his family, especially his sister, Jane Mecom, to whom he was always close.

The British began to impose taxes on the American colonists in 1764 to help pay off war debts from the French and Indian War. At first, Franklin thought this was reasonable. But Americans objected to the Stamp Act of 1765, which taxed certain documents and other items ranging from newspapers to dice. Franklin listened to the complaints of his countrymen, then made a dramatic appearance before Parliament. He explained that America insisted on governing and taxing itself but still wished to remain part of the British Empire. He managed to get the Stamp Act repealed in 1766.

Parliament continued trying to raise money in the colonies by passing several measures that Americans called oppressive. In London, Franklin was in the middle of all the political activity surrounding the issue. He tried to convince his friends in Parliament that Parliament's actions toward the colonies were wrongheaded. Over time he began to see that Parliament and King **George III** (see entry) were determined to have their way, regardless of the colonies' needs and desires. Meanwhile, by arguing against taxation, he had made enemies in Parliament. Soon Parliament passed the extremely oppressive measures that Americans called the Intolerable Acts, and sent troops to America to enforce the acts. Franklin saw that his efforts to find some way to avoid a break between Great Britain and the colonies were doomed.

In February 1775 Franklin received word that Deborah, his wife of forty-four years, had died. Grief-stricken, he left London for Philadelphia. By then he was thoroughly disgusted with British politicians.

Attends Second Continental Congress

The sixty-nine-year-old Franklin still had many contributions to make to his country. He arrived in Philadelphia on May 5, 1775, to hear the news that shots had been fired a few weeks earlier at Lexington and Concord, Massachusetts. On May 6 Franklin was chosen to represent Pennsylvania at the Second Continental Congress, which met to decide what steps to take against the British.

Franklin felt out of place at the Continental Congress. He was by far the oldest man there, and he knew few of the other delegates. He was in favor of declaring independence, but many others had not yet been convinced. He was embarrassed because everyone knew he could not convince his son, William, the British-appointed governor of New Jersey, to join the cause of independence. Over the course of the next several years, as America went to war with Great Britain, the rift between Franklin and his son grew wider; the two men were never fully reconciled.

Franklin was on the committee of five men, including **Thomas Jefferson** (see entry), who wrote the Declaration of Independence, adopted by the Congress in July 1776.

Contributions to war effort

Throughout the Revolutionary War Franklin served on congressional committees and attended every meeting of Congress, although he was often seen sleeping through them. He wrote newspaper articles designed to sway public opinion in favor of American independence. But his most important contribution was a secret one: to correspond with American sympathizers in other countries on the subject of aid for the American cause.

Franklin took direct steps to secure foreign aid when he and Thomas Jefferson sailed for France in September 1776. France was America's best hope for desperately needed protection against the mighty British navy. Franklin's family begged him not to go, reminding him that he was old, that he had already done more than enough for his country, and that he could be hanged for treason if his ship were overtaken by the British. He went anyway.

Throughout the Revolutionary War, Benjamin Franklin's most important contribution was a secret one: to correspond with American sympathizers in other countries on the subject of aid for the American cause.
Reproduced courtesy of the Library of Congress.

The Atlantic crossing was terribly uncomfortable; Franklin could barely stand by the time he arrived in France. His spirits picked up when the citizens of Paris greeted their distinguished visitor with open arms. Over the course of the next year, Franklin became a favorite of the beautiful upper-class ladies of Paris. In a time when Frenchmen wore lavish clothing and powdered wigs, the French saw the plainly dressed, bareheaded Franklin as an example of greatness combined with humble simplicity. By this time, Franklin had grown quite fat; his sparse hair was entirely grey. He suffered from bouts of dizziness and attacks of gout (a painful disease of the joints).

Becomes American diplomat in France

Franklin finally convinced the French to sign a treaty of friendship and trade in February 1778. He spent seven years in France, securing the naval assistance that helped win the American Revolution, and signing treaties of trade and friendship between the United States and any other foreign country that was interested. Franklin believed that the new nation would need the cooperation of the rest of the world in getting started.

When the Revolutionary War ended in 1783, Franklin helped negotiate the peace treaty that won very favorable terms for America (land and independence). On May 2, 1785, Franklin received the news that Congress had granted his request to come home. Overjoyed, he cried: "I shall now be free of Politicks for the rest of my Life." He spoke too soon.

The French were very sorry to see Franklin go. Now in poor health and nearly eighty years old, Franklin looked forward to the gratitude of his countrymen and spending the rest of his days quietly with his family. He occupied himself on the voyage home by writing three scientific papers.

At home in Philadelphia

In Philadelphia, Franklin was greeted warmly by a huge crowd, and his family wept for joy at his safe return. He soon learned that political squabbles had erupted in Pennsylvania while he was away. Hoping to ease the situation, he agreed to run for state office. On October 26, 1785, state legislators elected him President of the state of Pennsylvania; he would serve three one-year terms in that post.

Franklin hoped he could do something good for the people of Pennsylvania by serving in the legislature, but he did complain that his fellow citizens "engross the prime of my life. They have eaten my flesh, and seem resolved now to pick my bones."

In his spare time, Franklin devoted himself to inventing comforts for his old age. He lived with Sarah and her family in the home he had built nearly a quarter-century before. He invented a "long arm," a device for taking books down from high shelves. When his eyesight began to fail, he invented bifocal glasses. He invented an armchair with a fan attached to it, in which he sometimes took nude "air baths" in his garden.

Final days

In 1787 Franklin was a Pennsylvania delegate to the Federal Constitutional Convention, called to write a new con-

Writings of Benjamin Franklin

Benjamin Franklin, largely a self-educated man, was in his early twenties in 1729 when he began publishing *The Pennsylvania Gazette*. Colonial readers thirsted for news from Europe; they had already heard all of the local news. Franklin gave them what they wanted, but he often contributed humorous pieces he wrote himself. He also expressed his political views on issues of the day.

But Franklin knew that the real money was in almanacs, books published yearly and made up of bits and pieces of information in many unrelated fields. A majority of colonists owned only two books: the Bible and an almanac. As soon as he had his newspaper up and running, Franklin turned his attention to the almanac market.

Franklion began publishing the *Pennsylvania Almanack* in 1730. From 1732 to 1757 the book appeared under the name of *Poor Richard's Almanack*, the most famous work to come out of Franklin's long and productive writing career. What set his book apart from all other almanacs were his proverbs. According to biographer Alfred Owen Aldridge, those proverbs, or sayings, "represented Franklin's idea of the world's most witty and succinct comments on sex, religion, psychology and professions." Franklin put those comments in his own plain words. Among his many and lasting proverbs are these: "Eat to live, and not live to eat"; "He that lies down with Dogs, shall rise up with fleas"; "Little strokes fell big oaks"; and "Early to bed and early to rise / Makes a man healthy, wealthy, and wise."

Franklin's other famous work was his *Autobiography*, which contains most of what is known about his early life. Franklin began the book in 1771 and worked on it over the next eighteen years. He never completed it; the book ends with his 1757 trip to England. The book was published in England in 1793, and in America in 1818. Critics either loved the book or hated it. A 1905 *Harper's* magazine article noted: "Franklin's is one of the greatest autobiographies in literature, and towers over other autobiographies as Franklin towered over other men."

stitution for the United States. As the arguments went on around him at the convention, Franklin assumed the role of easing the tension. Although very ill, he told amusing stories but rarely joined the debate. He urged the members to ratify the Constitution; it was not perfect, he told them, but it established the best form of government then known.

In January 1788 Franklin fell and sprained his wrist and arm. He never fully recovered from the accident. By June 1789 he was in almost constant pain, reduced to nothing "but a Skeleton covered with a Skin," as he described himself.

Franklin died peacefully at home on April 17, 1790. He left behind his son, William; his daughter, Sarah; and eight grandchildren. He took pride in the fact that he had imparted to his family the necessity of standing on their own two feet and depending on no one else for their livelihood.

John Adams's assessment of Franklin

Like all politicians, Franklin had firm friends and bitter enemies. One who disliked him very much was founding father **John Adams** (see entry). Many who knew the two men suggested that Adams was jealous of Franklin. In spite of his dislike, Adams appreciated Franklin's "merits," which he described in a newspaper article written for the *Boston Patriot* in 1811, years after Franklin's death:

> Franklin had a great genius, original, [wise], and inventive, capable of discoveries in science no less than of improvements in the fine arts and the mechanic arts. He had a vast imagination ... wit ... [and] humor that, when he pleased, was delicate and delightful.... Had he been blessed with the same advantages of scholastic education in his early youth, and pursued a course of studies as unembarrassed with occupations of public and private life, as [scientist] Sir Isaac Newton, he might have emulated the first philosopher.... He has added much to the mass of natural knowledge, and contributed largely to the progress of the human mind.

For More Information

Adler, David A. *Benjamin Franklin—Printer, Inventor, Statesman.* New York: Holiday House, 1992.

Aldridge, Alfred Owen. *Benjamin Franklin: Philosopher and Man.* Philadelphia: J. B. Lippincott, 1965.

Clark, Ronald W. *Benjamin Franklin: A Biography.* New York: Random House, 1983.

Davidson, Margaret. *The Story of Benjamin Franklin: Amazing American.* Gareth Stevens Publishing, 1997.

Foster, Leila Merrell. *Benjamin Franklin, Founding Father and Inventor.* Enslow, 1997.

Franklin, Benjamin. *Benjamin Franklin's Autobiography: An Authoritative Text, Backgrounds, Criticism,* edited by J. A. Leo Lemay and P. M. Zall. New York: W.W. Norton & Company, 1986, pp. 244, 275, 278.

Deborah Read Franklin

Born c. 1707
Died December 19, 1774
Philadelphia, Pennsylvania

Businesswoman

Deborah Read Franklin played an important role in the founding of the United States simply by taking on the management of her family business. By doing so she allowed her husband, founding father **Benjamin Franklin** (see entry), the opportunity to actively pursue his role in state and national politics in the decades before and after the American Revolution.

Deborah Read was born about 1707 to John Read, a carpenter from London, England, and Sarah White Read of Birmingham, England. Whether the child was born while her parents still lived in Birmingham, or after they moved to Philadelphia, Pennsylvania, remains uncertain. The second of seven children, Read received little formal education; almost nothing else is known about her childhood.

In his biographical writings, Benjamin Franklin described Deborah Read's first glimpse of him when he was seventeen. Read watched the tall, husky youth pass her father's shop on Philadelphia's Market Street, chomping on a roll of bread. His pockets bulged with extra pairs of socks, and he carried two more rolls, one under each arm. As she watched, Deborah giggled out loud.

"She prov'd a good and faithful Helpmate, assisted me much by attending the Shop, we throve together, and have ever ... [tried] to make each other happy."

Benjamin Franklin

Portrait: Deborah Read Franklin. *Reproduced by permission of the Corbis Corportion (Bellevue).*

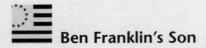

Ben Franklin's Son

William Franklin, born in 1731, was the son of Benjamin Franklin. William always claimed that Deborah Read Franklin was his mother, but many historians question whether or not that was true, even though he was raised in his father's home.

Until around age thirty, William Franklin stayed close to his father, assisting him in his political, financial, and scientific undertakings. Because of William Franklin's proximity to his father, he was present for Ben Franklin's famous kite and key electricity experiment. Around 1750 Benjamin Franklin helped William obtain the position of clerk of the Pennsylvania Assembly and later that of postmaster of Philadelphia. William accompanied his father to England, where he studied law and became a lawyer. While in England in 1762, he married Elizabeth Downes, a wealthy young Englishwoman.

William Franklin's friendship with England's Earl of Bute helped William become the royal governor of New Jersey in 1762. He held the post for thirteen years and performed his duties well. He helped bring about reforms such as the improvement of roads and the building of bridges, and he established the first Indian reservation in America. By 1775, with the beginning of the Revolutionary War, a break took place between William Franklin and his father, as each took separate sides in the conflict. William stayed loyal to England.

In June 1776 William Franklin was arrested by New Jersey patriots as an "enemy to the liberties" of America and was confined to his home. The Continental Congress soon sentenced him to a harsh prison in Connecticut. While he was in prison, his wife Elizabeth became sick and died. He was not permitted to visit her during her illness, and this left him very bitter.

William Franklin was involved in a prisoner-of-war exchange in 1778, in

Franklin soon became a lodger at the Read house in Philadelphia. The two young people grew to have affectionate feelings for one another, and Franklin asked Deborah Read to marry him. Her recently widowed mother objected to the match, however, because she thought that the couple was too young.

Franklin soon left on a two-year trip to England. He rarely wrote while he was gone, and in 1725 Deborah Read's mother persuaded her to marry John Rogers, a local potter, but the unhappy union soon ended when she left her husband.

which the British traded the patriot governor of Delaware for him. Franklin went to live in British-held New York City. He became president of an organization he founded called the Board of Associated Loyalists, a group that protected thousands of Loyalists in camps located on Long Island, New York. Criticized by some as a gang of thugs, they obtained information for the British and helped keep local citizens under control. In 1782 a citizen soldier from New Jersey named Joshua Huddy was illegally ordered executed by members of the Board of Associated Loyalists. **George Washington** (see entry) believed William Franklin was responsible for giving the order. The complicated political affair grew to involve not only the American colonies and Britain, but France as well. As a result, in order to avoid further embarrassment, the British ordered the group to disband.

In 1782 William Franklin permanently moved to England. For the loss of his home and financial holdings in America he received only the value of his furniture and a rather small annual payment from the British government. He and Benjamin Franklin met to try to reestablish a good relationship, but in time Franklin disinherited his son, writing in his will, "The part [William] acted against me in the late war ... will account for my leaving him no more of an estate [than] he [tried] to deprive me of."

In time William Franklin married a wealthy Irish widow and acted as an agent for Loyalist groups in London. William Franklin's own illegitimate son, William Temple Franklin, born in England in 1759, was raised partly by Benjamin Franklin, his grandfather. Young William served as Benjamin Franklin's secretary in Paris, France, and later edited the noted patriot's writings after his death.

There were rumors that Rogers already had a wife in England. He disappeared to the West Indies, where it was said he died in a fistfight.

Manages family and business

By 1730 Benjamin Franklin had returned to Philadelphia. He visited Deborah Read and again asked her to marry him. Although the young woman had grown fond of him, she said that a new marriage was out of the question as long as

Deborah Read Franklin, serving tea to a visitor. Benjamin Franklin sits to her left. She was supportive of her husband's social and political life but was herself less comfortable in these situations. *Reproduced by permission of the Corbis Corporation (Bellevue).*

there was any chance that Rogers might reappear. Had she and Franklin married, they could have been charged with bigamy (the crime of marrying another person when one is already married). On September 1, 1730, Deborah Read and Franklin entered into a common-law marriage, agreeing to live together as husband and wife without formal approval by religious or civil authorities. The couple's relatives and friends seemed to accept the unusual arrangement without objection.

The Franklins had two children (or possibly three; see box). Their first, Francis Folger Franklin, died in 1736 at age four of smallpox, a contagious disease that causes fever, vomiting, skin eruptions, and sometimes death. Their daughter, Sarah Franklin Bache, was born in 1743.

Deborah Franklin enjoyed being a homemaker and had a good head for business. While her husband ran their printing business, she was in charge of the couple's book and stationery shop as well as a general store. When Benjamin

Franklin began his frequent absences on government business, she managed all the businesses and sold such items as soap, medicines, chocolate, tea, cloth, feathers, and lottery tickets.

Spends life apart from husband

Deborah Franklin did not share many of Benjamin Franklin's intellectual, scientific, or political interests, and, unlike him, she was uncomfortable in social situations. She often referred to her husband as her "dear Child" or "Pappy." When Franklin spent the years of 1757 to 1762 and 1764 to 1775 in Europe as a representative of the government of Pennsylvania, Deborah Franklin stayed in Philadelphia. She had no wish to cross the ocean. Some say she feared that her plain appearance and simple ways would embarrass her husband in front of his elegant European companions.

In 1765 the British government, in an effort to raise money to pay off its war debts, imposed the Stamp Act on the American colonists, forcing them to pay a tax on each paper item they used. On September 17, 1765, a number of Philadelphia citizens threatened to attack Deborah Franklin's house, protesting that her politician husband had not fought against the Stamp Act vigorously enough. With the help of some armed relatives, she told the crowd she would not allow herself to be forced from her own home. Soon the angry mob retreated, leaving the house in peace.

Because of the great assistance Deborah provided him, Benjamin Franklin had the luxury of retiring from business early and devoting himself to a career in public life. But it also allowed him to spend many years in Europe without her. The couple sent frequent letters back and forth that mostly focused on personal matters. Only in their later years did the letters become quite brief and businesslike, reflecting their growing lack of closeness.

Death of Franklin

Around 1773 Deborah Read Franklin began experiencing health problems. Benjamin Franklin was in England, trying to help keep peace between America and England, and he was unable to return to the colonies. In 1774 he wrote her a letter in which, for the first time, he used the tender term "my dear Love," but she was too ill to respond or even acknowledge it. She died in Philadelphia in December 1774.

Three months later Benjamin Franklin returned to America, believing that a peaceful settlement to the British-American conflict was no longer possible. He wrote to a friend about his wife of many years: "I have lately lost my old and faithful Companion; and I every day become more sensible of the greatness of that Loss; which cannot now be repair'd." After his death in 1790 he was buried beside his mate at Christ Church Cemetery in Philadelphia.

For More Information

Boatner, Mark M. "Franklin, William" in *Encyclopedia of the American Revolution.* Mechanicsburg, PA: Stackpole Books, 1994, pp. 393–94.

Faragher, John Mack. "Deborah Read Franklin" in *The Encyclopedia of Colonial and Revolutionary America.* New York: Facts on File, 1990, p. 145.

Garraty, John A. and Marc C. Carnes, eds. "William Franklin" in *American National Biography,* Vol. 8. New York: Oxford University Press, pp. 401–03.

LaBaree, Leonard W. "Deborah Read Franklin" in *Notable American Women, 1607–1950: A Biographical Dictionary,* Vol. 1, edited by Edward T. James. Cambridge, MA: Belknap Press of Harvard University, pp. 663–64.

Lopez, Claude-Anne. "Deborah Read Franklin" in *American National Biography,* Vol. 8. New York: Oxford University Press, 1999, pp. 396–98.

Purcell, Edward, ed. *Who Was Who in the American Revolution?* New York: Facts on File, 1993, p. 170.

Randall, Willard Sterne. *A Little Revenge.* Boston: Little, Brown, 1984.

Elizabeth Freeman

Born c. 1744
Died December 1829
Stockbridge, Massachusetts

Slave, nurse, midwife

Elizabeth Freeman, who lived as a slave for thirty years, was known for her courage, wit, kindness, dignity, and intelligence. Her 1781 victory in obtaining freedom from slavery played a large part in putting an end to slavery in the state of Massachusetts.

Freeman was born around 1744, possibly on the estate of Pieter Hogeboom of Claverack, New York; this approximate birth date is based on the fact that she was said to have been about eighty-five years old when she died in 1829. Being a slave, she was not given a last name at birth. Known for most of her life as Mum Bett or Mumbet, a name that apparently came from Elizabeth, she adopted the last name Freeman upon being freed from slavery. Freeman and her sister lived as slaves on Hogeboom's estate. Around 1758 Hogeboom died, and the two girls passed into the possession of the Ashleys, one of the leading families of Sheffield, Massachusetts (Hogeboom's youngest daughter, Hannah, had married John Ashley in 1735).

For twenty years John Ashley was a judge of the Massachusetts Court of Common Pleas. He held other local and

"Anytime, anytime while I was a slave, if one minute's freedom had been offered to me, and I had been told I must die at the end of that minute, I would have taken it—just to stand on God's earth a free woman."

Portrait: Elizabeth Freeman.
Reproduced by permission of the Granger Collection, New York.

state government positions, including the chairmanship of a committee that discussed the growing oppression of the colonies by Great Britain during the 1760s. The committee drew up the Sheffield Declaration, which stated that members of humankind "are equal, free and independent of each other, and have a right to the undisturbed Enjoyment of their lives, their Liberty and Property." A young lawyer named Theodore Sedgwick Sr., was also on the committee.

Begins court case to gain freedom

According to an account of Elizabeth Freeman's life written in 1838 by English novelist and economist Harriet Martineau, "when [Freeman] was waiting a table, she heard gentlemen [saying] ... that all people were born free and equal, and she thought long about it, and resolved she would try whether she did not come in among them," that is, she decided she too was born free and equal. Although Freeman was unable to read and write, she heard the discussions of the men about the human right to freedom "by keepin' still and mindin' [paying attention to] things" and took them to heart.

One day Hannah Ashley, Freeman's mistress, became angry and tried to strike the slave's sister with a hot kitchen shovel. Freeman immediately stepped in to protect her sister and was struck on the arm with the shovel. From that time on her arm was badly scarred and she no longer had the full use of it. Cruelty to servants was unusual in the house, and Elizabeth was outraged by Hannah Ashley's act. She at once left the house and refused to return.

She persuaded a man named Brom (another of Ashley's slaves) to join her and then sought the help of Theodore Sedgwick Sr., a local lawyer whom she had met at the Ashley home. She told him she wanted to obtain freedom for herself and Brom.

Sedgwick believed that slavery was an illogical practice, especially at a time when Massachusetts was engaged in a fight for freedom, and he accepted Freeman's case. *Brom and Bett v. J. Ashley Esq.* came before the County Court of Common Pleas in Great Barrington, New York, in August 1781.

Victory sets course against slavery

During the court proceedings Freeman testified: "I heard that paper read yesterday, that says, 'all men are born equal, and that every man has a right to freedom.' I am not a dumb critter; won't the law give me my freedom?"

John Ashley objected to his slaves being freed, claiming they were his servants for life. But in the end the two slaves, represented by Sedgwick and a Connecticut lawyer named Tapping Reeve, won their case. Reeve was later to start the first law school in North America in Litchfield, Connecticut.

On August 22, 1781, the jury found that Freeman and Brom were freemen and that they had been illegally kept as slaves by the Ashleys. The court demanded that the family pay the two former slaves thirty shillings (British coins) in damages, a tiny sum of money. In addition, Freeman received payment for the years (since her twenty-first birthday) she had served the Ashleys.

Historians continue to argue whether Freeman's was the first court case against slavery in Massachusetts. In *Black Women in America,* historian Taunya Lovell Banks argued: "Historians overlook ... Freeman's contribution, citing instead the cases of two Black men [that were begun] and decided after Freeman's. However, Elizabeth Freeman's contribution is significant because ... the legal theory set forth in her suit had the potential to free not just [Freeman and Brom], but all enslaved Blacks in Massachusetts."

Goes to work for Sedgwicks

Freeman's suit was the first to base its challenge to slavery on a state constitution. The Massachusetts State Constitution of 1780 declared that "all men are born free and equal." However, Freeman's victory in her case did not result in the complete freedom of all black slaves in Massachusetts at the time.

At the end of the court case, Elizabeth chose Freeman as her last name. She turned down John Ashley's request to go back to work for him and instead went to work for the Sedgwicks as a paid housekeeper, remaining with the family for the rest of her life. In 1785 she moved with them to Stockbridge, Massachusetts. The family grew to love her, and she was espe-

Theodore Sedgwick Sr., Champion of Freedom

The lawyer who helped win Elizabeth Freeman's freedom and later became her employer was born in East Hartford, Connecticut, on May 9, 1746. Theodore Sedgwick Sr., attended Yale College, where he studied religion and law. He practiced law in Barrington and then Sheffield, Massachusetts.

Sedgwick fought for the patriots in battles in Canada during the Revolutionary War and also served in both the Massachusetts Senate and House of Representatives. In 1782 Sedgwick became a member of Benjamin Franklin's Abolition Society of Pennsylvania. The group helped fugitive slaves in their attempts to find freedom in the states that did not practice slavery. Other members of the society included **George Washington, Thomas Paine**, and the **Marquis de Lafayette** (see entries). Sedgwick also worked as a delegate to the Massachusetts state convention that adopted the Federal Constitution in 1788. He later served in both the U.S. House of Representatives and the Senate.

According to Richard E. Welch Jr., author of *Theodore Sedgwick: Federalist,* "Sedgwick was no friend of Slavery, but if he did not sympathize with the guarantees afforded that institution by the [U.S.] Constitution, he was prepared to respect and obey them. It was Sedgwick, as chairman of the committee appointed for the purpose, who virtually authored the first Fugitive Slave Law [in] November, 1791."

The Fugitive Slave Law, passed by the U.S. Congress in 1793, tried to make it easier to recapture runaway slaves and send them back to their owners. James M. Banner Jr., explained in his article on Sedgwick in *American National Biography* that Sedgwick "had a profound respect for the law and for legality. This was exhibited during his second year in Congress by his seemingly contradictory efforts to protect the Quakers' [members of the Society of Friends religious group, which opposed slavery] right of petition and the constitutional guarantees of their enemies, the slaveholders.... When in Congress, [Sedgwick] was the major force behind passage of the first fugitive slave law, which he justified as a legitimate protection of property, he also defended the rights of Quakers to petition for abolition of slavery."

Sedgwick's last professional post was that of judge on the Supreme Court of Massachusetts from 1802 to 1813. He served in this position until his death in Boston, Massachusetts, on January 24, 1813. Sedgwick was buried near Elizabeth Freeman in the Sedgwick family cemetery.

cially helpful in caring for Sedgwick's wife, who suffered at times from mental illness.

The Sedgwick's daughter, Catharine, became a popular novelist of the nineteenth century. She once wrote about Freeman, whom she affectionately called "Mumbet":

> One should have known this remarkable woman, the native majesty of her deportment [behavior] ... Mumbet was the only person who could [quiet] my mother when her mind was disordered—the only one of her friends who she liked to have about her—and why? [Freeman] treated her with the same respect she did when she was sane. As far as possible, she obeyed [mother's] commands and humored her [wishes]; in short, her superior instincts hit upon the mode of treatment that has since been adopted [for the mentally ill].

Marries, serves as nurse

Elizabeth Freeman married at some point, but according to Theodore Sedgwick Jr., her husband died in the Revolutionary War and Freeman never remarried. It is likely that the marriage did produce children; Freeman's 1829 will mentioned a daughter, Elizabeth (known as "Little Bet"), grandchildren, and great grandchildren.

During her lifetime Freeman acted as a nurse and a midwife (one who delivers babies) in her community. Careful with her money, she was able to support her large extended family on her wages. About her medical skills, Theodore Sedgwick Jr. wrote: "She had no competitor. I believe she never lost a child, when she had the care of its mother, at its birth. When a child, wailing in the arms of its mother, heard her steps on the stairway, or approaching the door, it ceased to cry."

Bravery under pressure

Freeman's courage and determination are shown by an incident that took place in 1786 during Shays's Rebellion (see **Daniel Shays** entry). Shays's Rebellion was an uprising of some farmers in western Massachusetts who were demanding relief money from the government following an economic downturn. With Theodore Sedgwick Sr. away, Freeman had to deal with the men who invaded the household. She was said to have hidden the family silver among her own possessions and then shamed the invaders into not searching them.

About the incident Theodore Sedgwick Jr., wrote: "She did not attempt to resist, by direct force [but] assumed a degree of authority; told the plunderers that they 'dare not strike a woman,' and attended them in their exploring the house to prevent [widespread] destruction." When one man broke off the neck of a bottle of wine to drink it, Freeman told him that if another bottle should be broken, she would lay flat with her shovel the man that broke it.

Final years

Freeman did not retire until she was an old woman. By that time she had saved enough money to buy a little house for herself, her daughter, and other family members. Catharine Sedgwick visited her every day as Freeman's death approached. "Even [long] suffering and mortal sickness ... could not break down [Freeman's] spirit," Catharine wrote.

Freeman died in December 1829, and was buried in Stockbridge at the center of the Sedgwick family plot. That Freeman was dearly loved by the Sedgwick family is shown by the fact that four of Theodore Sedgwick Sr.'s children created memorials to her, both during her lifetime and after her death. Susan Sedgwick's 1811 watercolor portrait of Freeman can be seen today at the Massachusetts Historical Society. Theodore Sedgwick Jr. used her as an example in his antislavery lectures. Catharine Sedgwick praised her in a book, and Charles Sedgwick had etched on her tombstone: "She could neither read nor write, yet in her own sphere she had no superior nor equal. She neither wasted time nor property. She never violated a trust, nor failed to perform a duty. In every situation of domestic trial, she was the most efficient helper, and the tenderest friend. Good Mother, farewell."

For More Information

Banks, Taunya Lovell. "Freeman, Elizabeth 'Mum Bett' (c. 1744–1829)." Darlene Clark Hine, ed. *Black Women in America.* Brooklyn, NY: Carlson Publishing, 1993, pp. 469–70.

Banner, James M., Jr. "Sedgwick, Theodore." *American National Biography,* Vol. 19. New York: Oxford University Press, 1999, pp. 583–84.

Felton, Harold W. *Mumbet: The Story of Elizabeth Freeman.* New York: Dodd, Mead & Company, 1970.

Johns, Robert L. "Elizabeth Freeman, 'Mum Bett.'" Jessie Carney Smith, ed. *Notable Black American Women*. Detroit: Gale, 1992, pp. 371–73.

Kaplan, Sidney, and Emma Nogrady Kaplan. *The Black Presence in the Era of the American Revolution 1770–1800*. Greenwich, CT: New York Graphic Society in association with the Smithsonian Institution Press, 1973, pp. 244–48.

Martineau, Harriet. *Retrospect of Western Travel,* Vol. 2. London: Saunders and Otley, 1838.

Nell, William C. *The Colored Patriots of the American Revolution*. Boston, MA: Robert F. Wallcut, 1855. Reprinted, New York: Arno Press and the New York Times, 1968, pp. 52–64.

Walter, Mildred Pitts. *Second Daughter: The Story of a Slave Girl*. New York: Scholastic, 1996.

Welch, Richard E., Jr. *Theodore Sedgwick, Federalist*. Middletown, CT: Wesleyan University Press, 1965.

Web Sites

The Story of Mumbet of Ashley Falls and Stockbridge, Massachusetts [Online] Available http://members.esslink.com/~channy/mumbet.html (accessed on 4/27/99).

Thomas Gage

Born c. 1721
Firle, England
Died April 2, 1787
Portland, England

Governor of Massachusetts, military leader

"Even the children here draw in a love of liberty in the air they breathe."

Portrait: Thomas Gage.
Reproduced courtesy of the Library of Congress.

Thomas Gage was the top British official in America at a time when the British were not popular. On the eve of the American Revolution, Gage was told by his superiors in England to make the colonists see reason and, if they would not, to put them down with the might of the British army. Gage kept the peace for as long as he could, finally giving the orders that led to the confrontation at Concord, Massachusetts, and the start of the American Revolution.

Thomas Gage was born at his family's estate, called High Meadow, in Firle, England, about 1721. He was the second son of Benedicta Hall and Thomas Gage, a member of Parliament's House of Lords (like the U.S. Senate) who also held the aristocratic titles of Viscount Gage of Castle Island and Baron Gage of Castlebar. These titles were passed from father to eldest son and, in the case of the Gages, were attached to property in Ireland. Thomas's older brother, William, succeeded to the titles and proved helpful in launching his brother's military career.

In 1728 Thomas and William Gage entered the Westminster School, which Thomas was to attend for eight years.

The school was for the sons of the wealthy and noblemen. While at school the Gage brothers met many young men who would later prove influential in setting and carrying out British political policy toward the American colonies.

Sees army service in European wars

After school, at about the age of sixteen, Thomas Gage entered the army, which was considered a suitable profession for a younger son of an aristocratic family. Gage's first commission (military rank) was that of ensign, a low-ranking officer. It was a fine time for a young man interested in promotion to be in the army, because Great Britain would be almost constantly at war with one nation or another for the next seventy-five years. Gage became a lieutenant in 1741 and a captain in 1743, serving in an Irish regiment. (Ireland was part of Great Britain.)

Gage served first in Great Britain's wars with her European neighbors. In 1745 he fought in Belgium in the War of Austrian Succession. In April 1746 Gage fought at Culloden Moor in Scotland, where the last of the exiled Stuart kings of England was defeated with his Scottish allies (see **Flora MacDonald** entry). Gage returned to Belgium (then called Flanders) and Holland in 1747 and spent the next two years there, as Great Britain continued to fight with her European enemies. He rose in the ranks, becoming first the major in 1748 and then the lieutenant colonel of the 44th Regiment (a fighting unit of about 1,000 men) in 1751.

Fights in French and Indian War in America

These European squabbles over territory and the rule of the seas eventually spilled over into their colonial possessions, including America and Canada. For years, Great Britain had challenged France for the control of Canada, a conflict that erupted into the French and Indian War (1754–63). In 1754 Gage and the 44th Regiment were shipped to America as part of General Edward Braddock's expedition (military mission). Their first clash with the French and their Indian allies was in 1755 in western Pennsylvania. The British lost the battle. Gage, slightly wounded, managed to direct his soldiers to carry the wounded Braddock to safety, but the general soon died. During the retreat, Gage befriended a young colonial officer whose Virginia militia (citizen soldiers) unit was reinforcing the British army. This young American was **George Washington** (1732–1799; see entry).

During August and September 1756 Gage served as second in command during the unsuccessful British push into the Mohawk Valley in upstate New York and in an expedition to Halifax, Nova Scotia.

Marries an American girl

At this point in his life Gage is described as a serious young man but a good companion and conversationalist. Unlike many other British officers, Gage did not pursue women, gamble, or drink to excess. Instead, he focused his energies on having the best regiment. He trained his men well, and kept their appearance orderly and smart. Gage was a good administrator (manager) but less inspired on the battlefield. He is described as a cautious commander, earning the names "Timid Tommy" and "The Old Woman" from his troops. In time, it would become clear that his real talent lay in running the territories gained for Great Britain by her armies. Friends described Gage as having a strong sense of fair play. Kinder nicknames bestowed on Gage include "Quiet Tommy," "Honest Tom," and the "Mild General."

In 1757 Gage was given permission to create a special unit of American troops who would be trained as a lightly armed regiment. While recruiting for this 80th Regiment late in 1757, Gage met a beautiful young American girl named Margaret Kemble. She was the daughter of Peter Kemble, a landowner and merchant who lived in the town of Mount Kemble, New Jersey. The Kemble family was of French, Greek, Dutch, and English ancestry. For the next year Gage courted Margaret Kemble through visits and letters.

On December 7, 1758, Gage married his American sweetheart in an Anglican (Church of England) ceremony at her home in Mount Kemble. Gage's new brother-in-law, Stephen, was an ensign in Gage's regiment. Acquaintances of hers described Margaret Kemble Gage as very proud, and conscious of her husband's place in the English aristocracy.

The Gages had a very happy marriage, one blessed with eleven children. Their first child, their son Henry, was born in 1761 while the Gages were posted to Montreal. When they were old enough Henry and his brother William attended Westminster, their father's old school in England, while their sister Maria Theresa attended a boarding school for girls. Among the Gages' six sons and five daughters were John, Louisa Elizabeth, and Harriet. Their daughter, Charlotte Margaret, was the only Gage child to be born in England rather than in America.

Serves in conquest of Canada

In 1758 Gage served as a colonel under Lord Abercrombie, head of the British army, in the attempt to capture the French-held fort at Ticonderoga, New York. He was slightly wounded in this action. In early 1759 Gage and his wife, Lady Gage, moved to Albany to be near the new commander-in-chief, Lord Amherst. As the British pushed to win Canada from the French, Gage was given command of a unit and told to take Fort La Galette on Lake Ontario on the way to taking the key city of Montreal. Gage got as far as Niagara and stopped because he thought he had too few men and supplies to complete his mission. Amherst was furious at Gage's decision but eventually their quarrel was made up. Amherst then drew upon Gage's military leadership when the British army took Quebec from the French in 1759.

In 1760 Gage served as a brigadier general under Lord Amherst, who was in charge when the French surrendered their vast Canadian empire to the English. Later that same year, Gage was named governor of Montreal, a city of 25,000 civilians. As governor, Gage proved capable of dealing with the many groups represented in Montreal, including the French Catholics, the Indians, the British military, and British civilians.

Gage was promoted to major general in 1761, given a regiment to command in 1762 and, in 1763, Gage succeeded Lord Amherst as commander-in-chief of the British forces in North America. Gage made his headquarters in New York City. He remained commander-in-chief for almost ten years, until 1772. Gage's responsibilities included overseeing the fifty British forts that protected the Canadian and American colonists from Newfoundland to Florida on the Atlantic seaboard, and from the island of Bermuda to the Mississippi River in the south.

These were turbulent years, as Britain passed law after law, and the colonists became more and more upset. Often these laws were passed on the recommendation of the British officers serving in America, officers like Thomas Gage. Many historians credit Gage with recommending the law that led to the closing of the port of Boston after the Boston Tea Party in 1773 and the Quartering Act, which allowed the British army to house their soldiers in civilian homes in Boston. As time went by he was losing sympathy with the Americans, as the colonists resorted to violence to make their point about wanting the power to rule themselves.

Named Governor of Massachusetts

In 1773, after seventeen years of service in America, Gage requested permission to return to England on family business. In June he and his wife and three of their children sailed to England. While in England Lady Gage was presented at court (introduced to the king and queen). Both the Gages found they liked London society life. But their visit was cut short in April 1774 when Gage was named Governor of Massachusetts and given orders to return to America.

It was hoped that Gage, with his knowledge of the American people and their politics, could calm the rebellious colonists. The politicians in Parliament gave Gage orders to end the rebellion without giving in to too many of the colonists' demands.

Gage returned to America in May 1774 as Governor in Chief and Captain-General of the Province of Massachusetts Bay, with headquarters in Boston. The next year he was made commander-in-chief of the British forces in North America. As Great Britain's military leader in the colonies, part of his job was to put down the rebellion brewing in the American colonies

King James II was forced to abdicate in favor of his daughter Mary and her Protestant husband William of Orange. The Gage family, which had a history of picking the wrong side in political struggles, supported King James II.
Reproduced courtesy of the Library of Congress.

The Gage Family and English Politics

By the time Thomas Gage, the last royal governor of Massachusetts, was born, his family was well established in the aristocracy (ruling class). But this was not always the case. In fact, it could be said that Gage's ancestors had a genius for picking the wrong side of any political or military fight.

Gage was the descendant of a French nobleman named di Gaugi who had come to England in 1066 with William the Conqueror, who would rule as King William I. Eventually, di Gaugi became the more English sounding "Gage." Thus far, life was good for the Gages. Then, in 1215, the Gages sided with King John, the English king who was eventually forced to give up some of his decision-making power to his nobles in a document called the Magna Carta.

In 1534 King Henry VIII broke away from the Catholic Church to form the Protestant Church of England. Nobles in the know quickly followed suit, becoming Protestants. Not the Gages.

They supported Queen Mary I (Bloody Mary), Henry's daughter and successor, who tried to reinstate Catholicism by force as the English state religion. For 150 years the Gages continued to practice Catholicism. It was a decision that cost them much loss of favor at many royal courts.

Then the Gages supported King Charles I, who eventually lost his head to start the English civil war in 1649. They then threw their support behind James II, who was forced to abdicate (step aside) in favor of his daughter, Mary, and her Protestant husband, William of Orange, in the Glorious Revolution of 1688.

The Gages only returned to royal favor in 1715, when Thomas Gage's father, also named Thomas Gage, converted to the Anglican church. The elder Gage was rewarded with an Irish aristocratic title, and eventually an English one. Thus Gage's family was finally in a position to support him politically and socially when he grew to manhood.

before the conflict erupted into a full-blown war. Since Boston was a rallying place for the rebels, Gage was to rule this key American city with a firm hand.

The American colonies in 1774 were simmering on the verge of outright rebellion against English rule. Gage, who for the most part still liked the American colonists, tried to cool tempers. He tried to lessen the importance of Boston by declaring Salem the capital of the Massachusetts colony, and spent the summer of 1774 there. He met with colonial leaders and tried to work out compromises to their grievances. All the time, Gage was receiving messages from England to take a harsher line with the Americans. It was a careful political balancing act for Gage.

Events lead up to Lexington and Concord

In response to England's orders, Gage tried to nip the American rebellion in its infancy. He knew that without weapons and leaders, the rebellion would falter. One of Gage's tactics was to seek out and seize the rebels' ammunition and weapons. Early in 1775 he sent British units to uncover rebel supplies in Jamaica Plains, Marshfield, and Salem, towns outside of Boston. Next he received word that the rebels had a stockpile of weapons at Concord, a town about twenty miles west of Boston. Gage planned to send a unit of seven hundred British soldiers to seize the weapons and to arrest two of the American rebel leaders, **John Hancock** and **Samuel Adams** (see entries). Gage had heard that Hancock and Adams were hiding in or around Concord.

Word of Gage's plans leaked to the Americans. Two messengers, **Paul Revere** (see entry) and William Dawes, rode through the countryside to alert the militia to assemble at Lexington, a small town on the way to Concord. There the American militia would try to stop the British advance.

In fact, the British broke through the American resistance at Lexington and pushed on the remaining six miles into Concord. There they began seizing cannons, muskets, and ammunition belonging to the colonial militia. As the British marched out of Concord, they were met by 150 Massachusetts militia men. The British were routed (driven off) and the supplies were recaptured. The Americans pushed the British all the way back into Boston, a twenty-mile march. The British had sustained a humiliating defeat.

British army trapped in Boston

Gage and his officers were surprised at the success of the American resistance. They still believed, however, that the British army was the best in the world and that the rebels would soon surrender. On June 12, 1775, Gage offered amnesty (pardon) for any rebel who took part in the action at Lexington or Concord. He excepted John Hancock and Samuel Adams from the amnesty, concerned at their ability to rouse the people to armed resistance.

On the night of June 16, the Americans sent troops onto two hills surrounding the city. When informed of the American move on the morning of June 17, Gage personally gave the order for the British forces to attack the American position on Breed's Hill. The action would soon include neighboring Bunker Hill, which gave its name to the first major conflict of the Revolutionary War. Gage then turned over command of the battle to General Sir **William Howe** (see entry), who had recently arrived from England. Gage, in his position as governor, wanted to concentrate on activity in the city. The British won the battle but at a heavy cost. Almost half their soldiers and officers were killed or wounded.

Relieved of American command

The government in England was appalled when Gage reported on the defeat at Lexington and then the siege of Boston and the Battle of Bunker Hill. In September 1775 they recalled Gage for a personal explanation of these events. Gage turned over military command to Howe in October 1775 and sailed for England.

In April 1776 Gage learned both that he had been relieved of his American command and that Howe had succeeded him as commander-in-chief there. Gage had lost his job and his pay. Five years later, in 1781, Gage was reappointed to the staff of his former commander, Lord Amherst. His assignment was to help the people of the county of Kent prepare against an invasion by England's old enemy, France. In 1782 Gage was named a full general. Gage did not live long to enjoy his final promotion. He died on April 2, 1787, at his home in Portland after a long and painful illness. Lady Gage survived her husband by thirty-seven years but never remarried.

For More Information

Armstrong, Jennifer. *Ann of the Wild Rose Inn*. New York: Bantam, 1994.

Boatner, Mark M., III.. "Gage, Thomas" in *Encyclopedia of the American Revolution*. Mechanicsburg, PA: Stackpole Books, 1994, pp. 405-09.

Forbes, Esther. *Johnny Tremain*. Boston: Houghton Mifflin Co., 1943.

Hawkins, Vincent B. "Gage, Thomas" in *The Harper Encyclopedia of Military Biography*. New York: HarperCollins, 1992, p. 270.

Rinaldi, Ann. *The Secret of Sarah Revere*. New York: Harcourt Brace, 1995.

Sanborn, Paul J. "Gage, Thomas" in *The American Revolution, 1775–1783: An Encyclopedia*, Vol. 1. Edited by Richard L. Blanco. New York: Garland Publishing, 1993, pp. 605-10.

Speare, Elizabeth George. *Calico Captive*. Boston: Houghton Mifflin Co. 1957.

Wilson, James Grant, and John Fiske. "Gage, Thomas" in *Appleton's Cyclopaedia of American Biography,* Vol. 2. New York: D. Appleton, 1888, pp. 569-70.

Bernardo de Gálvez

Born July 23, 1746
Macharaviaya, Spain
Died November 30, 1786
Mexico City, Mexico

Governor of the Spanish province of Louisiana,
viceroy of New Spain (Mexico)

Bernardo de Gálvez, an aristocrat born in Spain and trained for a military career, became governor of the Spanish colony of Louisiana in 1777. When Spain entered the Revolutionary War on the side of the American colonies, he helped fight the British in Louisiana, Alabama, and Florida. He kept the British busy in the South, and finally drove them from the area, freeing it up for American trading. For these successes, he was named a don (an aristocratic title similar to the British earl) by the Spanish government, and eventually was made viceroy (overall ruler) of New Spain (Mexico).

Bernardo de Gálvez was born in the Malaga province (state) on the southeast coast of Spain in 1746. His parents were Matías and Josepha Madrid y Gallardo de Gálvez. He came from a wealthy and highly regarded family, whose members served the kings of Spain as advisers, governors, and military leaders. His father, Don (Earl) Matías, was viceroy of Mexico, and his uncle, Don José, was minister of the West Indies, the highest position in the Spanish colonial empire. (The West Indies is an island chain extending from Florida to South America.)

"Whoever has honor and valour will follow me."

Portrait: Bernardo de Gálvez. *Reproduced courtesy of the Library of Congress.*

During de Gálvez's boyhood, European nations were frequently at war. Many had interests in other parts of the world, and sought to gain power, influence, and wealth through their colonies. In the conflicts, Spain was most often allied with France and an enemy of England. Not surprisingly, if a family was wealthy and important, some of its sons would be trained for military careers. Their job would be to expand their nation's empire and then rule its territories as their king's representatives.

De Gálvez attended a famous military school in Ávila in west central Spain, where he learned military tactics, Spanish history, how to lead and inspire his troops, and devotion to the Roman Catholic religion. His family was Catholic, as was much of the Spanish population, including the aristocracy and the Spanish king, Carlos III.

Begins military career

De Gálvez's first military campaign was in 1762, when he served as a lieutenant (pronounced loo-TEN-ent), fighting for his king's interests in Portugal. For his service, he was made captain of the military unit at La Coruña in northwest Spain. At this time, the way to further a young man's military career was to gain experience protecting or expanding the king's interests in the colonies. For a Spaniard, this meant service in New Spain, the territory now known as Mexico and the southwestern United States.

De Gálvez first journeyed to America with his uncle when Don José did a tour of inspection of New Spain. He was assigned to the northern frontier of New Spain in 1769, where he was in charge of Spain's military forces in the Mexican state bordering on what is now Arizona. While on this tour of duty, he fought Apache Indians, whose raids along the Pecos River in Texas and the Gila River in Arizona were interfering with trading in the area. De Gálvez demonstrated some of his diplomatic skills at this time by forming alliances with the Native Americans who were enemies of the Apaches. During this 1770–71 military campaign, he was wounded and decorated for bravery under fire. A ford (a shallow place for crossing) on the Pecos River was named Paso de Gálvez in his honor.

Further education in France

De Gálvez returned to Spain in 1772, and then traveled to France to learn about French military tactics. While there, he learned the language and an appreciation of French culture. When he returned to Spain in 1775, he participated in an assault on Algiers, in north Africa, as an infantry captain (infantry were foot soldiers). He was wounded, promoted, and sent to teach at his old military school in Ávila.

In 1776, de Gálvez was made a colonel (pronounced KER-nuhl) and sent to command the Spanish military post at New Orleans, Louisiana. He was named governor of Louisiana on January 1, 1777. He was just thirty-one years old at the time.

The king of France gave the territory of Louisiana to his friend and ally, King Charles III of Spain, as a gift. Most of the European settlers in Louisiana were of French descent, and they did not like the idea of Spanish rule. During his governorship, de Gálvez again demonstrated his genius for getting along with the local population. In colonial Louisiana, the local population was the Creoles. Creole, as it is used here, means a person of French heritage who was born in America. The Creoles kept their French language and customs, and resented any discourteous behavior by European-born visitors or rulers.

De Gálvez did more than make friends with the Creoles; he married one of them. His wife was Félicité de St. Maxent d'Estrehan, the daughter of an important Creole leader in New Orleans. Local merchants liked de Gálvez because he restored certain trading rights that had been taken away by a previous Spanish governor.

As governor of Louisiana, de Gálvez turned a blind eye to the American stockpiling of weapons in New Orleans warehouses. The Americans were preparing to declare war against Great Britain.

Europe watches the American revolution

At the time of the American Revolutionary War, most of what is now the United States was claimed by other countries. England had claims in the northeast, northwest, and what was called "the Floridas"—portions of the states of Florida, Georgia, and Alabama. The British had lined the east bank of the Mississippi River with a series of forts and trading towns to protect British interests.

Spain owned most of the territory west of the Mississippi River. (The vastness of this part of the Spanish American empire stretched uninterrupted from the middle of the present-day United States to the Rocky Mountains, into northern California, and then south through Mexico, down through Central America, and into most of South America). In contrast, by the mid-1700s, France had lost much of its Canadian territory to England as part of the settlement of an earlier war. However, France still had hopes of regaining this territory and did have an interest in the Canadian area called Quebec. Its French citizens in eastern Canada were forcibly evicted by the new British rulers. These French Canadians trekked southward into Louisiana, and became known as Acadians.

England, Spain, and France were all interested in keeping or expanding their lands in North America. The British were horrified when their American colonies declared war in 1776, but the French and Spanish waited to see how severe this threat would be to England's empire. The French and Spanish were not passive, however. During the years leading up to the American Revolution, France and Spain helped the rebels by providing information about British movements, and by giving them supplies and ammunition.

During the time before Spain officially entered the war, de Gálvez tried to help the American cause. As a Spanish aristocrat, he did not believe strongly in the American goal of liberty from its colonial parent or in equality for all people. Rather, he saw the revolution as a way to help Spain's interests—including regaining the territories of Florida and parts of Alabama, which had once belonged to Spain. One of his first moves was to make sure that the port city of New Orleans would be open only to Spanish, American, and French ships. He cut off the British from this key supply route into the American heartland. He also stored Spanish supplies so they would be ready for the Americans when Spain entered the war.

Once Spain and France were satisfied that the Americans were serious about separating from England, these two European powers saw a chance to deal England a smashing blow. Spain was an ally of France, and followed its lead in declaring war on Great Britain and officially entering on the side of the American revolutionaries on June 21, 1779. With both Spain and France as allies, the Americans had a better chance of winning their freedom from England. Spain and France had large fleets of warships, which could interrupt British shipments of soldiers and supplies across the Atlantic Ocean. These European allies could also supply the Americans with much needed war supplies such as gunpowder, guns, medicine, food, cloth for uniforms, and information about British plans.

Saving the South for the Americans

De Gálvez helped the Americans by shipping supplies and weapons up the Mississippi River to American troops in Pennsylvania. He used his own army to attack British forts and trading towns on the Mississippi River. Because the British were busy sending men to protect these forts, there were fewer British soldiers to fight the American armies.

De Gálvez's army of fourteen hundred men was made up of his Spanish soldiers from the Louisiana fort, as well as volunteers who were Creoles, Acadians (French Canadians), Choctaw Indians, and free African Americans.

De Gálvez next planned to push the British eastward, back toward the Atlantic Ocean. His army marched eastward to take the British Fort Charlotte at Mobile (in what is now Alabama). This key British fort was also the closest port to New Orleans, and could be a future threat to Spain unless it was captured. By the time of the Mobile campaign in March 1780, de Gálvez's army had swelled to two thousand men, and was supported by Spanish naval forces from their base in Havana, Cuba (a large island off the southern coast of Florida and an important Spanish naval base).

The next fort to fall to de Gálvez's army was Fort George in Pensacola, in the Florida panhandle. This was an important victory, because Pensacola was the capital of British West Florida. In May 1781 de Gálvez took the city through a combined army-navy siege, which lasted two months. (A siege is when an enemy force surrounds a city or fort, cutting the defenders off from all supplies and reinforcements.) His forces now numbered seven thousand men. The guns at the British fort were firing on the Spanish navy ships, and the Spanish commander refused to risk his ships by sailing into Pensacola. De Gálvez took over the commander's ship and sailed it into

An Inspiring Leader of Men

Bernardo de Gálvez was one of the first leaders of an international army. When he marched on British possessions in the American South in 1779, his army included soldiers from many different backgrounds. There were the Spanish soldiers (called "regulars") who were posted at the fort in Louisiana. They were joined by Acadians (the French Canadians who had been expelled by the English and who had migrated to Louisiana, then a French territory). Armed by their hatred of the British, the Choctaw Indians further swelled de Gálvez's force. Local militiamen (citizen soldiers, not professionals) joined, and included New Orleans Creoles, free blacks, and American frontiersmen.

By the time de Gálvez was ready to march on the British islands in the Atlantic Ocean in 1782, his forces included Spanish and local marines from Havana, Cuba. Another regiment under de Gálvez's command included the Irish Brigade, made up of Irish soldiers who offered their services to the Spanish because the Irish resented British control of Ireland. More than five hundred French soldiers also fought under de Gálvez.

De Gálvez's gift for finding common ties among groups of people was a valuable asset throughout his military and political life, but never more so than when he commanded his international army. His skill as a leader helped ensure the American victory during the Revolutionary War (1775–83).

the bay despite being wounded in the stomach and in the hand. His bravery ensured the victory and earned him the respect and loyalty of both soldiers and sailors.

De Gálvez's overall victories in the southern United States meant that Spain controlled both banks of the Mississippi River and the five thousand miles of shoreline around the Gulf of Mexico. It also meant that just as the British were taking the war into the American South, their lines of supply were cut off. Their lack of support was a major turning point in the war. (In the long run, the removal of the British from the Floridas also helped pave the way for American expansion into the southeast. The United States eventually gained the Florida territory through purchase, not war.)

The war moves to the islands

In May 1782 de Gálvez's forces took their fight into the Bahamas, a group of islands in the Atlantic Ocean off the southeast coast of Florida. The islands were held by the British. De Gálvez and his combined army-navy force captured the British navy's key supply city of New Providence. De Gálvez next turned his attention to the nearby island of Jamaica, also held by the British. However, the Revolutionary War ended before he could launch his campaign against this British stronghold.

For his efforts on behalf of the American cause, the U.S. Congress gave de Gálvez a citation (a document honoring him) and asked for his advice in writing some of the terms of the treaty with England that ended the war. Always a Spanish patriot, de Gálvez made sure that the Floridas returned to Spanish control as part of the treaty. This same treaty made the Mississippi River the western border of the United States, giving the new American republic much more land than Great Britain had originally planned.

Promotion and rewards follow

De Gálvez returned to Spain with his Creole wife and two small children at the conclusion of the American Revolutionary War in 1783. In 1783–84, he served as an adviser to the king on Spanish policies toward the Florida and Louisiana territories. For his war efforts and in recognition of his continuing service to the crown, de Gálvez was awarded the title of "don," an aristocratic title similar to a French count or an English earl. He also was named a major general in the Spanish army, and made captain general of the Floridas and Louisiana.

In 1784 de Gálvez was named captain general of Cuba. His headquarters were in Havana, from which he commanded all Spanish military forces in the Caribbean and the Gulf of Mexico.

In 1785 de Gálvez succeeded his father as viceroy of New Spain and took up residence in Mexico City. (Viceroy is the Spanish title given to the governor of a country or province who rules in the name of his king.) As viceroy, de Gálvez again demonstrated his ability to help opposing parties reach agreements. He involved local politicians in decision-making and was a very popular leader. One of his acts as viceroy was to order maps to be made of New Spain. In his honor, one of his mapmakers named a bay off the coast of east Texas "Bahía de Galvezton" (or Galveston Bay in English). The Texas city of Galveston is also named for de Gálvez.

Barely a year later, in November 1786, de Gálvez died of a fever and was buried at the Church of San Fernando, next to his father, the former viceroy. Shortly after de Gálvez's death, his widow gave birth to their third child. Some historians believe de Gálvez died of an epidemic that swept through Mexico City, while others believe that he finally fell victim to the malaria that he first contracted during his service in Louisiana.

For More Information

Blanco, Richard L. "Galvez, Bernardo de" in *The American Revolution: 1775–1783, An Encyclopedia,* vol. A–L. New York: Garland Publishing, 1993, pp. 613–15.

Fleming, Thomas. "Bernardo de Gálvez: The Forgotten Revolutionary Conquistador Who Saved Louisiana" in *American Heritage,* vol. 33. (April–May 1982): 30–39.

Fleming, Thomas. "I, Alone." *Boys' Life,* vol. 70. (November 1980): pp. 22–24, 69.

Sinnott, Susan. *Extraordinary Hispanic Americans.* Chicago: Childrens Press, 1991, pp. 68–70.

Tyler, Ron., ed. "Gálvez, Bernardo de" in *The New Handbook of Texas.* Austin: Texas State Historical Association, 1996, pp. 73–74.

Web Sites

Diaz, Héctor. *Hispanics in American History* [Online] Available http://www.coloquio.com/galvez.html (accessed on March 12, 1999).

PBS. "Bernardo de Galvez and Spain." [Online] Available http://www.pbs.org/ktca/liberty/chronicle/galvez-spain.html (accessed on March 21, 1999).

George III

Born June 4, 1738
London, England
Died January 29, 1820
London, England

King of Great Britain and Ireland

K ing George III is widely blamed for Great Britain's loss of the American colonies in the Revolutionary War (1775–83). In some ways, George III was a capable king who stubbornly controlled the British government as best he could. But in the last decades of his life, George III suffered from a mental disorder that caused him to lose his hold on reality.

George III was the son of Frederick Louis, prince of Wales, who was the eldest son of King George II. Frederick Louis died in 1751, while George II was still king, leaving behind Augusta, his German-born wife, and their twelve-year-old son, who later was crowned King George III.

George III was an emotionally immature boy and a poor student. His suspicious mother did her best to keep him from contact with other young people. She thought most of them had bad morals and would corrupt her children. The shy and somewhat lazy George grew up over-protected from the real world. He looked up to his tutor, John Stuart, the earl of Bute (pronounced BOOT), who would later serve as one of his prime ministers.

"[Fighting] must decide whether they [the American colonies] are to be subject to this country [England] or be independent."

Portrait: George III.
Reproduced by permission of the National Archives and Records Administration.

History of the Hanovers

George III's family, the Hanovers, originally came from Hanover, an area in northwestern Germany. In 1714, when Anne, queen of Great Britain and Ireland, died without any descendants to inherit the throne, the British, eager to have a Protestant king, invited George I of the German Hanovers to become their king. The Hanovers were distantly related to the Stuart family who had once ruled Great Britain.

The Hanovers' German ancestry is why English king George I was unable to speak English. His son, George II, who spoke with a heavy German accent, was, like his father, more interested in events in Germany than in England. This was the background in which George III grew up.

George III, the new ruler

In 1759 Britain enjoyed military victories in a number of battles around the world. That year, British general James Wolf began the destruction of French power in North America with the takeover of Canada's Quebec province. Americans, who feared falling under the French flag, were delighted at the victory. In 1760 George III became king of Great Britain at age twenty-two. His subjects, including the Americans, looked upon the young king with great enthusiasm.

Auburn-haired George III was a tall and well-built man with a long nose and a serious expression. He was also shy, insecure, and overly trusting of others. Some referred to his way of speaking rapidly and repeating himself as a "gobble." George III was a hard worker who did not drink liquor and prohibited the use of bad language in his court.

For a time George III was a capable leader, devoting himself to controlling Parliament, the British law-making body. He perfected the art of politics, playing one group against the other to achieve his desired ends and befriending people who would be helpful to him.

Members of the Whig Party were George III's chief opponents in Parliament. He weakened their power through the use of bribery (offering money to gain an advantage) and by bestowing honors on individuals who served him well. He could be flexible about minor matters, but when it came to matters of great importance to him, George firmly held his ground.

The king's personal life

In 1761 George III married a German Protestant, Princess Charlotte Sophia of Mecklenburg-Strelitz. Although the new queen could not speak English, she learned the words to "God Save the King," the British national anthem, and sang them for the royal family upon first meeting them. George was devoted to his wife and the couple produced nine sons and six daughters. Once a week the entire family paraded around the palace garden so that the general public could view them.

The king enjoyed such hobbies as making metal buttons, writing articles on farming, playing cards, collecting coins and ship models, hunting, and playing musical instruments. George was also a supporter of the artists and writers of his day.

American attitudes toward the king

From 1763 to 1775, the American colonists increasingly balked at England's efforts to control and tax them. The harder England tried to bring them back in line, the more they rebelled.

At first, the anger of the American colonists was not toward the king, but toward the members of Parliament and their taxes and policies. Americans did not seem to understand that Parliament was carrying out George's wishes. They thought of themselves as his loyal subjects, but believed that he was being badly advised by his ministers (advisers) in government.

Finally, in 1776, America declared its independence. Long after Americans recognized George as their enemy, he continued to try to control them. George apparently never considered that the Americans' complaints might be justified. He once said, "I wish nothing but good, therefore everyone who does not agree with me is a traitor or a scoundrel."

George's right-hand men deal with the Americans

In ten years, George went through five prime ministers, who helped him to shape his policies towards the American colonies. Among them were George Grenville, the mar-

George III (seated) receiving the Turkish ambassador (right, bowing). Initially, the king was well liked by Americans. *Reproduced by permission of the Corbis Corporation (Bellevue).*

quess of Rockingham (pronounced MAR-kwis; a nobleman; Rockingham is pronounced with a silent "ha;" ROK-ing-m), and Charles Townshend.

George Grenville, who served as prime minster from 1763 to 1765, proposed taxing the colonists in America to raise money to support British troops there. This made Americans angry, especially at the Stamp Act of 1765, which required them to pay a tax on legal documents and other paper items. Facing fierce opposition, the British repealed the Stamp Act a year later and Grenville soon after left office over another matter.

In 1765 thirty-five-year-old Charles Watson-Wentworth, the marquess of Rockingham, was appointed to the position. With the Stamp Act gone, Watson-Wentworth put in place the Declaratory Act, in which the British government stated its right to tax Americans "in all cases whatsoever." Watson-Wentworth lost the job when his opponents, led by Grenville, persuaded the king to get rid of him.

Charles Townshend was then placed in charge of the British Empire's finances. In 1767 Townshend drew up the Townshend Act, requiring American businessmen and shop owners to pay new taxes on lead paint, glass, paper, and tea. Soon after, Townshend died from influenza, a dangerous and easily contagious disease.

George finally found a minister he really liked in Sir Frederick North, usually called Lord North. North was appointed first lord of the Treasury, and served from 1770 to 1782.

The era of Lord North

For the first fifteen years of his reign, George responsibly performed his royal duties. He put his seal on official documents, gave out titles and medals, oversaw how money was spent, and listened to the opinions of an endless stream of advisers. With the help of Lord North, the king also had to deal with the rebellion of the American colonies.

George III liked and trusted Lord North. He persuaded North to hold the job of prime minister for twelve years, even though most historians agree that North did not do a very admirable job. Historian Mark M. Boatner, for instance, wrote in the *Encyclopedia of the American Revolution,* "In 1770 the King found a [prime minister] who was to be as loyal as a dog, but fortunately for America he was no more qualified [than a dog] for the office."

A large, friendly man who had been a childhood friend of George III, Lord North neither strongly opposed nor supported America's interests. He was carrying out George's orders.

Americans unite to oppose Britain

In 1773, Prime Minister North helped pass the Tea Act, which Americans believed would allow the East India Company to have a monopoly on the tea market in North America. The Americans' response to this development was the Boston Tea Party, which took place in December 1773 in Boston, Massachusetts. Americans expressed their rage over North's policies by dumping hundreds of pounds of tea into Boston Harbor. This event was a major milestone on the road leading to the American Revolution.

America's Attitude toward George III

Shortly after George III became king of England, American patriot John Hancock wrote after meeting him, "The new king was good-natured and well liked." The positive regard Americans had for George III proved to be short-lived. The king is probably best remembered in the United States as a tyrant whose unpopular taxes brought about the American Revolution. Thomas Jefferson's description of George III in the Declaration of Independence ensured that Americans would long remember the king unkindly.

The colonists laid the necessity for the American Revolution at the feet of George III. As John Brooke pointed out in his biography *King George III,* the monarch was considered by Americans as a "would-be tyrant whose wicked plans were foiled by the courage and resistance of the American people." Americans claimed that as the king strove to become an absolute despot (tyrant), it became their duty to protect themselves against further aggressions on his part.

In the Declaration of Independence, Jefferson wrote: "The history of the present King of Great Britain, is a history of repeated injuries and usurpations [improper takeover of power. The document then pointed out eighteen of them]. He has refused his assent to laws the most wholesome and necessary for the public good.... He has obstructed the administration of justice.... He has plundered our seas, ravaged our coasts, burnt our towns.... He has excited domestic insurrections amongst us [caused us to fight among ourselves]."

These are but a few of the crimes for which the king was held to be accountable. As a result, wrote Jefferson, "a prince, whose character is thus marked by every act which may define a tyrant, is unfit to be the ruler of a free people."

The British punished Bostonians by passing a series of acts that the Americans came to call the "Intolerable Acts." These acts included closing the port of Boston until Americans paid for the ruined tea, taking away certain rights of self-government of the people of Massachusetts, and housing British soldiers in occupied buildings in Boston (including people's private homes). Americans, who previously had not acted as a unified people, responded to the harsh punishment of Boston with offers of help and food. The Intolerable Acts brought Americans closer together in opposition to Great Britain.

Americans were a people of independent spirit, self-reliance, and self-respect, who rejected notions of privilege received merely by birth and inherited wealth. The energetic, enterprising colonists began to have less and less in common with England, where following accepted customs and displaying formal manners guided the upper classes.

At the First Continental Congress (the legislative body of the American colonies) in 1774, thirteen acts that had been put in place by the British government beginning in 1763 were declared illegal by colonial delegates. They issued a document stating Americans' rights, wrote a petition to the king, and agreed not to import British goods. In 1776 the United States declared its independence, but the Revolutionary War between England and America had already begun.

Revolutionary War period

At first, George III was eager for war and wanted to show the world that England would not tolerate disobedience anywhere in its empire. He saw himself as a "kindly father" trying to deal with his disobedient American children. Once the Americans were brought back into line, he intended to tell them that he would impose no fresh taxes.

But when the Revolutionary War started to go badly for Great Britain, many members of the British upper classes came to oppose it and to disrespect King George. George III resisted ending the fighting, even following the big American victory at the Battle of Yorktown in 1781 that devastated the British army.

After the defeat at Yorktown, George III said to those who expressed fear that the war was lost, "I prohibit you from thinking of peace." The king carried on the disastrous war for two more years, following a course of action that most Englishmen knew to be self-defeating even as they followed it. The king's enemies in Parliament succeeded in making Lord North resign in 1782. In 1783 George III signed the Treaty of Paris that finally ended the Revolutionary War, with Britain finally recognizing the United States of America as an independent nation. For the first time in modern history, a dependent nation had thrown off a king and replaced him with a government of ordinary people.

Post-war problems

Following the Revolutionary War, political pressures forced George III to put men he detested in the post of prime minister. Finally, in 1783, William Pitt the Younger took the post. This brought about long-term stability in the government but also decreased the king's political influence as Pitt assumed greater power.

Pitt the Younger proved successful at the job, and devoted his efforts to reforming the country's finances and political system. George III faded into the background and paid more attention to his personal life. However, Pitt's punishing policies toward Catholics in Ireland and the resulting outcry from his opponents resulted in his 1801 resignation from office. George III then reclaimed some of his power.

Beset by mental illness

George III was struck with a bout of severe mental illness at age fifty and his mental stability began to fall apart rapidly. It caused him to experience emotional extremes, especially sadness. Medical experts have said that George's illness was caused by a rare hereditary disorder called porphyria (pronounced por-FEAR-ee-uh), from which several of his European cousins also suffered. His mental condition was made worse by political scandals involving members of his family and dejection over the loss of the war to America.

George III experienced four major attacks of mental illness. They lasted from less than one year to a final illness that extended from October 1810 until his death ten years later. During his final years he was a peculiar looking person with wild white hair and a beard, and he frequently appeared in a purple bathrobe. Near the end, George III was both blind and deaf, and became an object of sympathy among the British people. He died in 1820 at the age of eighty-two.

In 1811 George III's son, Prince George, had become prince regent, which meant that he took charge of governing Great Britain though he was not yet king. The prince regent suffered under the pressures of trying to run the empire according to the desires of his increasingly unbalanced father. His reign as King George IV, which lasted from 1820 until 1830, was to be a time of elegance in art and architecture, but of self-indulgence and immorality in his personal life.

For More Information

Ayling, Stanley E. *George the Third*. New York: Alfred A. Knopf, 1972.

Boatner, Mark M. "George III" in *Encyclopedia of the American Revolution*. Mechanicsburg, PA: Stackpole Books, 1994, pp. 416–20.

Bourgoin, Suzanne M., and Paula Kay Byers, eds. "George IV" in *Encyclopedia of World Biography*, 2nd ed. Detroit: Gale, 1998, pp. 270–72.

Brooke, John. *King George III*. New York: McGraw-Hill Book Co., 1972.

Fleming, Thomas. *Liberty! The American Revolution*. New York: Penguin-Putnam, 1997, pp. 11–89.

Fritz, Jean. *Can't You Make Them Behave, King George?* New York: Coward-McCann, 1977.

Hibbert, Christopher. *George III, A Personal History*. New York: Basic Books, 1999.

Lloyd, Alan. *The King Who Lost America: A Portrait of the Life and Times of George III*. Garden City, NY: Doubleday & Co., 1971.

Purcell, L. Edward, ed. "George III" in *Who Was Who in the American Revolution*. New York: Facts on File, 1993, pp. 182–83.

Stokesbury, James L. *A Short History of the American Revolution*. New York: William Morrow and Company, 1991, pp. 33, 47, 67, 86, 130.

Web Sites

[Online] "George III." From *Monarch of Britain*. [Online]. Available http://www.britannia.com/history/monarchs/mon55.html (accessed on May 25, 1999).

Simon Girty

Born 1741
Chambers' Mill, near Harrisburg, Pennsylvania
Died February 18, 1818
Malden, near Amherstburg, Ontario

Frontiersman, interpreter of Indian languages, scout, raider

"You will die, some time, but we will make your life so awful that you will beg a thousand time[s] to die.... I must think up some new way of burning a man to death by little inches, dear Tom, just for your own special case."

Words attributed to Simon Girty by Tom Johnson, taken captive by Girty and a band of Indians.

Illustration: Simon Girty.
Reproduced courtesy of the Library of Congress.

Simon Girty, roughneck son of the American wilderness, spent nearly his entire life involved in warfare. He was first caught up as a child in Indian-white struggles over land on the frontier. At fifteen he was captured by Indians and lived among them, learning their language, their ways, and their deep distrust of white settlers. During the American Revolution, he fought for both the British and the Americans and led Indian raids against white pioneers. His name is so closely linked with stories of savage brutality against American pioneers that it is difficult to separate the truth from the frightful legends that grew up around him.

In 1741, Simon Girty was the second of four sons born to Simon Girty, an Irish immigrant, and Mary Newton Girty, an Englishwoman. His birthplace in western Pennsylvania was on the American frontier. Biographer Thomas Boyd described it as "a huddle of rough log houses, a stockade named Fort Hunter, a mill and a tavern."

The Indians of western Pennsylvania came to Fort Hunter to trade furs for whiskey, weapons, and cloth. Girty's father supported his family by trading illegally (without a license) with them.

The Girty boys received no formal education and could neither read nor write. Their life in the backcountry was hard. Diseases were common, medical treatment was primitive, and the diet was monotonous and unhealthy. The boys mingled freely with the Indians who came to the fort, but everyone on the frontier lived under the constant threat of Indian attack. (The Indians objected to the increasing numbers of white settlers trespassing on their hunting grounds.)

Like most pioneers of his time, Simon Girty Sr., wanted to own land, and it made no difference that the Indians had a prior claim. In 1750 he moved his family about six miles westward, across the Blue Mountains into Indian territory. Other families settled around him. The Indians protested to white government authorities, and this time the law favored the Indians. The settlers were evicted, their homes were set on fire, and they were forced to pay fines. The Girtys moved back east of the Blue Mountains.

This may have been young Simon Girty's first serious encounter with the white man's law. While many pioneer children emerged from childhoods like his to become law-abiding citizens, Girty developed a contempt for authority that lasted the rest of his life.

Taken captive by Indians

The senior Girty liked to entertain his Indian trading partners in his small home; they played cards and drank heavily. One day when young Simon was about ten years old, the party got out of control, and an angry Indian warrior by the name of the Fish sank his tomahawk into the skull of old Simon. Another partygoer named John Turner then killed the Fish. Shortly thereafter, John Turner married Mary Girty and became stepfather to the four Girty boys.

According to biographer Thomas Boyd, under Turner's parenting, young Simon Girty spent the next four years "learning to bawl out roaring curses and take his liquor like a man." John Turner soon discovered he could not support his large family. In 1755, he learned that the Penn brothers (relatives of William, founder of Pennsylvania) had bought land from the

Indians, including the land old Simon Girty had tried to settle. The Girty-Turner family moved west of the Blue Mountains and built a farm.

In 1756, the already chaotic lives of the Girty-Turner family took a dramatic turn when they became victims of the French and Indian War (1756–63) on the American frontier.

The French and Indian War was the American part of a global struggle between France and England. England had her colonies on America's eastern seaboard. France claimed the land west of the Appalachian Mountains and had built a line of forts to protect it, extending from Lake Erie to what is now western Pennsylvania. **George Washington** (see entry) was sent to protest the construction and manning of the forts, but the French refused to leave.

In July 1755, Washington and his militia men (pro-nounced ma-LISHA; citizen soldiers) joined 1,400 British soldiers under the command of General Edward Braddock to drive the French out of the disputed territory. The party was ambushed by the French and their Indian allies. Braddock was killed, and Washington and the rest of the soldiers were forced back into Virginia.

Urged on by the French, the Indians then went on a rampage through the Pennsylvania-Virginia frontier, murdering and scalping white settlers, burning their cabins, and killing their livestock. Sometime in 1756, the Girtys were taken prisoner by the Indians. As his family looked on, John Turner was tortured and scalped; after three hours of torment, a tomahawk was buried in his skull, ending his misery. Several tribes then divided the rest of the family among themselves. Simon Girty went to live with the Seneca tribe.

Lives with Indians; returns to white world

Simon Girty was adopted into a Seneca family and treated like any other member of the tribe. For perhaps three years, he hunted with the Senecas, learned their language and customs, and became a Seneca warrior. For a young man like Girty, who was not interested in owning land, it was probably a rich experience.

Girty might have remained with the Senecas forever, but events in the white world intruded. In 1758, a treaty was signed that required certain Indian tribes to give up all their prisoners. The next year, Girty was reunited with his family at Fort Pitt (on the site of present-day Pittsburgh, Pennsylvania).

Some legends say that Simon Girty became a savage during his captivity, but biographer Consul Willshire Butterfield disagreed. Girty became a productive citizen. Because he spoke an Indian language, he was ideally suited for a job as an interpreter (translator) for white and Indian traders. He proved to have a flair for Indian languages and learned several. He became so popular among the Indians that a Delaware chief took for himself the name "Simon Girty." To anyone who dealt with the Indians, a man like Girty was a necessity. According to writer James K. Richards, "he could take you among the [quarrelsome] tribes, help you conduct your business, and get you out again with a whole skin and your hair in place."

Girty became a responsible citizen and voted in the first election held in western Pennsylvania. But he did not like to take orders, and he was usually unpopular with his bosses.

Joins Lord Dunmore's War

From 1758 to 1773, Simon Girty worked mostly for the British government, acting as an interpreter and earning a dollar a day. During that time, a boundary dispute simmered between Pennsylvania and Virginia; both claimed the region west of the Allegheny Mountains that now falls in Pennsylvania and West Virginia. The dispute came to blows in 1774 when Lord Dunmore, Royal Governor of Virginia (appointed by the British government), sent a man named John Connolly to take Fort Pitt from the Pennsylvanians. Connolly took it and renamed it Fort Dunmore.

Meanwhile, there was trouble brewing with the Indians of the region, who had recently stepped up their attacks against white settlers. Connolly and Lord Dunmore led a series of counterattacks in what became known as Lord Dunmore's War. Simon Girty, who favored Virginia in the boundary dispute even though he was a Pennsylvanian, agreed to serve as a scout and interpreter for Lord Dunmore (scouts were men who knew the land and the people and could serve as advisers).

Many famous frontiersmen served as Lord Dunmore's scouts, including George Rogers Clark and Simon Kenton, who would later play a role in the Simon Girty legend. They would go down in history as heroes, but Girty is reported to have shown an enthusiasm for killing that became the basis of his evil legend.

Girty got along well with Lord Dunmore. One night during the campaign, when Dunmore grew bored, he asked Girty and the other scouts to put on a performance of Indian songs, dances, and war cries. Dunmore was delighted with the performance. Lord Dunmore's War ended in 1774 with the signing of a series of treaties with several Indian tribes. Simon Girty was present when Chief Logan of the Mingo tribe refused to sign a treaty (see box).

Lord Dunmore was so pleased with Girty's assistance that he named him a lieutenant (pronounced lew-TEN-ant) in the Virginia militia at Fort Dunmore. As part of his new job, on February 22, 1775, Simon Girty took an oath of allegiance to King **George III** (see entry) of England. Two months later, the first shots of the American Revolution were fired in Massachusetts.

Girty aids patriots in American Revolution

At first Girty supported Great Britain in the struggle, but he soon changed sides, for reasons that can only be guessed at. Perhaps he was inflamed by the anti-British talk he was hearing, about the British denying colonists their rights and overtaxing them.

In May 1775, representatives from all the colonies met at the Second Continental Congress in Philadelphia, Pennsylvania, to prepare for war with England. One item on their agenda was what to do about the Indians on the frontier. The Congressmen knew that in case of war, the Indians would be more sympathetic to the British than to the American colonists, who cheated them and trespassed on their land. Knowing they would not get cooperation from the Indians in a war, they hoped to at least get neutrality (non-involvement) from them.

In July 1775, Captain James Wood undertook the dangerous mission of visiting Ohio tribes to request neutrality. Simon Girty went with him as interpreter and guide. For nearly three years, Girty worked for the patriot cause, as an interpreter, militia man, and recruiter for the frontier militia (convincing people to join). Despite his efforts, his superiors never trusted him; they always suspected him of loyalty to the British. When they did not give Girty an army promotion in 1777, he got angry and resigned.

In late 1777, some of the Indian tribes Girty was known to have visited entered the war on the British side. Girty was placed under arrest for suspicion of being a British sympathizer. He escaped easily, returned to face the charges, and was set free without being convicted of any crime. He was bitter about the incident.

In February 1778, Girty was sent as a guide on a mission to seize weapons the British supposedly had stored in an Indian village somewhere in Ohio. The mission was a disaster; it resulted in nothing but the slaughter of several innocent Indian women and children by white soldiers.

Girty changes sides; supports British

In March 1778, soon after the failed action in Ohio, Girty and several other men deserted to the British. Historians cannot say for sure what his reasons were. Perhaps he believed that the American cause was doomed. Maybe his companions in flight were unusually persuasive. Whatever his reasons (and in later years he gave many different ones), he made his way to the British fort at Detroit, where he was hired as an interpreter at a wage of two dollars a day.

Girty used his influence to talk the Indians out of their neutrality and into joining the British side. He promised the Indians that land already taken from them by white settlers would be returned to them if they fought on the side of the

Chief Logan Gives a Famous Speech

Logan (c. 1725–80), sometimes called James Logan, was a chief of the small Mingo tribe of Ohio. Logan is said to have been friendly to white settlers until his family, including a pregnant sister, was slaughtered in 1774 during Lord Dunmore's War. This was one in a series of brutal acts committed by whites against Indians that contributed to the violence of the time.

Chief Logan refused to participate in the peace treaties that ended Lord Dunmore's War. Under the shade of a huge elm tree, Chief Logan delivered a famous speech said to have been translated into English by Simon Girty. Chief Logan said in part: "I appeal to any white man to say that he ever entered Logan's cabin, but I gave him meat; that he ever came naked, but I clothed him.... He will not turn his heel to save his life. Who is there to mourn for Logan? No one."

British and won. He spent the next few years going from one Indian village to another, convincing the tribes to join the British cause. Along with British soldiers and their Indian allies, Girty also took part in raids on the frontier, from Fort Pitt to the Kentucky River. The intention was to destroy American supplies and divert American soldiers from General George Washington's main army in the East. Washington was forced to send badly needed troops to protect American settlers on the frontier.

Girty's legend grows

The raids that Girty and others took part in were astoundingly brutal. Scalping, rape, the cold–blooded murder of innocents, torture, and burnings at the stake were common. Before long, Simon Girty was being called "The White Savage." No one knows what motivated him; he never wrote anything down. At the time, most people believed he enjoyed the violence. It has been said that he was a champion of the Indian cause and was fighting for Indian rights. According to James K. Richards: "A mystery that will never be solved is Girty's perception of the Indians themselves; whether or not he felt any affection for them, any empathy for their plight, or sympathy for their cause, or was simply doing a job he was good at ... in spite of an undercurrent of contempt" for them.

In one famous incident, Girty was able to talk the Indian captors of his old friend, Simon Kenton, out of burning him at the stake (Kenton was accused of stealing Indian horses). This was done at the risk of Girty's own safety. Kenton became famous as a Kentucky frontiersman, and he often afterwards spoke of Girty's kindness. But he was one of the few who ever had a good word to say on Girty's behalf.

In 1780 Girty was charged by the state of Pennsylvania with treason and a price was put on his head. He evaded capture and continued his journeys through Indian country, stirring up the Indians to higher levels of brutality against the Americans. In 1781, legend says, he got involved in a drunken fight with the Mohawk Chief **Joseph Brant** (see entry), who struck him on the head with his sword and gave him an ugly wound. The resulting scar only added to his reputation as a human nightmare.

By 1782, Revolutionary War fighting had mostly ended in the East but it continued on the frontier. Girty was part of a white-Indian force that captured American Colonel (pronounced KER–nuhl) William Crawford in Ohio in June 1782. Crawford suffered a horrible torture and death; it is said that Girty refused to do anything to help and may even have been amused at the scene—he is reported to have directed jokes at the dying man. The grisly story spread and became the most famous evil deed attributed to Girty. Some historians have pointed out that Girty would have put his own life at risk if he attempted to save Crawford's, and probably would have failed.

Last days

Girty was given a pension by the British after the war (an annual payment for his military services). He moved to Amherstburg, Ontario, Canada, across the Detroit River from Detroit. In 1784 Girty married Catherine Malott, a former Indian captive who may have been rescued by Girty. She was less than half his age. The couple took up farming and eventually had at least three children.

Simon Girty was too restless for farm life, though. He often left home to visit Indian villages and stir up the residents against the increasing numbers of white settlers. He took part in a few more battles against American forces during outbreaks of white-Indian violence on the frontier. By 1794, it was obvious to the Indians that the British support Girty had promised them would not be coming. His usefulness to the Indians ended, and Girty retired to his farm.

Girty's health and eyesight began to fail; he became crippled after he broke his ankle in 1800. He liked to sit in the local bar and tell tales of his exploits. His wife left him for a time; his enemies liked to say it was because of his evil temper and drunken abuses. Girty died quietly at home in 1818.

About Girty's lasting reputation as a man of unmatched viciousness, James Leighton wrote in an encyclopedia article: "These tales were spread by people who could not see that hostilities between the western tribes and the new [American government] were caused, not by the behavior of men like Girty, but by the white settlers' insatiable hunger for land and their government's failure to honor its agreements with Indians."

For More Information

Boatner, Mark M. "Crawford's Death." "Indians in the Colonial Wars and in the Revolution." "Western Operations." *Encyclopedia of the American Revolution.* Mechanicsburg, PA: Stackpole Books, 1994, pp. 306-7; 541-3; 1188-94.

Boyd, Thomas. *Simon Girty: The White Savage.* New York: Minton, Balch & Company, 1928.

Butterfield, Consul Willshire. *History of the Girtys.* Cincinnati: Robert Clarke & Co., 1890. Reprinted by Long's College Book Co., Columbus, Ohio, 1950.

Grey, Zane. *The Spirit of the Border: A Romance of the Early Settlers in the Ohio Valley.* Originally published in 1906. Reprinted, University of Nebraska Press, 1996.

Johnson, Tom. Reminiscences regarding the renegade, Simon Girty. In the Henry T. Thomas Papers, MSS 645. Courtesy of the Ohio Historical Society.

Leighton, Douglas. "Girty, Simon." *Dictionary of Canadian Biography.* Toronto: University of Toronto Press, 1983, pp. 345-6.

Richards, James K. "A Clash of Cultures: Simon Girty and the Struggle for the Frontier." *Timeline* (a publication of the Ohio Historical Society), June-July 1985, pp. 2-17.

Web Sites

Ohio Historical Society. [Online] Available http://www.ohiohistory.org/index.html (accessed on October 4, 1999).

Mary Katherine Goddard

Born June 16, 1738
Groton, Connecticut
Died August 12, 1816
Baltimore, Maryland

Publisher, postmaster, printer of the "authentic copy" of the Declaration of Independence

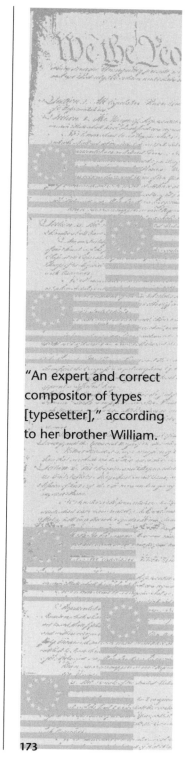

"An expert and correct compositor of types [typesetter]," according to her brother William.

Mary Katherine Goddard was a successful businessperson of the eighteenth century who turned enterprises begun by her undependable brother into financial successes. She was the most acclaimed female publisher during the American Revolution. Her reputation for quality work spread far beyond the cities where her newspapers were produced. In the end, she was forced to live in near-poverty when she lost her government job because of limitations set on women of her day.

Mary Katherine Goddard was the daughter of Dr. Giles Goddard and printer Sarah Updike Goddard (see box). She was born in Groton, Connecticut. She and her brother William were the only two of the couple's four children who lived to maturity. Goddard received her schooling from her educated mother. Few facts are known about her early life, except that the family moved from Groton to nearby New London, Connecticut, where her father practiced medicine and served as postmaster.

In 1762, after the death of her father, Goddard joined her mother in the printing business in Providence, Rhode Island (owned by her brother). It was during this period that Goddard learned the printing business.

When William moved to Philadelphia, Pennsylvania, to open a new printing business, Goddard and her mother stayed behind to manage the Providence shop and print the weekly newspaper, the *Providence Gazette*. Faced with money problems, William had to sell the Providence business in 1768; the two women then joined him in Philadelphia.

Becomes publisher in Baltimore, Maryland

After her mother died, Goddard became the office manager, helping her brother produce the *Pennsylvania Chronicle* newspaper. In 1773 the ever-restless William moved once again, this time to Baltimore, Maryland, to launch a new business venture. Goddard stayed in Philadelphia, running the printing shop until it was sold in early 1774. She then went on to Baltimore to join William.

In 1775, at the beginning of the Revolutionary War, the Continental Congress (the legislative body of the American colonies) began work on establishing a national postal service. William was asked to help, and he put his sister in charge of the Baltimore business. She became publisher of Baltimore's first newspaper, the *Maryland Journal,* and she performed the task so well that her reputation as a newspaperwoman was made.

Goddard continued printing the *Journal* during the years of the American Revolution. When standard size paper was difficult to find because of wartime shortages, she sometimes had to produce the *Journal* on small sheets of paper, the only paper available to her. Throughout the war years other newspapers had similar problems, but only Goddard consistently managed to publish a newspaper. She kept American patriots informed about the latest war news, and she made a major contribution to the cause of independence by publishing facts, not rumors. When she retired as its editor in 1784, the *Journal* had become one of the most widely read publications in the United States.

Prints Declaration, gains reputation for excellence

Goddard's most famous contribution to the war effort occurred on January 18, 1777. She was chosen by the Continental Congress to print the first copies of the Decla-

Sarah Updike Goddard, Colonial Printer

Mary Katherine Goddard's mother, Sarah Updike Goddard, was also a remarkable woman. She was born around 1700 near Wickford, Rhode Island, to a family whose ancestors had emigrated from Germany in the 1600s. Her mother was Abigail Newton Updike, and her father, Lodowick Updike, was a public office holder and a landowner of some wealth.

Goddard studied French, Latin, and other subjects at her home under the guidance of a French tutor. She married Dr. Giles Goddard of Connecticut in 1735 and moved with him to New London, Connecticut. After the death of her husband in 1757, Sarah Goddard paid for her son, William, to be trained as a printer and to begin a printing business in Providence, Rhode Island. There she and her daughter Mary Katherine helped him run the newspaper he had established, the

Providence Gazette. The paper printed a number of articles speaking out in favor of colonial rights in pre-Revolutionary times. A special issue in 1765 rallied its readers in opposition to the Stamp Act, a British measure that required that colonists pay for specially stamped paper to be used for all official documents.

After her son moved to New York, Goddard continued to supervise the printing office, publishing the newspaper, the annual *West's Almanack,* and various pamphlets. She reorganized the business under the name Sarah Goddard and Company, working with her daughter and other assistants. When times were hard, she sometimes traded copies of the paper for food and other goods. Along with her daughter, she was forced out of the printing business by her son William in November 1768. She died in Philadelphia in 1770, at the age of seventy.

ration of Independence that included all the names of the document's signers.

The first printing of the document, on July 4, 1776, had contained only the names of **John Hancock** and Charles Thomson; the names of the other signers were kept secret for a time because of fear that the British would take revenge on them. By its order of January 18, 1777, Congress required that "an authentic copy of the Declaration of Independence, with the names of the members of Congress subscribing to the same [supporting the document], be sent to each of the United States."

The complete copy was then printed, with all the signers' names, by Mary Katherine Goddard in Baltimore. The importance of this event did not escape Goddard; she signed the piece with her full name, rather than her customary initials. Each of the thirteen states in the union received a copy.

Unfortunately for historians, none of Goddard's personal letters have survived. Goddard's Baltimore printing business prospered during the ten years she was in charge of it. William helped only occasionally, as he pursued his other business interests. Mary Katherine Goddard remained a respected member of the Baltimore community, even though her brother was twice threatened by local mobs because of newspaper articles he had written that were thought to be unpatriotic.

Begins new career as postmaster

Near the end of Goddard's time as publisher, the two Goddard siblings often disagreed. Mary Katherine finally became completely alienated from William after a bitter battle between the two. William had decided to take over the paper from his sister and paid her a pitiful sum for her share of it. Forever after, she would have nothing to do with her brother, and she even refused to attend his wedding. The falling out marked the end of Mary Katherine Goddard's career as a printer.

Fortunately, Goddard had other interests she could fall back on. For years, she had been binding books (attaching the covers and backing on books), and she proceeded to further develop this business. In 1775 Goddard had accepted a position as postmaster of Baltimore, the first woman to hold such a position in the United States, and one of the few to be granted any type of public appointment in the 1700s. In 1781, as a patriotic service, she published *An Almanac and Ephemeris* (a calendar), which featured the schedule of court sessions in Maryland, Pennsylvania, and Virginia.

Goddard kept the postmaster's job for fourteen years, until it began to require widespread travel—respectable women of the time did not travel alone. In a remarkable development, more than two hundred businessmen signed a petition that she be allowed to keep the position. But their protests fell on deaf ears within the federal government. Against her will, she was retired from her post in October 1789.

Runs bookstore, dies

Following the loss of her job, Goddard continued to live in Baltimore, where she ran a book shop on the city's Market Square from 1784 until about 1810. Mary Katherine Goddard, who never married, died in Baltimore on August 12, 1816, at the age of seventy-eight. She was buried in the cemetery of Baltimore's St. Paul's Church.

Goddard's will freed the female slave who had been her assistant during her later years. The woman, Belinda Starling, also inherited Goddard's meager estate. Some years later, Goddard's memory was honored when the Omaha, Nebraska, members of the Daughters of the American Revolution, a group of women who can trace their ancestry back to the earliest days of America, named its chapter for her.

For More Information

Claghorn, Charles E. "Goddard, Mary Katherine" in *Women Patriots of the American Revolution, A Biographical Dictionary.* Metuchen, NJ: Scarecrow Press, 1991, pp. 87–88.

Farragher, John Mack, ed. "Goddard, Mary Katherine" in *Encyclopedia of Colonial and Revolutionary America.* New York: Facts on File, 1990, p. 171.

Henry, Susan. "Sarah Goddard, Gentlewoman Printer." *Journalism Quarterly* 57 (Spring 1980), pp. 23–30.

Humphrey, Carol Sue. "Goddard, Mary Katherine" in *American National Biography.* John A. Garraty and Mark C. Carnes, eds. New York: Oxford University Press, 1999, vol. 9, pp. 136–37.

Miner, Ward L. "Goddard, Mary Katherine" in *Notable American Women.* Cambridge, MA: The Belknap Press of the Harvard University Press, 1971, vol. 2, pp. 55–56.

Zeinert, Karen. *Those Remarkable Women of the American Revolution.* Brookfield, CT: The Millbrook Press, 1996, p. 47–48.

Nathan Hale

Born June 6, 1755
Coventry, Connecticut
Died September 22, 1776
New York, New York

Military leader, spy, schoolmaster

> "I only regret that I have but one life to lose for my country."

Portrait: Nathan Hale.
Reproduced by permission of AP/Wide World Photos.

Nathan Hale was a schoolteacher who became an officer in the Continental (American) army during the American Revolution (1775–83). When General **George Washington** (see entry) needed information about the British military plans to take New York City, Hale volunteered to go behind the British lines as a spy. He was captured and killed by hanging, but his brave words have inspired generations of soldiers and schoolchildren ever since.

Nathan Hale was born on June 6, 1755, in Coventry, Connecticut, the son of Richard Hale and Elizabeth Strong. He was one of twelve children born to the couple, and one of nine sons. (Six of those nine sons would fight for the patriot cause in the American Revolution.) The Hales were well-to-do farmers and the family was devoted to the cause of American independence.

Nathan Hale was a sickly baby and not expected to survive. He did, however, and as he grew up he found that he had a natural talent for sports. He loved to play outdoors and soon grew tall and strong. At school, Hale discovered he also had a talent for learning. In grammar (elementary) school, Hale probably studied the typical topics taught in colonial schools: reading, writing, arithmetic, and religion. When he grew older, his father suggested that Hale become a minister. The boy then began to study with the Reverend Joseph Huntington, the minister of the church in Coventry and a respected classics scholar. Under his direction, Hale studied "the classics," subjects that included languages (Greek and Latin, the language of the ancient Romans), mathematics, philosophy (the study of the nature of life and the universe), Greek and Roman history and literature, and oratory (the art of developing and making speeches).

Huntington and Hale's friends described Hale as tall and blue-eyed, with light brown hair. He was muscular and well coordinated because of his devotion to sports. He was neatly dressed, well spoken, and a great favorite with the young ladies of his home town.

Studies the classics at Yale University

In 1769 Hale entered Yale University in New Haven, Connecticut. There he continued his study of the classics. He also helped organize a library for the Linonia Society, a secret club for students who loved literature. Hale was an excellent student, admired by teachers and classmates alike. His roommates were William Hull and Benjamin Tallmadge; both would later serve under General Washington, Hull as an army captain and Tallmadge as head of the secret service (spy operation).

While at school, Hale was exposed to much political discussion. Naturally, much of the talk centered around whether the American colonies should break away from England. Already a patriot, Hale became devoted to the cause of American freedom. He also learned how to form arguments, how to debate (a discussion that addresses two sides of a question), and how to give well-received public speeches.

When he graduated in 1773, Hale and several other students staged a public debate on the question of whether the education of daughters was more neglected than the education of sons in most families. Hale argued that girls were shortchanged when it came to education, and he won the debate easily.

After graduation, Hale took a job as a schoolmaster. He worked first in East Haddam, Connecticut, from October 1773 until March 1774, and then in New London, Connecticut, from March 1774 until July 1775. Hale was a good teacher who made learning interesting for his students. He was a natural leader, able to maintain discipline in his classroom without sacrificing his students' fondness for him.

Enlists in Connecticut militia

By July 1775 the American colonies were at war with Great Britain. Hale completed his teaching commitment and responded to General Washington's request for recruits by joining the local unit of the Connecticut militia (pronounced ma-LISH-a). Each colony had its own local army, called a militia. Some militia men would eventually join the American force called the Continental army.

Hale joined the Seventh Connecticut Regiment as a first lieutenant (pronounced loo-TEN-ant) under the command of Colonel Charles Webb. Perhaps because of his skill in making speeches, Hale was sent from town to town to recruit other men into the rebellion against Great Britain. In one of his speeches Hale said, "Let us march immediately, and never lay down our arms until we have obtained our independence."

In September 1775 Hale was promoted to captain and his regiment was ordered to Cambridge, across the Charles River from Boston, Massachusetts. Washington's troops were hoping to provide relief to the citizens of Boston, whose city was occupied by the British army under General **Thomas Gage** (see entry). The British had entered Boston, a major city in the northern colonies, as they retreated eastward from their defeats at Lexington and Concord.

Hale's militia unit's term of service ended in late 1775. Hale then transferred into the Nineteenth Regiment of the Continental army in January 1776 as a captain. In March the British left Boston and went to Halifax, Nova Scotia, in Canada. Canada was still a loyal part of the British empire, and the plan was to use Halifax as a staging point for the invasion and capture of New York City. Since the British had failed to end the war with the capture of Boston, they hoped to end it by taking New York.

In April both the Continental and British armies were encamped in the vicinity of New York City, but no major battles were fought until August. In mid-May, Hale and a small group of patriot soldiers captured a sloop (a small British boat) loaded with supplies. They made their daring raid at night, despite the presence of a British man-of-war (a battleship) called *Asia*. The much-needed supplies from the sloop were divided among the American soldiers.

Recruited into Knowlton's Rangers

By the summer of 1776 the British forces of thirty-two thousand outnumbered Washington's army of twenty thousand poorly equipped men. The Americans went on to fight a series of battles with the British. Then came the Battle of Long Island in August 1776, and an American defeat. Desperate to preserve his smaller army and to learn of the enemy's plans, General Washington created a new unit of soldiers called rangers. Their job was to gather intelligence about enemy troop movements, the size of their armies, and where their defenses were positioned. The rangers would ride ahead of the army and scout for information that would be useful to the Americans in making military plans.

The new unit was called "The Connecticut Rangers" or "Knowlton's Rangers," after its leader, Lieutenant Colonel (pronounced loo-TEN-ant KERN-uhl) Thomas Knowlton. The colonel was allowed to hand-pick the men for his battalion. He was looking for men who were smart, could think independently, and were resourceful in obtaining information. Nathan Hale was one of the 120 men who formed this special unit. Knowlton selected Hale as a captain to lead one of his ranger companies. Washington was relying on Knowlton's Rangers to provide him with information about British plans for capturing New York City.

Accepts spy mission

At the request of General Washington, Colonel Knowlton approached his troops and asked for a volunteer to go behind the British lines (the territory under British control). The main force of the British army was on Long Island at this point. The volunteer would not wear his soldier's uniform but would be disguised as a civilian. His task would be to discover the strength of the British troops and determine where they

would strike next. Washington could then plan how to meet this British offensive (attack).

The mission posed serious risks, which is why Knowlton asked for a volunteer. For an American soldier to travel out of uniform behind the British lines meant only one thing; if captured, that man would be considered a spy, not a soldier. Spies faced execution. Soldiers captured in battle, on the other hand, were exchanged for enemy soldiers or held in prisoner of war camps.

No one responded to Knowlton's first call for volunteers. When he asked again, Hale accepted the mission. As Hale explained to William Hull, then a captain in Washington's army: "I wish to be useful and every kind of service, necessary to the public good, becomes honorable by being necessary." Hale, dressed in civilian clothes and carrying his Yale diploma, planned to pose as a schoolmaster looking for work. He left the American camp on September 12, 1776, and traveled by boat to Long Island.

By most accounts, Hale was a poor choice for this or any spy mission. He was given no cover story to try and fool the British if he were captured. He had no training in the tools of spying, such as disappearing ink, false-bottomed carrying cases, or coded messages. Instead, he had to rely on sketchy instructions and his own bravery and intelligence.

For almost two weeks, Hale moved about behind the British lines, visiting every British camp on Long Island. During this time, he made sketches of the British fortifications (defensive positions) and kept count of the types and numbers of British soldiers he saw. He kept these documents hidden in his shoes. By September 15, he was ready to return to General Washington with his news.

Captured and executed

But fate intervened. On September 20, the city of New York was set on fire. By the time the fire was put out, about a fourth of the city's buildings had been burned beyond repair. In the excitement, Hale hoped to escape past the British sentries (guard soldiers) around the city. But the British suspected that the Americans had set the fire to keep the British from having the city's resources. So the British were out in force, looking for American plotters and arsonists (people who set fires deliberately). One of the suspicious characters they took into custody on September 21 was Hale. The place and story of his capture are unclear. However, whatever the actual circumstances, Hale found himself a prisoner of the British, who soon found the documents hidden in his shoes.

The British brought Hale to their main camp. Some historians believe that Hale was betrayed by his cousin, Samuel Hale, who was a Loyalist (an American loyal to England). Samuel Hale was working for the British army as the deputy commissioner of prisoners. However, when confronted with the evidence in his shoes, Hale admitted that he was an American soldier on a spy mission. With that admission, Hale sealed his fate.

General Sir **William Howe** (see entry), commander-in-chief of the British army in the colonies, ordered Hale's execution by hanging. Hale was given no trial at which he could have defended his actions. The crime of spying was judged so awful that Howe felt justified in denying the trial. Some historians believe that Howe's hasty decision about Hale was based in part on Howe's anger at the Americans for their suspected part in the burning of New York. Whatever Howe's motivation, Hale was sentenced to hang at dawn the next morning. He was placed in the care of William Cunningham, Howe's provost marshal (head of military police).

Hale spent the night in the greenhouse at Howe's headquarters, under close guard. Cunningham had no sympathy for Hale, who was both a rebel and a spy. When Hale asked for a Bible to read, Cunningham denied the request. He later denied Hale a visit from a chaplain (a military priest), even though such visits were standard procedure for condemned men.

At dawn on Sunday, September 22, Hale was taken to the gallows that had been built in the apple orchard at what is now Market Street and East Broadway in New York City. Then a delay occurred. While he was waiting to be executed, Hale was befriended by a British officer, Captain John Montresor, who was General Howe's chief engineer (an officer who planned forts and groundworks). Montresor took Hale into his tent and provided him with pen and ink so Hale could write to his family. Hale wrote two letters, one to his brother Enoch and the other to Colonel Knowlton (unknown to Hale, Knowlton had been killed six days earlier).

At eleven o'clock, Hale was led to the gallows and a noose was placed around his neck. He was just twenty-one years old. Before his eyes were blindfolded, Hale was allowed to make a last comment. It was then that he made the statement that is still remembered today. Turning to the crowd of British soldiers and officers who had come to witness his death, Hale said, "You are shedding the blood of the innocent; if I had ten thousand lives, I would lay them down in defense of my injured, bleeding country." He closed with his famous statement, "I only regret that I have but one life to lose for my country."

Legacy of heroism and courage

After his death, Hale's body was not buried but left hanging as a warning to other spies. His last letters were never delivered, because Captain Montresor had entrusted them to Cunningham, the provost marshal. Cunningham was anxious that little word of the Hale incident should reach the Americans. He did not want either the Americans or the British to know that Hale had died bravely and without regret.

General Washington learned of Hale's fate a week later, when Captain Montresor met with two American officers to discuss the exchange of prisoners. One of these officers was William Hull, Hale's college roommate. The other was **Alexander Hamilton** (see entry), who would go on to become the first secretary of the U.S. Treasury. It was through Montresor's testimony that Hale's companions heard the true nature of his capture, execution without trial, and brave last words.

Today, Nathan Hale is renowned as a patriot who bravely gave his life when his country asked for his services. Statues to Hale were erected in City Hall Park in New York City, and in Hartford, the capital of Connecticut. A memorial stands in Coventry, his birth place; and Fort Hale in New Haven harbor bears his name. A monument near Huntingdon, New York, marks the spot where it is believed Hale was captured by the British. His execution has been depicted in paintings and in magazine illustrations.

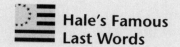

Hale's Famous Last Words

Like many scholars, Nathan Hale memorized favorite parts from plays, poems, and essays. One play that impressed him during his college years was about a famous ancient Roman statesman named Marcus Porcius Cato (95–46 B.C.). Cato, a leader in the fight against Julius Caesar's dictatorship, died rather than submit to Caesar's rule. This tragic figure was celebrated in *Cato*, a play written by British writer and statesman Joseph Addison (1672–1719). In Act 4, Scene 4, in the play, Cato says, "What a pity it is that we can die but once to save our country!"

Nathan Hale undoubtedly remembered these words when he made his final remarks. Like Cato, he was a patriot who considered it an honor to die for the cause of liberty. Today, Hale is often referred to as America's "martyr spy" because he responded to his country's call without thinking of his own safety.

For More Information

Lambeck, Mark. "Hail to the Hero." *Yankee.* Vol. 51 (May 1987): pp. 16–18.

Martens, Anne Coulter. *One Life to Lose: What Makes an American Hero?* (A children's play about Nathan Hale, American revolutionist.) *Plays.* Vol. 55, no. 6 (April 1996): pp. 111.

Rogers, Kerri, and Shon Hedges. "A Prison Keeper's Tale." (A short story about Nathan Hale.) *Stone Soup* Vol. 24, no. 3. (January 1996): pp. 33–45.

Sanborn, Paul F. "Nathan Hale" in *The American Revolution, 1775–1783: An Encyclopedia,* vol. 1: A–L. Edited by Richard L. Blanco. New York: Garland Publishing, 1993, pp. 719–22.

Wilson, James Grant, and John Fiske, eds. "Nathan Hale" in *Appleton's Cyclopaedia of American Biography,* vol. 3. New York: D. Appleton and Co., 1888, pp. 30–31.

Alexander Hamilton

Born January 11, 1755
Nevis, British West Indies
Died July 12, 1804
New York, New York

Secretary of the treasury, political leader, lawyer, soldier, journalist

A lexander Hamilton served as a trusted secretary to General **George Washington** (see entry) during the American Revolution (1775–83) and fought in the famous battle at Yorktown that ended the war. He is best known for his economic policies after the war, and for his role as the main author of the *Federalist Papers*. A brave soldier and talented writer and speaker, he seemed to have a solution for every problem he encountered.

Alexander Hamilton was born on January 11, 1755, in the town of Charleston on the island of Nevis (pronounced NEE-vus) in the West Indies, a group of islands that are located between the United States and South America. He was born to Rachel Fawcitt Lavien, daughter of a French doctor and planter, and James Hamilton, an unsuccessful Scottish businessman. At the time of Hamilton's birth, his mother was actually married to someone else, a man named John Lavien. She divorced Lavien in 1758, but the court that granted the divorce prohibited her from remarrying.

In 1765, shortly after the Hamiltons moved to the island of St. Croix (pronounced Saint-CROY), James Hamilton

"Give all power to the many and they will oppress the few. Give all power to the few, they will oppress the many. Both therefore ought to have power, that each may defend itself against the other."

Portrait: Alexander Hamilton. *Reproduced by permission of the Smithsonian Institution.*

187

Throughout college Hamilton openly defended the rights of colonists. When the Revolutionary War began in 1775, Hamilton quit college and joined a military unit in New York. *Reproduced by permission of Archive Photos, Inc.*

lost all his money then abandoned his family. At age eleven, Alexander Hamilton had to take a job as a clerk at a local trading post, where he later worked as bookkeeper and briefly as a manager. His mother died in 1768.

Alexander Hamilton was a bright boy and it was his dream to go to college. In 1772 some townspeople raised the funds to send him away to school. He journeyed to America, briefly attended school in New Jersey, then went to New York City, where he entered what is now Columbia University in 1774.

Attends college, joins military

While a student in New York, Hamilton read the works of American patriots James Otis, **John Adams**, and **John Dickinson** (see entries), in which they defended the rights of Americans against oppressive British taxation policies. He was so moved by what he read that he decided to support the patriots' cause. Hamilton took part in his first public act of resistance against the British when he spoke out at a rally in a New York City park. His speech defended the Boston Tea Party (1773), in which citizens of Boston protested British taxation by throwing hundreds of cases of tea into Boston Harbor. He also spoke in favor of the upcoming First Continental Congress, which would bring together representatives from twelve of the thirteen colonies in Philadelphia, Pennsylvania, in 1774. They met to discuss ways of dealing with what they considered unfair treatment by the British.

During his college years, Hamilton wrote well-reasoned political pamphlets defending the rights of the colonists as English citizens. At first, Hamilton wrote in favor of binding the United States and England together as equal partners. But when England showed its unwillingness to share power, Hamilton and other patriots came to realize America would have to declare independence.

At the outbreak of the Revolutionary War in 1775, Hamilton quit college and joined a military unit in New York, where he was appointed a captain. It was a volunteer army and Hamilton had to gather together at least thirty men to serve under him. Hamilton's military company had to follow the same regulations as the Continental army, but members received lower pay. In a short time, Hamilton and his troops served at the battles of Long Island and White Plains, New York, and at Trenton and Princeton, New Jersey.

In 1777, after two years in combat, Hamilton became the assistant and secretary to Commander in Chief George Washington, holding the rank of lieutenant colonel (pronounced loo-TEN-uhnt KER-nuhl). He wrote reports on the defects of the American military system and offered suggestions to correct them. While serving in the post, Hamilton earned the respect and admiration of Washington. He also met a number of other high-level soldiers and well-known people who would later help him advance his career. They came to respect him for his well-spoken manner, writing abilities, leadership skills, and first-hand knowledge of what was going on with the war.

Marries into wealthy family, splits with Washington

On December 14, 1780, Hamilton married Elizabeth Schuyler (pronounced SKY-ler), daughter of the well-known General Philip John Schuyler, who was a member of a wealthy and important New York family. Richard Brookhiser, in his biography *Alexander Hamilton, American,* described Hamilton's appearance at about this time: "[He] had wavy chestnut brown hair, a classical [straight] nose, and deep-set violet eyes.... He was five feet seven, not short by the standards of the day.... But he was slim when many men ... were stout. [There] was something youthful about him, younger even than his years; lively, open, [and impulsive]." The couple produced eight children during their long and happy marriage.

According to some historians, on February 16, 1781, Hamilton had an argument with General Washington that resulted in Hamilton's resignation. In July, after his replace-ment had been found, Hamilton took command of his own battalion (military unit). He played an important role in the Yorktown (Pennsylvania) Campaign, the last battle of the Rev-olutionary War. Hamilton was made colonel on September 30, 1783, but left military service at the end of the year.

Serves in Congress, attends Constitutional Convention

Hamilton was elected New York's representative to the Continental Congress (legislative body of the United States) for the 1782–83 term. He kept his hand in politics but also became one of the most-well known lawyers in New York City. In 1787 Hamilton was elected to the New York Legislature, the state's lawmaking body.

Hamilton had begun his career in national politics a year earlier in 1786, when he attended a convention in Mary-land to discuss national governmental issues that were not cov-ered by the Articles of Confederation. The Articles had served as the basis of America's government since 1777, but they were no longer adequate in a growing and developing nation. At the Maryland convention, Hamilton suggested that a Constitu-tional Convention be held the following year in Philadelphia to revise the Articles of Confederation and discuss major issues relating to the government of the United States.

Supports strong central government

Hamilton did not have a good opinion of human nature, and his ideas about government reflected that view. He believed that most people looked out only for themselves, and that there were few men who had the wisdom and foresight to govern a nation—he called them "the wise and good and rich."

In 1787 Hamilton attended the Constitutional Con-vention in Philadelphia. He spoke out for a strong central gov-ernment for the country, instead of a system in which indi-vidual states held equal power. Historian Brookhiser explained the core of the plan proposed by Hamilton in his biography. Brookhiser wrote, "The power ... in Hamilton's plan would be wielded by a Senate [an upper house], elected from special elec-tion districts" by the citizens. The senators could serve for life if they behaved properly. The citizens would also elect representatives to a lower house, an Assembly whose members would serve for three years. Brookhiser explained, "The balance wheel between [the Senate and Assembly] would be a governor, chosen by special electors [voters] from the senatorial election districts. Like the senators, the national governor would serve [on the basis of] good behavior; he would also appoint the governors of the states."

Hamilton proposed that the federal government should act boldly in economic and military affairs and should have the power to overturn the decisions of state governments. Some of his ideas disturbed his fellow delegates, who feared the loss of state-held powers.

The *Federalist Papers*

To support their version of a proposed new U.S. Constitution, Hamilton, **John Jay**, and **James Madison** (see entries) wrote a series of essays called the *Federalist Papers*. Historians believe Hamilton wrote at least fifty-one of the eighty-five essays, which provided arguments that supporters of a Constitution could use in debating the issue. The *Federalist Papers* also provided explanations of how a proposed new government could operate.

After much debate by representatives at the Continental Congress, a proposed constitution for the United States was drawn up. It reflected many of Hamilton's views about government, particularly that of making the federal government more powerful than the state governments. The proposed work was sent to the legislatures of each state for a vote for or against passage. Hamilton was present at the New York Convention in 1787, where state representatives met to decide whether or not New York would ratify (pass) the proposed constitution. There, Hamilton made speeches, talked with individuals, and helped get the document passed.

The U.S. Constitution, which was adopted by the whole country in 1789, did not create a federal government as powerful as Hamilton would have liked. Still, he supported the Constitution because he believed it provided the country with its best hope for an effective union.

Serves as secretary of the Treasury

With the new U.S. Constitution in place, George Washington was elected the first U.S. president in 1789. When the new Congress established the Treasury Department to oversee the nation's financial affairs, Washington appointed Hamilton, his former military aide, as secretary of the Treasury.

Despite their earlier differences, Washington had always retained affection and respect for the younger man. Robert Hendrickson explained in his book on Hamilton that once Hamilton had stopped serving as Washington's aide, "he and Washington were free to form a new relationship.... The old relationship of master to servant ... changed to that of senior to junior partner, but partners nevertheless in public service to the nation in war and peace."

Hamilton served at the helm of the Treasury Department from 1789 to 1795. During that time he proposed many innovative measures that contributed to the security of the new nation. For example, during his first month in office, Hamilton proposed the establishment of a seagoing branch of the military. Hamilton's proposal led to the establishment of the U.S. Navy, and to the creation of the U.S. Naval Academy to train young officers.

Perhaps Hamilton's greatest contribution as Treasury secretary was the "Hamiltonian System." It was developed after Congress asked him to find a way to deal with the huge debts left over from the Revolutionary War. Hamilton published his solution in the 1790 "Report on the Public Credit." It described a model for a stable but flexible money system for the country that has survived to the present day. Hamilton proposed that the federal government assume the responsibility of paying the states' war debts.

Republican opposition

Hamilton's views were controversial and often faced opposition. His chief critics were **Thomas Jefferson** (see entry) and his Republican Party. The Republicans criticized Hamilton for being arrogant and favoring the interests of the wealthy over those of farm workers and other ordinary people. Many Republicans feared that Hamilton sought the destruction of the federal form of government and all state governments, and that he was leading the country toward rule by kings and queens.

To this charge Hamilton replied, "To this there is no other answer than a flat denial, except this: that the [notion], from its absurdity, refutes [disproves] itself." The Republicans also accused him of using his office to add to his own wealth (a charge for which there was no proof).

When Republicans opposed Hamilton's 1790 financial recommendations, the parties ironed out their differences at a private meeting. At the meeting, Hamilton agreed to support Jefferson's proposal to place the new capitol of the United States on Virginia's Potomac River in exchange for Jefferson's support of Hamilton's measures (Jefferson was from Virginia). When put to a vote, Hamilton's plan passed overwhelmingly in the U.S. Congress.

Other contributions to a strong, new nation

Hamilton had a very active and creative mind, and during his term as Treasury secretary, he offered many proposals to the new Congress. For example, Hamilton developed a plan to establish the first Bank of the United States. Government funds would be deposited in the bank, and the bank would encourage American manufacturing by paying cash rewards for productivity. He also suggested charging taxes on American imports and exports (goods shipped into and out of the country) to provide new sources of funds to run the government.

The always confident Hamilton grew so powerful that eventually he managed more than one thousand federal employees. He was an excellent financial planner. He prepared long, detailed financial reports for Congress, and he spoke out on nearly all major political issues, especially those regarding finance.

Hamilton's financial methods faced new opposition in 1794, when a group of whiskey makers rebelled against his efforts to collect taxes on liquor produced in the United States. Their protest resulted in outbreaks of violence in western Pennsylvania and Virginia, called the "Whiskey Rebellion." Hamilton was a great believer in the rule of law. He responded to the rebellion by joining General Henry Lee and his soldiers as an adviser when they were sent by President Washington to put down the rebellion.

Resumes private life; alienates John Adams

In 1795, Hamilton resigned from his office as Treasury secretary, mostly because he could not live on the salary it paid. He resumed the practice of law, which nearly tripled his salary to $12,000 a year. He worked mainly on cases involving business and insurance. But Hamilton's resignation did not mark the end of his public life. He stayed close to President George Washington, as both a friend and an adviser, and even helped to write his old friend's well-known Farewell Address at the end of his presidency.

Hamilton also assumed a leadership role at the Federalist Party convention of 1796 (see **John Adams** entry). Hamilton's dealings there led to bad feelings between him and party leader John Adams. Hamilton hoped to get Thomas Pinckney elected president, a job Adams wanted for himself. Hamilton's plan backfired, and Adams became the second president of the United States.

John Adams resented Hamilton's interference in the convention proceedings. But at the insistence of George Washington, in 1798 Adams reluctantly appointed Hamilton inspector general of the U.S. Army when war threatened to break out between France and the United States. Hamilton served for two years, then published an attack on Adams's presidency.

Some years later, Adams showed his great dislike of Hamilton and the people who held him in extremely high esteem. In a January 25, 1806, letter to his friend **Benjamin Rush** (see entry), Adams wrote of Hamilton, "He was in an [excited madness] of ambition: he ... had fixed his eye on the [presidency] and he hated every man young or old who stood in his way." The feud between Hamilton and Adams finally split their Federalist Party and contributed to its defeat in the presidential election of 1800.

Despite Hamilton's objections, Burr becomes vice-president

When Republicans Aaron Burr and Thomas Jefferson tied that year for the office of president, Hamilton used all of his influence to get his long-time enemy Jefferson elected, although he deeply disliked him. Hamilton trusted Jefferson far more than he did Burr, who was a successful New York lawyer, like Hamilton himself, and had served as a U.S. senator from New York.

In a series of letters he wrote to other Federalist Party members, Hamilton said "Burr has no principle, public or private" and "will listen to no monitor but his own ambition.... He is cold-blooded enough to hope everything, daring enough to attempt everything, wicked enough [never to have his conscience bother him about anything]." Hamilton also voiced his fear that Burr would sell out to foreigners for his own financial advantage.

When the votes were counted, Jefferson became president and Burr vice-president. Elections at that time were determined by representatives of the different areas of the country. Hamilton's fears that Burr would behave unfairly as vice president proved unfounded, and Burr was praised by both parties for how well he presided over the Senate. Still, Hamilton never got over his deep distaste for Burr. In 1804, Hamilton succeeded in getting Burr defeated when Burr ran for governor of New York.

Hamilton and Burr duel

Burr was angry at Hamilton's efforts to keep him out of public office. When Burr read in a New York newspaper that Hamilton had called him "a dangerous man and one who ought not to be trusted with the reigns of government," it was the last straw for Burr. He challenged Hamilton to a duel. A duel is a formal fight between two people armed with deadly weapons.

On July 11, 1804, Hamilton and Burr met in the countryside of Weehawken, New Jersey (dueling was illegal in the state of New York). Hamilton had recently experienced a religious awakening. Some historians claim that he decided to meet Burr for the duel but withhold his gunfire, so that Burr would have time to pause and reflect before acting. But Burr did not hesitate to fire. He hit Hamilton in the abdomen, with a bullet that finally lodged in his spine. Hamilton was rushed to the home of a friend in New York City, where he died thirty-one hours later in extreme pain. He was forty-seven years old. As for Burr, he fled shortly after the shooting, but soon returned to Washington and resumed his vice presidential duties.

The night before the duel, Hamilton wrote in a letter to his wife, "If it had been possible for me to have avoided the [duel], my love for you and my precious children would have been alone a decisive motive. But it was not possible without sacrifices which would have rendered me unworthy of your esteem."

Hamilton widely mourned

Hamilton's death shocked the nation. The Common Council of New York City voted to hold a public funeral at city expense, and citizens were asked to wear black armbands for thirty days in his honor. Merchants in his hometown of New York City voted to shut down their shops to march in the funeral procession, and flags were hung at half-mast. Hamilton was buried the next day in Manhattan's Trinity Churchyard.

Governor William Morris of New Jersey, his friend of thirty years, spoke at Hamilton's funeral. He recalled how George Washington had sought out Hamilton for his "splendid talents, extensive information and incorruptible integrity." Morris pointed out that Hamilton's policies resulted in "a rapid advance in power and prosperity, of which there is no example in any other age or nation. The part which Hamilton bore is universally known."

Strangely enough, Alexander Hamilton had lost his nineteen-year-old son, Philip, in a duel three years earlier. Overcome by grief at Philip's death, Hamilton's daughter, Angelica, became mentally ill. In time, his five other sons became lawyers and his daughter, Eliza, married and had a family. She also took care of her mother, Elizabeth, who lived to be ninety-five years old.

For More Information

Boatner, Mark M. "Hamilton, Alexander" in *Encyclopedia of the American Revolution*. Mechanicsburg, PA: Stackpole Books, 1994, pp. 477–81.

Brookhiser, Richard. *Alexander Hamilton: American*. New York: The Free Press, 1999.

Hendrickson, Robert A. *The Rise and Fall of Alexander Hamilton*. New York: Van Nostrand Reinhold Co., 1981.

McDonald, Forrest. "Hamilton, Alexander" in *Encyclopedia of American Biography, 2nd ed.* John A. Garraty and Jerome L. Sternstein, eds. New York: HarperCollins Publishers, 1995, pp. 490–92.

Web Sites

"Biographical Sketch of Alexander Hamilton." *Department of the Treasury: The Learning Vault.* [Online] Available http://www.treas.gov/opc/opc0010.html (accessed on August 16, 1999).

Finseth, Ian. "The Rise and Fall of Alexander Hamilton." [Online] Available http://xroads.virginia.edu/~CAP/ham/hamilton.html (accessed on August 16, 1999).

"Who Served Here?: Major General Alexander Hamilton." Independence Hall Association. [Online] Available http://www.libertynet.org/iha/valleyforge/served/hamilton.html (accessed on August 16, 1999).

John Hancock

Born January 23, 1737
Quincy, Massachusetts
Died October 8, 1793
Quincy, Massachusetts

Political leader, businessman

"The [Revolutionary] Cause is certainly a most glorious one, and I trust that every man ... is determined to see it gloriously ended, or perish in the ruins of it."

Portrait: John Hancock.
Reproduced by permission of the National Archives and Records Administration.

John Hancock played an important role in American life during the early days of the Revolution. He served as a unifying force among men who displayed a wide variety of opinions about the wisdom of declaring independence. Although criticized for his vanity and self-interest, he showed strong abilities as the president of the Second Continental Congress. But after 1776, Hancock spent most of his time attending to the affairs of his home state of Massachusetts, where he was immensely popular.

John Hancock was born in 1737 in what is now Quincy, Massachusetts. He was the second of three children born to John Hancock, a Protestant minister, and his wife, Mary Hawke Thaxter Hancock. When young John Hancock was seven years old, his father died of a heart attack. His mother then sent him to live with his uncle, Thomas Hancock, one of Boston's wealthiest businessmen. John Hancock attended Boston Latin School, then graduated in 1754 from what is now Harvard University in Cambridge, Massachusetts. He immediately went to work as a clerk in his uncle's shipping business.

In 1760 young Hancock went to London, England, to learn more about his uncle's foreign business affairs. There he met and socialized with high-ranking members of European society and witnessed the crowning of the new British king, **George III** (see entry), who granted him the honor of a brief meeting.

Hancock returned to Boston after a year abroad. Two years later, in 1763, he became a partner in his uncle's successful shipping business. When his uncle died in 1764, Hancock inherited the business and his childless uncle's large estate. He became, at age twenty-seven, the richest man in Boston and probably all of New England. Hancock continued to prosper, in time owning twenty ships that carried whale oil, whalebone, lumber, and codfish from New England to Europe and elsewhere. They were traded for such items as tea, paper, furniture, wine, leather, and swords that were then brought back and sold in America.

Hancock's biographer, William M. Fowler Jr., described the handsome young man in *The Baron of Beacon Hill*. (A baron is a powerful businessman and Beacon Hill was the elite section of Boston where Hancock lived.) Fowler wrote: "Though not tall, Hancock was slender and well proportioned. He had dark brown hair, which he usually hid under a short white wig, and bushy eyebrows sitting atop dark, almond-shaped eyes." He also had a long, straight nose and a large dimple in his chin.

Opposes Stamp Act taxation

Hancock greatly enjoyed his life of luxury. He traveled in a carriage drawn by six horses, and held lavish parties that featured expensive imported wines. Writer Jean Fritz described his fashionable way of dressing in her book *Will You Sign Here, John Hancock?* She wrote: "Generally, John's [vests] were of embroidered satin, his [trousers] were of velvet, and his shoes had gold or silver buckles on them. He liked a touch of lavender or purple about his neck and he was wild about lace."

The first sign of trouble in Hancock's prosperous world came in 1765, when the British imposed a new form of taxation on the colonists by way of the Stamp Act. The act's purpose was to help pay for the cost of maintaining British troops in America. The Stamp Act taxed many paper items such as newspapers, business and legal documents, and even dice and playing cards.

Along with other colonial merchants who would be affected by the tax, Hancock deeply resented the Stamp Act. In a letter to businessman John Barnard, Hancock protested the fact that the colonists were being taxed but were not represented in the Parliament, the British law-making body. He wrote, "I will not be a slave. I have a right to the libertys and privileges of the English constitution."

Strong opposition to the Stamp Act by the colonists and their supporters in Parliament led to its repeal in 1766. Upon hearing the news, America celebrated. In Boston, Hancock held a huge banquet. Lamps were placed in all fifty-four windows of his Beacon Hill mansion. He endeared himself to ordinary citizens when he provided them with casks of wine on Boston Common as part of the celebration. At the end of the evening, hundreds of men, women, and children gathered in Boston Common to hang lanterns in the Liberty Tree, Boston's symbol of freedom. That same year, 1766, Hancock's popularity resulted in his election to serve on the Massachusetts General Court, a position he held for eight years.

The *Liberty* affair

By the late 1760s, tensions were high between the American colonists and their British rulers over British taxation policies. In time, a large number of British troops were stationed in Boston under General **Thomas Gage** (see entry) for the purpose of keeping the rebellious colonists under control.

During that time, Hancock began using his ships for smuggling. (Smuggling is bringing goods secretly or illegally into or out of a country without paying the required taxes.) British tax collectors in Boston objected to Hancock's open display of contempt towards them. But since they could not find any evidence to charge him with smuggling, they were unable to punish him. Then, in June 1768, tax officials used an oddity in the tax law as an excuse to seize one of Hancock's vessels, the *Liberty*.

Hancock was by then a very popular man among the citizens of Boston. When the British towed Hancock's ship into the harbor and anchored it right next to a British ship, riots broke out among the angry Bostonians. They were already seething with resentment against British taxation policies. Fearing attack, tax officials fled in terror to an island in Boston Harbor. Hancock was threatened with huge fines for the *Liberty* affair. But Boston patriot **Samuel Adams** (see entry) spoke so eloquently in Hancock's defense in court that the British dropped the smuggling charges against him.

"Johnny Dupe"

Hancock soon became friends with patriots Samuel Adams and his cousin, **John Adams** (see entry). The two men realized the value of having such a wealthy, well-known, and well-liked comrade. Soon Samuel Adams and Hancock began to be seen together at political clubs and meetings throughout Boston. Hancock was proud to associate with the esteemed patriot, and Samuel Adams used Hancock's popularity to influence more people to support the revolutionary cause.

Hancock and Samuel Adams became such constant companions that their enemies started calling Hancock "Johnny Dupe." A dupe is a person who is easily fooled or influenced. They joked that Adams "led him around like an ape." They also referred to the vain and self-involved Hancock as "Hancocky" (cocky means conceited).

Hancock begins his political rise

The years just before the start of the Revolutionary War were a time of much disagreement and turmoil among the American colonists. While some wanted to break away from England and declare their independence, others wanted to remain part of Great Britain.

Hancock wavered for a time before announcing that he was totally committed to the patriot cause, even if it cost him his life and all his money. Some historians have suggested he was waiting to see which way the public was leaning before he made his own decision. Before long, his reputation as a patriot grew. In his article on Hancock in the *Encyclopedia of American Biography,* Richard D. Brown refers to the Bostonian as "remarkable for his deliberate decision to build a public career based on popularity."

Hancock enhanced his image by giving gifts to the city such as church steeples, library books, and even a fire engine. Using their own influence, the Adamses helped him to become a powerful figure beyond the boundaries of Boston, among those people throughout the colonies who favored revolution. Whether or not he really deserved all the acclaim he received as a force for liberty is a question still debated by historians. Still, it took courage to defy the British Empire in as public a way as Hancock did.

In Massachusetts, it was the British-appointed governor who decided issues that involved the whole colony, but each town had its own "selectmen," who decided local issues and oversaw the town business. Hancock's reputation as a voice for American freedom got a big boost in 1770 when he was elected to one of Boston's most important offices, moderator of the Boston Town Meeting. At that time Boston citizens were very upset over an incident called the Boston Massacre, in which five colonists were killed by British soldiers during a mob action. In his new position as moderator, Hancock and other committee members went to the British-appointed authorities to demand the removal of British troops from the city of Boston because their presence was causing so much trouble. Their demands were ignored.

By 1774, the citizens of Boston were growing more and more angry with Great Britain for ignoring their protests. The anger boiled over when a series of measures was passed that colonists called the Intolerable Acts. The acts punished Boston for the Boston Tea Party, a protest in which Bostonians threw hundreds of pounds of English tea into Boston Harbor to protest British taxation policies. The Intolerable Acts punished Boston's rebellious behavior by closing Boston Harbor and ending the Massachusetts charter government, which had been in place for nearly a century. (A charter is a document setting forth a group's or nation's aims and principles.)

First Continental Congress

In April 1774, General Thomas Gage was appointed by King George III to be the British governor of Massachusetts. When a military man is appointed governor, it usually means that citizens have become very unruly. Gage had problems trying to restore order, especially among the citizens of Boston, who were considered the most rebellious of all the Americans.

In September 1774, the First Continental Congress met in Philadelphia, Pennsylvania, to discuss what to do in the face of what they considered unfair taxation and other measures imposed on them by the British. The Congress was made up of representatives of all the colonies except Georgia. The congressmen called for a boycott on British goods, to begin in December. Boycotting meant they refused to buy from or sell products to the British. This measure would hurt British merchants; if they were hurt badly enough, Congress thought, merchants would protest to Parliament for a change. Hancock was not present at the First Continental Congress, but he did participate in Massachusetts meetings leading up to the Second Continental Congress.

Hancock presides over Massachusetts Provincial Congress

Meetings were held in cities and towns throughout the colonies to discuss how to enforce the boycott and what else could be done. In Suffolk County, which included the town of Boston, representatives met and criticized the Intolerable Acts. They called Gage and his aides "enemies of the country." They then asked each town in Massachusetts to elect delegates to a statewide provincial congress to meet in October 1774.

The actual formation of the Provincial Congress marked the beginning of independent government in Massachusetts. John Hancock was elected its president. He was also made chairman of the Committee of Safety; the committee's job was to oversee the security and defense of the province of Massachusetts in case of armed conflicts with the British. Hancock was given power to call out the militia (a group of citizen soldiers) to deal with any troubles that occurred.

By the end of 1774, two governments operated in Massachusetts. One was under the command of General

John Hancock holding the Resolutions of the Continental Congress.
Reproduced by permission of AP/Wide World Photos.

(and Governor) Gage and held power in Boston. The other, the Provincial Congress with Hancock at its head, met in Salem.

By 1775 outbreaks of mob violence against the British were common in Massachusetts. In February, Parliament declared the colony to be in a state of rebellion. By then, Hancock was recognized as one of the foremost American radicals (those who favor a complete change in the government). In August 1775, King George issued a proclamation declaring all the colonies to be in a state of rebellion.

Flees to Philadelphia, attends Continental Congress

In April 1775, Governor Gage decided to seize Hancock and Samuel Adams for disloyalty to Great Britain. Hearing this, Hancock and Adams fled from Boston to Lexington, Massachusetts, to hide. Boston patriot **Paul Revere** (see entry) rode to Lexington and warned them that the British were on the way to capture them. The two escaped to Philadelphia, where they were to serve as representatives at the May meeting of the Second Continental Congress.

Governor Gage never forgave the two American patriots for the trouble they had caused him, including their escape. Two months later, when the governor made yet another effort to restore peaceful relations with the colonies, he offered a general pardon to anyone who had acted against the British government. Hancock and Adams were the only ones excluded from the pardon.

Leaders from all thirteen colonies met in Philadelphia in May 1775 for the Second Continental Congress, and Hancock and Samuel Adams were among them. King George had ignored the documents sent to him by the First Continental Congress, and he had stated that fighting would decide whether the colonies would be subject to his country or become independent. Now, delegates had to decide how to deal with Great Britain. Though still not ready to make a complete break with England, they did take action to put the colonies in a state of readiness for possible war.

Hancock briefly heads Congress

John Hancock was elected president of the Second Continental Congress, replacing Peyton Randolph who resigned due to ill health. Some members of the Congress were so pleased with themselves that a major enemy of King George III had been elected, that they happily picked Hancock up and set him in the president's chair. Hancock ran the meetings and performed such other duties as writing letters, ordering supplies, giving directions for moving troops and building forts, and signing laws.

But during his short term of office, Hancock's superior attitude earned him some enemies. He alienated many New England radical comrades, especially Samuel Adams, when he made friends with men such as **John Dickinson** (see entry) and Benjamin Harrison, who favored a less extreme course of action in dealing with Great Britain than did the radicals. When a proposal to thank Hancock for his services did not come to a vote in Congress in 1777, Hancock blamed Adams. Their relationship was never fully mended.

Hancock presided over Congress when it adopted the Declaration of Independence on July 4, 1776. His signature dwarfs that of all others on the Declaration. A famous story quotes Hancock as saying that he signed his name in such large letters because he wanted King George III of England to be able to read Hancock's name without his eyeglasses.

Marriage and military action

In 1777 Hancock resigned from the presidency of the Continental Congress, perhaps out of anger and disappointment that the congressmen had not voted to thank him for his service. When he was again elected to the Congress and chosen its president, he never appeared in person to take his seat, causing both confusion and embarrassment for the group. Hancock became less involved in national politics and began spending more and more of his time in his hometown of Boston, where his popularity grew.

In August 1777, Hancock married Dorothy Quincy in Fairfield, Connecticut. In a portrait by renowned artist John Singleton Copley, Mrs. Hancock appears as a slender, thoughtful-looking young woman with dark hair and eyes. The couple had two children: a daughter who died as an infant, and a son who died at the age of nine after falling and hitting his head while iceskating. The Hancocks managed to accept the tragedies and go on with their lives.

John Hancock was a person who constantly sought public acclaim, and he longed for military glory. He had been gravely disappointed when, in 1775, he was denied command of the new Continental army due to his lack of military experience. The position he desperately wanted went instead to **George Washington** (see entry).

Hancock's only chance to earn military fame came in 1778 in the unsuccessful American attempt to recapture Newport, Rhode Island, from the British. As leader of the five-thousand-member Massachusetts unit, his service was unremarkable.

Excels in Boston politics; shows evidence of character flaws

Away from the Continental Congress and national affairs, Hancock demonstrated a talent for politics. He used his wealth to make himself popular, even among the poorest groups of Boston citizens, who were not the natural supporters of such a wealthy man. According to historian Dennis Fradin in his biography of Samuel Adams, Hancock "was as known for his generosity as his showy way of life. Each winter he donated food and firewood to Boston's poor," and he was quick to offer help to widows, orphans, and other needy citizens of Boston. He also helped the first American black poet, **Phillis Wheatley** (see entry), to get her book of poems published.

Of course, like everyone else, Hancock also had his flaws. He loved to be idolized, as when crowds ran along his carriage shouting "King Hancock!" In addition, he sometimes behaved in an immature way and could be easily insulted. This was demonstrated in his handling of a treasurer's post at Harvard College.

In the fall of 1773, Harvard elected Hancock to serve as its treasurer. The college did so partly out of patriotism and partly to encourage him to be even more generous with his contributions. It would have been embarrassing for everyone if Hancock had refused. But his acceptance of the post caused endless problems for both him and his college. Very busy with his work leading up to the American Revolution, he ignored his treasurer's duties and did not manage the college's funds properly. Finally, Harvard asked him to resign and appointed a new treasurer. Hancock felt resentful because he believed he had been shown disrespect. When he died in 1793, he still owed Harvard money, which had to be repaid by his heirs.

Becomes nine-time governor

In spite of his damaged reputation over the Harvard incident, the people of Massachusetts still loved Hancock. In 1780, they elected him as their first governor. Massachusetts's elections for governor took place every year and Hancock was reelected five years in a row.

In 1785, Hancock voluntarily retired from the position, claiming ill health. He suffered from bad headaches and gout, a disease that resulted in painful, swollen legs. But his retirement came at a time of financial crisis for Massachusetts. Critics said that Hancock knew this and resigned to avoid the resulting political storm, caused in part by his poor handling of state funds.

Hancock left to his successor and rival, Governor James Bowdoin (pronounced BOW-dun), the task of dealing with an uprising of farmers, known as Shays's Rebellion, which took place in 1786–87 (see **Daniel Shays** entry). The farmers were protesting what they considered unfair taxation. After the crisis quieted down, Hancock again ran for governor, beating out Bowdoin.

Helps passage of U.S. Constitution

In 1787 Hancock was elected president of the Massachusetts State Convention, which had been formed to decide whether or not Massachusetts would accept a proposed U.S. Constitution. At that time, opinion was divided on the issue of how the document should be worded and the delegates argued over every paragraph.

According to one story, Hancock offered a compromise to get Massachusetts delegates to accept the Constitution, thinking he might become the nation's first president for his efforts. His compromise was accepted. Massachusetts voted to accept the new Constitution, but his hopes of ruling the country never came to pass.

It is possible that the Constitution would not have passed in Massachusetts without his support. And had Massachusetts not passed it, the entire constitutional effort might have failed. Hancock emerged with a reputation as a peacemaker, gaining more prestige than ever.

Final years

John Hancock spent the rest of his life serving as the governor of Massachusetts, although his poor health sometimes prevented his full participation in political events. He died during his ninth term of office on October 8, 1793, at the age of fifty-six.

Hancock's funeral in Boston was one of the largest and most impressive events ever held in New England up until that time. Twenty thousand people marched four abreast in a procession that extended more than a mile. He was laid to his final rest at Boston's Old Granary Burying Ground, where people still come to look at the grave of the famous revolutionary.

In 1789 Massachusetts politician James Sullivan, a friend of John Hancock, sent a letter to fellow politician Elbridge Gerry, in which he referred to Hancock as "the centre of union." Though many historians do not consider Hancock a brilliant thinker, he was a flexible and masterful politician who could bring together people with strong opposing political opinions. As a result, Hancock helped to hold his new country together at a time when revolutionary fervor threatened to tear it apart.

For More Information

Allison, Robert T. *American Eras: The Revolutionary Era*. Detroit: Gale, 1998, pp. 78–79, 202–3.

Baxter, W. T. *The House of Hancock: Business in Boston, 1724–1775*. Cambridge, MA: Harvard University Press, 1945.

Boatner, Mark M. "Hancock, John" in *Encyclopedia of the American Revolution*. Mechanicsburg, PA: Stackpole Books, 1994, pp. 483–84.

Bourgoin, Suzanne M., and Paula Byers, eds. "Hancock, John" in *Encyclopedia of World Biography*. Detroit: Gale, 1998, pp. 114–16.

Brown, Richard D. "Hancock, John" in *Encyclopedia of American Biography*. John A. Garraty and Jerome L. Sternstein, eds. New York: Harper-Collins Publishers, 1996, pp. 496–97.

Faragher, John Mack, general ed. "Hancock, John" in *Encyclopedia of Colonial and Revolutionary America*. New York: Facts on File, 1990, p. 183.

Ferris, Robert G., ed. *Signers of the Declaration of Independence*. Washington, D.C.: U.S. Government Printing Office, 1973, pp. 67–69.

Fowler, William M., Jr. *The Baron of Beacon Hill: A Biography of John Hancock*. Boston: Houghton Mifflin Co., 1980.

Fowler, William M., Jr. "Hancock, John" in *American National Biography*. John A. Garraty and Mark C. Carnes, eds. New York: Oxford University Press, 1999, vol. 9, pp. 969–70.

Fradin, Dennis. *Samuel Adams: The Father of American Independence*. New York: Clarion Books, 1998, pp. 46–7, 51.

Johnson, Allen, and Dumas Malone, eds. *Dictionary of American Biography*. New York: Charles Scribners Sons, 1932, vol. IV, pp. 218–19.

Purcell, Edward L. *Who Was Who in the American Revolution*. New York: Facts on File, 1993, pp. 211–12.

Nancy Morgan Hart

Born c. 1744
North Carolina or Pennsylvania
Died c. 1841
Henderson County, Kentucky

Farmer, spy

It is difficult to separate the facts from the myths about Nancy Morgan Hart, a patriot from the American South who captured and killed Tories (colonists who were loyal to England) during the Revolutionary War (1775–83). Although some people question whether Hart ever existed, there are memorials throughout Georgia honoring her, the South's most famous Revolutionary War heroine.

Nancy Morgan was born in the 1740s, probably in North Carolina or Pennsylvania. The identity of her parents has never been confirmed. Named Ann at birth, she was always known as Nancy. Nancy Morgan married Benjamin Hart (who was related to Thomas Hart Benton [1782–1858], a famous American senator, and to the wife of Henry Clay [1777–1852], who was an American secretary of state) and the couple settled in the Broad River area of Georgia around 1771. They were living there in 1775 when the Revolutionary War broke out as America fought to gain its independence from England. After the war, they moved to Brunswick, in Glynn County, Georgia.

"War woman"

Ben and Nancy Hart were hardworking farmers who had at least eight children. They owned more than four hundred acres of land on the banks of the Wahatchee Creek, where Nancy first gained fame for her exploits. The Indian word Wahatchee means "war woman." The creek was given its name by local Indians in honor of Hart, whom they both feared and respected.

Nancy Hart has been described as a cross-eyed, red-headed woman who stood over six feet tall and smoked a pipe. She contracted smallpox as a child, and her face was pitted with scars from the illness. Writer Edith Patterson Meyer says that Hart was once described as "a two-gun woman who drank and swore [and was] admittedly ignorant of all refinements."

Captured and killed Tories

When fighting broke out in Georgia's back country during the American Revolution, Hart worked at becoming an excellent shooter. Both she and her husband were present for a battle at a place called Kettle Creek. Fighting between the patriots and the Tories, as the Loyalists were also known, was so fierce at Kettle Creek that it has been called the "War of Extermination."

During this period, outlaws and Tories wandered the Georgia countryside, stealing from and killing patriots. Men who were loyal to the cause of American independence were often forced to go into hiding. Women and children were generally spared, but they had to take care of their homes and crops in the absence of the men. While her husband was hiding from the Tories, Hart ran the family farm.

Hart was fiercely patriotic. She has been credited with capturing and killing many Tories she met on roads, in cabins, and in the forests near where she lived. According to one story, she once met some young Tories when she was on horseback, taking a sack of corn to the mill. For amusement they startled her horse, and she was thrown off. She did not respond to their act with vile language as they had expected, but soon afterward the young man who had startled her horse got a bullet in his shoulder along with a warning never to play such a trick again.

Another famous tale describes an incident that took place one afternoon when Hart and her children were making soap in her kitchen. The process involved boiling the soap mixture in a big pot. While Hart was stirring the soap mixture, one of her children noticed an eye pressed against a crack in the wall of their log cabin and discreetly alerted Hart. Hart went quietly along with her work then, suddenly, she turned and threw a ladle full of boiling soap at the crack, and a man cried out in pain. When Hart and her children rushed outside, they found a Tory neighbor who had been spying. Hart doctored his wounds and turned him over to local patriotic officials.

Spy stories

Hart was good at using herbs from her garden to cure all sorts of common ailments. She had also become a terrific shooter, and it is said the walls of her log cabin were covered with the antlers of deer she had killed. Her family dined frequently on the wild game she hunted.

There are many stories of Hart serving the Continental army by spying on Tories. One story recounts how she pretended to be a mentally deranged seller of eggs and household items when in fact, she was collecting information for the patriots. According to another tale, Georgia patriots badly needed information about what was happening on the Carolina side of the Savannah River. Hart was said to have tied a few logs together with grapevines, crossed the river, and obtained the needed information.

In the nineteenth and early twentieth centuries, southerners did not agree about Hart's exploits and questioned her existence. Some historians dismissed accounts of her life as fiction. Her descendants said otherwise.

Famous Nancy Hart tales

In 1901 Loula Kendall Rogers wrote in the *Atlanta Evening Journal* about another popular Hart story: "Many Tories lived on the other side of the river, opposite [Nancy's] cabin.... There was a large oaken stump near her home in which she cut a notch for her gun. Concealing herself in the undergrowth around, she watched for Tories as they crossed the river, and without [any guilt or regret] shot them down, and [made a

loud noise by blowing] the conch (pronounced KONK; a sea animal) shell for her husband to deliver their bodies over to the proper authorities."

The most famous story about Hart recounts when she was doing farm chores at home with her thirteen-year-old daughter, Sukey. A group of five Tory soldiers arrived at her cabin on horseback from Augusta, Georgia, and demanded that she serve them a meal. She explained she had only one tough old turkey because Tory groups had taken the others earlier. The soldiers shot the turkey and told her to cook it. She was pleasant to them, cooked dinner, and entertained them with stories. All the while she made sure they were drinking plenty of alcohol. When she felt the soldiers were relaxed enough, she sent her daughter to the well for water.

As Sukey left on her mission, Hart told her to blow in the big conch shell that was kept by the well. The sound it trumpeted out would let the neighbors know she needed help.

When a group of Tory soldiers arrived at Nancy Hart's home demanding dinner, she fed them. While they ate and drank plenty of alcohol, Hart hid their weapons and used one soldier's rifle to hold the soldiers at gunpoint. *Reproduced by permission of Archive Photos, Inc.*

The blare of the conch shell brought her husband as well as neighbors who were working nearby. Back at the cabin, while this was going on, Hart gathered up the soldiers' guns and hid them under her skirts. One by one she slid the rifles out the holes left in the walls for shooting at enemies, but her activities were detected before she could collect all the guns. She immediately picked up a rifle and held her "guests" at gunpoint. Legend has it that two soldiers went for their guns, but because of her crossed eyes the soldiers could not tell in what direction she was looking, and Hart shot them both before they could react.

The neighbors responded to the conch call and wanted to shoot the rest of the Tories at her table. Hart, who had learned that the soldiers had killed a local patriot, said that shooting them would be too good for them. Instead, the Tories were hanged from a tree behind her house. Hart is said to have sung choruses of the patriotic song "Yankee Doodle" as she watched them die.

Hart legend grows

Nancy Morgan Hart could neither read nor write, and the incident concerning the five Tories was never written down by any of the eyewitnesses. In addition, there were no newspapers published in the backwoods of Georgia to preserve tales of heroic acts. When Revolutionary War battles were fought in small communities, there were few amateur historians recording everyday events.

But historian Sallie Smith Booth pointed out: "After the war, citizens all along the Georgia frontier were relating tales concerning Nancy Hart and the stories were remarkably similar in detail.... Although Nancy may not have actually performed the deeds attributed to her, many of [those who lived at the same time as Hart] firmly believed that she did."

During the 1820s, newspapers in Georgia began printing accounts of Nancy's brave deeds. During the American Civil War (1861–65), a group of women in LaGrange, Georgia, who did not have men to depend on for protection from Northern soldiers, organized themselves into a society to protect one another. They called themselves the "Nancy Harts." The state of Georgia erected a statue of Nancy Morgan Hart

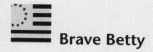

Brave Betty

In *Petticoat Patriots of the American Revolution*, writer Edith Patterson Meyer retells a popular tale about another brave frontierswoman named Betty Zane. Born around 1766 in West Virginia, Elizabeth "Betty" Zane was just a young girl when her parents died. After attending a girls' school in Philadelphia, Pennsylvania, Zane moved with her four older brothers to West Virginia. There her brother Ebenezer founded the present-day city of Wheeling. She lived there with her brother in a sturdy cabin that contained a storage place for gunpowder.

During the Revolutionary War, Zane's brother Silas was in charge of Fort Henry, which was located near the family's cabin. One day when Zane was at home, Fort Henry was attacked by nearly five hundred Tories and their Indian allies. They came so swiftly that the settlers barely had time to reach the fort. When the fort's supply of gunpowder ran low, a decision had to be made as to who would venture out to the Zane cabin to get more.

Betty Zane, who could run as fast as most men, volunteered. She took off her long skirt and petticoat, sneaked out of the fort, and made her way toward the cabin. The attackers were so astounded to see a half-clothed woman approaching that Zane was able to reach the cabin before they recovered enough to fire a shot.

Inside the cabin, Ebenezer, who had returned after the rest of the settlers fled to the fort, filled a sack with gunpowder. As Betty Zane slipped out the door with the ammunition, the enemy opened fire. Four sharpshooters from the fort covered her, firing against the Tories and Indians while trying not to endanger Zane. Although she stumbled once, she was able to make it back to the fort with her precious package. The men and women inside cheered as she entered unharmed.

The powder held out for another night and day until the siege ended, and the inhabitants of the fort were safe. In comparing Zane's action with that of other Revolution-era heroines, one historian wrote that "none [was] equal to this."

near the town of Hartwell and named a section of highway in her honor. Hart County in Georgia was also named after her.

The reputation of Hart's husband, Ben, seems to have suffered as his wife became famous. A story circulated that Ben Hart was a lazy man, totally dependent upon his wife for his well-being. In fact, Ben Hart took an active part in the Revolutionary War as an officer in the army. In the late 1790s, when the family moved to Brunswick, Georgia, Ben served as a judge there.

After her husband's death around 1800, Nancy Hart moved to Clarke County, Georgia, where she lived near her son, John. About 1802 she and John moved to Henderson County, Kentucky, where she remained until her death at about age ninety-three.

Remains provide evidence of Hart tale

Until 1912, the story about Hart shooting two Tories and watching as three others died by hanging was thought by many to be only a legend. But that year, when land was being leveled off for the Elberton & Eastern Railroad line, the remains of five bodies were found. This seemed to prove that the often-repeated story was true. When the skeletons were unearthed on December 22, 1912, the *Atlanta Constitution* reported that "the bones and teeth were in a splendid state of preservation."

In 1932 the site of the Harts' cabin and the burial site of the Tories in north Georgia were turned into a five-acre park called the Nancy Hart Historical Park. The family cabin was reconstructed on the site of the original cabin, using stones from the fireplace and the chimney of the Harts' early home. Funds for the project were supplied by the State of Georgia and the local chapter of the Daughters of the American Revolution, an organization for descendants of people who fought in the Revolutionary War. The park is now the site of an annual Pioneer Day, where the festivities include a re-creation of the events of Hart's life, a Nancy Hart look-alike contest, and demonstrations of pioneer life.

For More Information

Anticaglia, Elizabeth. *Heroines of '76*. New York: Walker and Company, 1975.

Booth, Sally Smith. *The Women of '76*. New York: Hastings House, 1973.

Garrison, Webb. *A Treasury of Georgia Tales*. Nashville: Rutledge Hill Press, 1987.

Kaufhold, Shirley, ed. *The Harts of Georgia: A History of Hart County*. Newnan, GA: W. H. Wolfe, 1992.

Meyer, Edith Patterson. *Petticoat Patriots of the American Revolution*. New York: The Vanguard Press, 1976.

"Nancy Hart and the Skeletons of Six Tories." *Atlanta Constitution*. December 22, 1912.

Rogers, Loula Kendall. "A True Story of Nancy Hart." *Atlanta Evening Journal*. October 14, 1901.

Patrick Henry

Born May 29, 1736
Studley, Virginia
Died June 6, 1799
Charlotte County, Virginia

Politician, lawyer, public speaker

"If we wish to be free
we must fight....
Gentlemen may cry
peace! peace! but there
is no peace! The war
is actually begun!"

Portrait: Patrick Henry.
Reproduced by permission of
AP/Wide World Photos.

During Revolutionary times most Americans got their information by the spoken word. Patrick Henry's fiery speeches
inspired the American colonies to turn their dreams of freedom from England into reality. His ability to relate to the common man as well as lawmakers allowed him to capture the loyalty of a wide audience and become one of the major heroes of
the American Revolution.

Patrick Henry was the son of John Henry, a wealthy
planter, and his wife, Sarah Winston Syme Henry. He was born
on May 29, 1736, in Hanover County, Virginia. For a few years
he attended the local schools, but he was mostly taught by his
father, who had attended college in his Scottish homeland.

At sixteen he and his older brother, William, opened
their own store. Despite their hard work, the store soon failed.
In 1754, young Patrick Henry married Sarah Shelton, the
daughter of a prosperous family who lived nearby. In time the
Henrys had six children.

Henry's father-in-law gave the young couple a three-
hundred-acre farm and slaves to work the land. In those days,

most large farms were worked by slaves. Henry ran the farm until a fire destroyed his house. Then he went to work again as a storekeeper, also working for a time in his father-in-law's tavern.

Begins practicing law

In 1760 at age twenty-three, Henry decided to become a lawyer. Over the next several years, the intelligent young man built a successful law practice. Henry first gained a reputation as a champion of the common man in December 1763. He was defending some local churchgoers in a lawsuit over money matters filed by the church's minister. During the case, the eloquent Henry displayed deep concern about injustices done to common people.

Early political involvement

Henry began his political career in 1765 when he won a seat in the House of Burgesses (pronounced BER-juss-es), the lower house of the Virginia legislature (its lawmaking body). The red-headed young man brought an outspoken, direct style to the House that impressed his listeners.

Henry's reputation spread beyond Virginia when he took part in protests against taxes the British imposed on the colonies. One such tax, the Stamp Act of 1765, required that Americans purchase stamps and specially stamped paper to be used for all documents. As a lawyer, Henry would be affected by such a tax on legal documents; so would his clients.

In May 1765 the House of Burgesses passed Patrick Henry's Stamp Act Resolves. The document branded the Stamp Act unfair and illegal. It also included a resolution claiming the colony of Virginia had the legal right to make laws on its own, without England's approval. To openly make such claims was an act that took courage; Henry could be severely punished by Great Britain for this kind of talk. He soon became known around America as a strong opponent of the policies of the British Empire.

During the 1760s Henry was kept busy raising his young family and furthering his legal career. In 1769 he received official approval to practice law before the General Court, Virginia's highest court.

As tensions mounted between the colonists and the British government, Henry remained a member of the House of Burgesses. Opinion was divided on the question of how to handle the quarrel with England. Henry joined other members of the House who spoke out early in favor of a complete break with England. He also favored the establishment of a new type of government in the colonies that would give more power to the average citizen. Among Henry's allies were **Thomas Jefferson** (see entry), who later became a U.S. president, and Virginia patriot Richard Henry Lee (see box).

Supports development of American political organizations

In 1773 Henry helped establish committees of correspondence in the colonies. These were groups that aroused public opinion and organized acts of defiance against Great Britain. Soon England began punishing the colonies for their acts of resistance. Harsher laws and restrictions on trade were put in place by British authorities. But as a result of this crackdown, the colonies drew closer together in their opposition to Great Britain.

In 1775 Royal Governor John Dunmore of Virginia (he was appointed by the king of England) dissolved the meeting of the Virginia House of Burgesses because lawmakers there proposed a day of mourning over unfair British taxation policies.

In response to Dunmore's actions, Henry held illegal and informal sessions of the House at a tavern in Richmond, Virginia. He called for members to support a constitutional convention for Virginia to organize a new system of government. He also called for a continental congress, a meeting where representatives of all the colonies would gather to decide what to do about America's political future.

Delivers stirring speech in Congress

The First Continental Congress met in Philadelphia, Pennsylvania, in September 1774. Representatives of twelve of the thirteen colonies met there to express grievances against British taxation policies. Henry served as one of the seven delegates from Virginia.

The members of the First Continental Congress could basically be divided into two groups: conservatives, who hoped to patch up the quarrel with England, and radicals—like Henry—who were determined to resist.

Henry was well known among those in attendance and he received several important committee assignments. He gave a speech that impressed his listeners when he declared, "The distinctions between Virginians, Pennsylvanians, New Yorkers, and New Englanders, are no more. I am not a Virginian, but an American."

According to historian George F. Willison, at this time Henry was "some six feet tall, [and] trim.... [He] was not a handsome man, but personable and engaging. His manner toward all men, from the humblest to the highest, was quiet, friendly, and unaffected.... Henry when speaking publicly was often something of an actor.... Even so, his words and his posturing [often] carried the day."

The First Continental Congress prepared several petitions, which they sent to King **George III** (see entry) in 1774. The petitions included complaints about British oppression and objections to the Intolerable Acts, measures put in place by the British to punish the colonists for acts of rebellion. The Congress then adjourned, agreeing to meet again in May 1775 if King George had not responded satisfactorily to their petitions.

Calls for an army kept ready for action

By the winter of 1774–75, Henry saw a war as unavoidable. He organized a militia (pronounced ma-LISH-a; a volunteer group of citizen-soldiers) to defend his home county of Hanover against the British. Tragedy struck the Henry family early in 1775 when Sarah, who had shown signs of serious mental illness, died from unknown causes. Henry was left to raise their children on his own.

In 1775 Henry assumed a leadership role in Virginia's Revolutionary government, called the Convention of Virginia. It replaced the lawmaking body approved by the British government, the Virginia House of Burgesses. At the first meeting of the Convention in March 1775, there was much disagreement as to whether the Virginia colonists should seek a peaceful solution to their problems with England.

Patrick Henry was an accomplished speaker. His ability to relate to the common man as well as lawmakers allowed him to capture the loyalty of a wide audience and become one of the major heroes of the American Revolution. *Reproduced courtesy of the Library of Congress.*

This meeting marked the high point of Henry's fame. It was here that he uttered his legendary remarks in support of preparing for war. He was reported to have said, "Is life so dear or peace so sweet, as to be purchased at the price of chains and slavery? Forbid it almighty God! I know not what course others may take; but as for me, give me liberty or give me death!" Virginians decided to arm themselves in preparation for a possible war of independence.

When Governor Dunmore heard what had taken place at the Virginia Convention, he sent a small group of British soldiers to seize arms and ammunition the revolutionaries had stored in Williamsburg, Virginia. The soldiers were only partly successful; their mission was discovered before they could complete it.

The colonists protested the governor's actions and threatened him with violence. An angry Henry planned to set out from Hanover to Williamsburg with his local militia unit to demand payment for the seized guns and gunpowder. It took several men to persuade Henry and his troops not to march forward and carry out their plan.

Henry attends Second Continental Congress

On May 18, 1775, Henry attended the Second Continental Congress in Philadelphia. Just one month before, the Concord, Massachusetts, militia had exchanged gunfire with British troops, then forced them back to Boston. In part because of this event, Henry urged that local militias be formed, equipped, and trained to defend the colonies if it became necessary.

While Henry was away in Philadelphia, the Virginia Convention formed two military units. By a slim vote, the convention elected Henry to command one of the units and act as senior officer to both divisions, even though he had little military experience. Henry was quite successful at getting recruits for the unit he commanded. But there were people in power who did not care for him. On December 9, 1775, those people sent Henry's second unit out to fight against Governor Dunmore without Henry as senior officer. Then, in early 1776, both militia units were combined and made part of the newly formed Continental army. Henry was to serve as a colonel (pronounced KER-nuhl) in his old regiment, under the command of men he had formerly led.

Enraged at the insults, Henry declined to serve. To protest this poor treatment of their commander, his entire unit nearly quit. But Henry displayed real character when, despite his personal disappointment, he urged his men to stay and serve under the new officers.

Serves as governor

His military career went nowhere, but Patrick Henry's political career flourished. On May 6, 1776, Henry once again was elected to the Virginia Convention. He successfully urged his fellow delegates there to adopt Richard Henry Lee's resolutions to be presented at the next session of the Second Continental Congress. The resolutions were a bold call for independence from England and the creation of a declaration of independence. At the Virginia Convention, Henry also drafted

Richard Henry Lee, Henry's Rebellious Companion

Richard Henry Lee (1732–1794) was a member of the distinguished Lee family of Virginia. From 1758 to 1775, Lee served in the House of Burgesses until that body was dissolved by the British.

Along with Patrick Henry and Thomas Jefferson, Lee became widely known as an early defender of the rights of the colonies against England. In 1773 Lee and others proposed founding committees of correspondence, bodies that organized resistance in the colonies to British policies they saw as unfair. In 1773 Lee joined the newly formed Virginia Committee of Correspondence.

Lee served in the Continental Congress from 1774 to 1780. In June of 1776 he offered a famous resolution there that gave rise to the Declaration of Independence, which he later signed. His stirring resolution stated: "Resolved, that these United Colonies are, and of right ought to be, free and independent States, that they are absolved from all allegiance to the British Crown, and that all political connection between them and the state of Great Britain is, and ought to be, totally dissolved."

Lee again served in Congress from 1784 to 1787, acting as its president from 1784 to 1785. Like Henry, Lee was an opponent of the early version of the U.S. Constitution, which he believed infringed on the rights of the individual states. He proposed a change in the document that was adopted, almost in his exact words, as the Tenth Amendment of the Constitution. It states, "The powers not delegated to the United States by the Constitution, nor prohibited by it to the States, are reserved to the States respectively, or to the people." He served as a U.S. senator from Virginia from 1789 to 1792. Lee died on June 19, 1794, on his plantation near Stratford, Virginia.

and had adopted a constitution for the new Commonwealth of Virginia. (Some states prefer to call themselves commonwealths rather than states.)

Virginia voters elected Henry as their first governor and he began serving his term in July 1776. Henry found that the Virginia governorship was a largely ceremonial office with very little power. He had problems raising and equipping an army to serve in the Revolutionary War (1775–83), but he did the best he could. He did manage to set up a court system and get some government offices up and running.

In October 1777 Henry married Dorothea Dandridge, a woman from an old and wealthy Virginia family. The couple went on to have ten children. Henry would find it a struggle trying to support the many children from his two marriages. In time the Henrys relocated to a ten-thousand-acre plantation in faraway Henry County, named for Patrick Henry.

Opposes Jefferson-Madison group

In 1779 Henry left the Virginia governorship. In 1780 he won a seat to the House of Delegates, the lower house of the Virginia legislature known as the General Assembly. The Assembly had been established by the new Virginia Constitution four years earlier. He served there until 1784. Even though his attendance was irregular, he soon became one of its most important members.

Henry was always looking out for the common man. He supported tax reduction and financial relief for people in debt. Other men in the legislature had different ideas about government. Henry's chief opponent in the house was **James Madison** (see entry), a supporter of then-Virginia governor Thomas Jefferson. Henry and his followers managed to block almost every bill proposed by the Jefferson-Madison group.

In 1784 Virginia voters once again elected Henry governor. With his family he returned to Richmond, where he served as governor until his resignation in 1786. He then bought a farm in Prince Edward County, where he and his family lived for the next six years. He represented the county in the Virginia legislature.

Opposes U.S. Constitution

The Treaty of Paris ending the Revolutionary War was signed in 1783. It soon became obvious that the Articles of Confederation, adopted in 1777, were not adequate to govern an independent and expanding United States. A new constitution was needed. A Federal Constitutional Convention met in Philadelphia in May 1787 to draft a new U.S. Constitution. Conventions were then held in each of the states to vote on whether to accept the document.

When representatives from Virginia met at their state constitutional convention in 1788, Henry opposed the adoption of the proposed Constitution of the United States. His chief objection was that it had no bill of rights to safeguard individual citizens. He also complained that the proposed Constitution made the federal government too strong and took away states' rights. Henry wanted the United States to remain a loose union of states allied with one another. He feared that the adoption of the Constitution would turn it into "one great consolidated national government of the people of all the States."

Despite his opposition, the Constitution met with overwhelming support. But thanks in part to Henry, the final version of the Constitution did contain a Bill of Rights (the name given to the first ten amendments to the Constitution). The Bill of Rights protects the basic rights of individuals against the power of a strong federal government.

Retirement years

In the 1780s and 1790s, Henry turned down all offers to run for state or national government posts. He preferred to engage in his own law work. In 1790, now sixty-four and in declining health, Henry retired to Red Hill, a plantation near Brookneal, Virginia, part of his expanding real estate holdings. He worked hard at his law practice and earned huge fees as he won case after case. He also became one of the largest landholders in Virginia and surrounding states.

In the early 1790s, Henry surprised everyone when he abruptly left the Republican Party. The fiery young revolutionary had grown into a man who supported order in government. He believed the Republican Party had become too disruptive under the leadership of his old opponents, Jefferson and Madison. At the invitation of **George Washington** (see entry) and Richard Henry Lee, Henry joined the Federalist Party (see box in John Adams entry).

Henry ran for the state legislature in 1799 as a Federalist and easily won. But he was never to serve again. He died of cancer on June 6, 1799, at his Red Hill home in Charlotte County, Virginia. The enormous Henry family attended his funeral and he was laid to rest under a plain stone. The epitaph (a short composition written in memory of a person who has died) read: "His fame his best epitaph."

Thomas Jefferson remembered Henry as "the idol of his country beyond any man who ever lived." He later added, "It is not now easy to say what we [Americans] should have done without Patrick Henry."

For More Information

Allison, Robert J. "Patrick Henry" in *American Eras: The Revolutionary Era, 1754–1783*. Detroit: Gale, 1998, pp. 221–22.

Boatner, Mark M. "Henry, Patrick" in *Encyclopedia of the American Revolution*. Mechanicsburg, PA: Stackpole Books, 1994, pp. 500–501.

Bourgoin, Suzanne M., and Paula K. Byers. "Henry, Patrick" in *Encyclopedia of World Biography*. Detroit: Gale, 1998, vol. 7, pp. 309–11.

Meade, Robert Douthat. *Patrick Henry: Practical Revolutionary*. Philadelphia: J. B. Lippincott Co., 1969.

Risjord, Norman K. "Henry, Patrick" in *Encyclopedia of American Biography*. John A. Garraty and Jerome L. Sternstein, eds. New York: Harper-Collins, 1996, pp. 538–39.

Willison, George F. *Patrick Henry and His World*. Garden City, NY: Doubleday and Company, 1969.

William Howe

Born August 10, 1729
London, England
Died July 12, 1814
Plymouth, England

Commander-in-chief of the
British army in North America

"My going thither [to America] was not of my seeking. I was ordered, and could not refuse, without incurring the odious name of backwardness to serve my country in distress."

Portrait: William Howe.
Reproduced courtesy of the Library of Congress.

William Howe was the British general given credit *not* for losing the war against the American rebels, but for failing to win it. Howe was an excellent soldier but a less-than-adequate commander-in-chief. On many occasions he won battles against the Americans but failed to suppress the rebellion early in the war when he did not pursue and decisively defeat the army of General **George Washington** (see entry).

William Howe was born on August 10, 1729, in London to Emanuel Scrope Howe and his wife, Mary Sophia, the eldest daughter of Baron Kielmansegge. William was their third son, and they had at least one daughter, Caroline, who was a famous letter writer.

Although the Howes lived in England, the oldest son of the family held an Irish aristocratic title, viscount (pronounced VY-count) Howe. William's father was the second viscount Howe. William's oldest brother, George Augustus, inherited the title to become the third viscount Howe. (The Howes proved an unfortunate family in respect to this title. George died as a young man, leaving the second son, Richard, to become the fourth viscount Howe. Richard also held an English title, earl Howe. When Richard died, William became the fifth viscount Howe and, as he died without children, the Irish title of viscount Howe lapsed.)

The Howe family was believed to be of royal blood. William's grandmother had been a mistress (lover, not a wife) of King George I and bore him a child, from whom William and his brothers and sisters were descended. This made William, Richard, and George Howe the uncles of King **George III** (1738–1820; see entry), who held the British throne at the time of the American Revolutionary War (1775–83). In later years, when Richard was made an admiral in the navy and William a general in the army, some of their critics claimed that they received their positions as a result of the king's favor.

As a child, William Howe was tutored at home and then attended Eton, an exclusive private school. While at school, he met and became friends with many of the men who would run the British government and military during the war with the American colonies.

Joins the army

As a younger son, William Howe needed a profession to support himself. He chose the army, and soon proved that he was a talented soldier. His family purchased a commission for him (they bought a military rank and regiment for him to serve in, a common practice at the time). In 1746, at the age of seventeen, he entered the army as a cornet (a low-ranking officer). He was a dragoon, an infantry or foot soldier who also fought on horseback. By the time he was twenty-nine, Howe had attained the rank of lieutenant colonel and was serving in Ireland. Along the way, he became friends with James Wolfe, a brilliant young major in his regiment.

Service in French and Indian War

In 1760 Howe and his regiment left Ireland for America to support the colonists in the French and Indian War (1754–63). This war was part of a larger European struggle called the Seven Years War (1756–63). This struggle, mainly between England and France, spilled over into their colonial possessions, and many English regiments were sent to Canada and the American colonies to answer the French threat there. (In the Americas, the French enlisted the aid of their Native American allies; from that came the name French and Indian War.)

Howe gained a reputation for bravery during the battle to take the Canadian city of Quebec, in September 1759. His commanding officer was his old friend, James Wolfe, now a successful general. Howe led a small force of twenty-four men who helped clear a path for the British army to move across the Heights of Abraham, the plain overlooking Quebec. This daring act put the British in a position to take the city from the French. In 1760 the British army swept into Montreal, completing the defeat of the French in Canada. During this action, Howe commanded a brigade (a fighting unit of both foot and horse soldiers).

Howe returned briefly to England, to help in the war effort there. He commanded a brigade at the siege of Belle Isle, off the coast of Brittany, France, in 1761. By 1762 he was back across the ocean in time to serve with the British army in their conquest of Havana, on the island of Cuba off the Florida coast.

Holds seat in Parliament

At the end of the Seven Years War, Howe's military future looked very promising. Upon returning home, he was first made colonel of a regiment stationed in Ireland. In 1765 he married Frances Conolly, the fourth daughter of William Conolly and his wife, Lady Anne Wentworth. Frances and her family lived in Castletown, in county Kildare, where Howe's regiment was stationed. Howe may have loved Frances Conolly when they married, but he would prove himself incapable of remaining a faithful husband. He loved going to parties, flirting with beautiful women, and dining well. His officers loved him and he proved his bravery on the battlefield many times. Both friends and critics described Howe as a tall, stout man with a dark complexion. He seems to have been good tempered, but when angered would explode.

Although Howe stayed in the military, the lack of fighting gave him a chance to pursue a political career. He was named governor of the Isle of Wight in 1768. A seat in Parliament (Great Britain's lawmaking body) in the House of Commons (similar to the U.S. House of Representatives) became vacant when Howe's brother, George Augustus, also a British officer serving in the French and Indian War, died in a battle in 1758. William Howe was elected to his brother's seat in 1759, and continued to sit in Parliament until 1780. When he stood to address Parliament, his subject was often the harsh measures Britain was using to subdue its rebellious citizens in America. Howe had served in America and liked the people there.

But politics did not absorb all of Howe's time. In 1772 he was promoted to major general, another step on the way to becoming a full general. In 1774 he was put in charge of training army units in a new style of fighting called light infantry drill. Then, in February 1775, Howe received orders that would take him to America and the coming revolution there. Howe had said publicly that he liked Americans, and had no interest in fighting them. However, as a soldier, Howe felt he had to obey the orders sending him to Boston to help General **Thomas Gage** (see entry).

Battle of Bunker Hill

Howe sailed on the *Cerebus,* along with two other generals who would gain fame in the Revolution, General Henry Clinton and General **John Burgoyne** (see entry). Howe and his companions arrived in Boston Harbor on May 25. By mid-June, he had assessed the military situation, and he took command at the urging of Gage, Britain's military governor in Boston. After clashing with the American militia (the Minutemen) at Concord, the British had retreated into Boston. George Washington, in charge of the American (or Continental) army, had camped around the city to keep the British contained.

Howe advised that the British army leave Boston to assault (charge) the American positions on Bunker and Breed's hills, just outside the city. This was the first major battle of the American Revolution. It took three assaults, but the British finally broke through the American lines. The cost was staggering, with the British losing almost half their attack force. The sight of the wounded and dead left a huge impact on Howe, and made him more thoughtful in risking his men's lives.

In October 1776 Howe assumed total control of the British army in the American colonies. From then on his title was "His Excellency, General William Howe, the commander-in-chief of His Britannic Majesty's expeditionary forces in

America." One of Howe's first moves as commander-in-chief was to determine that it was unprofitable to the British to try to hold on to Boston. In March 1776 he evacuated (left) Boston, along with his army and many Loyalists (Tories or Americans loyal to Britain), for Halifax, Nova Scotia. This Canadian city was still a British stronghold. One of the Loyalists to leave Boston in General Howe's evacuation fleet was Elizabeth Loring, the wife of Joshua Loring. Howe fell in love with Mrs. Loring, and their open love affair fueled criticism of both Howe and his lover. She was nicknamed "lovely Lizzie Loring," and poems that made fun of her and the general would appear in American newspapers until Howe left the country. Her husband, Joshua, was left behind in New York City, but Howe consoled him by making him commissary of prisoners (person in charge of the store that sold goods to prisoners).

Takes New York City

From Halifax, Howe took his army of thirty-two thousand soldiers and camped around New York City in June 1776. His goal was to capture this important port city and break the American resistance. Aiding Howe in this goal was his brother, Richard, now an admiral and in charge of the British fleet in America. After a series of battles, including British army victories at White Plains and Long Island, the Howes succeeded in taking New York in November 1776, and occupied the city that winter. That same year, William Howe was knighted for his service to the British crown, becoming General Sir William Howe. He and Richard were also named peace commissioners by the king, and urged to try to find a peaceful solution to the rebellion (the king wanted the American rebels to surrender).

Throughout the winter, both William and Richard Howe tried to negotiate with the rebels, but their peace overtures were not accepted. Instead, the Americans published their Declaration of Independence, which would gain them European allies with whom to continue their fight against Britain. William Howe realized then that his strategy was not working (he was trying to show the Americans the strength of the British army in the hopes that the rebels would back down). In fact, the Americans surprised Howe by winning battles at Trenton and Princeton, New Jersey, in December 1776 and January 1777. Then Washington went into winter quarters at Valley Forge, in

Pennsylvania. Howe again had a chance to smash Washington's smaller and weaker army, but he stayed in New York.

Captures American capital of Philadelphia

Howe now decided that he would need to break Washington's army in order to end the rebellion. He requested thousands of British and Loyalist reinforcements. He would use these soldiers to hold New York while he went south to take the American capital of Philadelphia. The reinforcements never came but Howe was committed to taking Philadelphia. He packed up most of his army and sailed into Chesapeake Bay in August of 1777. He left behind General Henry Clinton and a skeleton force to hold New York City. His move southward also left General **John Burgoyne** (see entry) without support as he tried to invade upstate New York from Canada. (This lack of support would earn Howe much criticism, as Burgoyne eventually lost the Battle of Saratoga and surrendered his army to the Americans.)

On his march into Philadelphia, Howe defeated Washington at Brandywine Creek, where the Continental army tried to stop the British advance. By September, Howe had taken Philadelphia. Many in Philadelphia welcomed the British with open arms, especially the Loyalists, who were glad to have the British in their city. Others in the city remained indifferent to the American struggle for independence. An even smaller group actively worked to oust the British first from Philadelphia and then from America itself. This group of patriots continually spied on Howe and his staff, and even on Mrs. Loring. But Howe had a hard time believing that the friendly American faces around him were really those of his enemies. After a time, even his own officers began to question his judgment about Americans.

In October 1778 Howe defeated an American attempt to retake Philadelphia at the Battle of Germantown. Then Howe once again went into winter quarters, taking the best house in Philadelphia for his headquarters. He spent the winter taking Lizzie Loring to parties, and only occasionally made war on the American-held forts along the Delaware River that blocked the British fleet from supplying Philadelphia. Howe also responded to criticism about how he was running the war by offering to quit. That fall, he submitted his letter of resignation.

Did General Howe Lose the War?

Critics for more than two hundred years have charged that William Howe's lack of aggression cost Britain its richest possession, the American colonies. Howe proved himself an able commander, defeating George Washington's army time and again. However, many wonder why Howe did not pursue the fleeing rebels and destroy their army.

Why did Howe hesitate? Some historians believe that Howe was a good soldier but did not have the necessary skills to be commander-in-chief. They say that Howe could plot a single battle but could not develop a strategy (long-term plan) for winning the war.

Other historians cite Howe's fondness for the American people. It is true that Howe was moved when the people of Massachusetts raised money for a monument in honor of his brother, George, who was killed in the French and Indian War defending the colonists. It is true that Howe was publicly in love with an American woman, Elizabeth Loring. It is true that he argued in Parliament for a peaceful settlement of the quarrel with America.

However, Howe was first and foremost an English aristocrat and a soldier. He was bred, educated, and trained to serve Great Britain and to defend his country and its possessions. It is unlikely that Howe would put these claims aside, however much he may have liked the Americans. A more likely explanation is Howe's apparent inability to trounce the rebels. Armies were hard to raise and expensive to provide for, and few military leaders were willing to take on the risks unless a victory was assured. Howe had to preserve his army, because few replacements were coming out from England. The Loyalists whom Howe had expected to flock to his aid had turned out in disappointingly small numbers. And then Howe had to make his supplies and ammunition last, because his supply line stretched back across the Atlantic Ocean to England.

Geography also played a part. It was impossible for Howe to capture a major city, leave it controlled by his soldiers, and then go on to take another city. America was simply too big and he had too few soldiers. Given these problems, it is unlikely that any British commander could have avoided losing the war in America.

Howe, however, could have broken the American resistance early in the war had he pursued and smashed the Continental army. Why he chose not to do so, on repeated occasions, remains one of the most perplexing questions of American Revolutionary War history.

Resigns and returns to England

In April 1778 Howe learned that his resignation had been accepted, and that he and Richard Howe were to return to England. When word of Howe's departure spread through his staff, many were disappointed to lose such a popular commander. One of his favorite aides, Major John André, organized a huge farewell party called a *mischianza,* which is Italian for medley or mix of entertainment. The officers dressed up as knights and fought a tournament on horseback. The party also included an elaborate dinner, fireworks, and dancing. Many who criticized Howe's love of luxury pointed to this party as an example of how he wasted time and money when he should have been waging war. General Henry Clinton arrived in May 1778 to officially take over the British command from Howe.

When Howe arrived in England in July 1778, he found that many in Parliament and throughout the British upper classes were openly questioning how he and his brother Richard had organized the war effort in America. By early 1778, the Howe brothers demanded that Parliament open a public inquiry into how the war in America was being conducted. The hearing was held, and included evidence both supporting and criticizing the Howes. One critic was Henry Clinton, who wrote bitterly that Howe had failed in his mission to put down the American rebellion. The hearing closed in 1779 without finding the Howe brothers either guilty or innocent. William Howe responded in 1780 by publishing a pamphlet in his own defense called *Narrative of Sir William Howe before a Committee of the House of Commons.* Responding to critics who said that his military strategy in America had not been bold enough, Howe wrote, "As my opinion has always been, that the defeat of the rebel regular army is the surest road to peace, I invariably pursued the most profitable means of forcing its commander to action under circumstances least hazardous to the royal army."

Serves in war against France

While the Howes' reputation may have suffered, the setback was temporary and both men's careers soon were back on track. Some believe that the Howes survived the storm of criticism because the king intervened on his uncles' behalf.

Whatever the reason, beginning in 1782, William Howe was promoted several times and in 1793 he became a full general, in charge of England's northern defense in 1795 when war broke out with France. In 1795, Howe was named governor of Berwick-on-Tweed, an English city.

When his brother Richard died in 1799 without children, William Howe inherited the Irish title and became the fifth viscount Howe. By 1803, Howe's health was so bad that he resigned his military post and took up residence in the port city of Plymouth. He was made governor of the city in 1805. Howe was also named a privy councillor, one of a group of personal advisers to the king. He died in Plymouth on July 12, 1814, after a long illness.

For More Information

Anderson, Troyer Steele. *The Command of the Howe Brothers during the American Revolution.* Temecula, CA: Reprint Services Corp., 1993.

Cornwell, Bernard. *Redcoat.* New York: HarperPaperbacks, 1987.

Cullen, Joseph P. "Brandywine Creek." *American History Illustrated.* Vol. 15, August 1980, pp. 8–18.

Galloway, Joseph. *A Reply to the Observations of Lieut. Gen. Sir William Howe, on a Pamphlet, Entitled Letters to a Nobleman.* New York: Irvington Publishers, 1972.

Gruber, Ira D. *The Howe Brothers and the American Revolution.* New York: W. W. Norton, 1972.

Inguanzo, Anthony P. "Howe, William" in *The American Revolution, 1775–1783: An Encyclopedia,* vol. 1: A–L. Richard L. Blanco, editor. New York: Garland Publishing, 1993, pp. 785–88.

Leckie, Robert. *George Washington's War: The Saga of the American Revolution.* New York: HarperCollins, 1992, pp. 463–66.

MacGregor, Bruce. "A Failure to Communicate: the British and Saratoga." *American History Illustrated.* Vol. 20, October 1985, pp. 12–20.

Purcell, L. Edward. "William Howe" in *Who Was Who in the American Revolution.* New York: Facts on File, 1993, pp. 239–40.

John Jay

Born December 12, 1745
New York, New York
Died May 17, 1829
Bedford, New York

First chief justice of the U.S. Supreme Court, lawyer, diplomat

John Jay was a highly respected lawyer who distinguished himself in several different high state and federal offices, before, during, and after the Revolutionary War (1775–83). He helped negotiate two major treaties with foreign nations that were of tremendous benefit to the newly formed United States. As chief justice, his fairness and courage in making unpopular decisions secured the public's respect for the U.S. Supreme Court.

John Jay was born in 1745 in New York City. He was the eighth child of Peter Jay, a merchant, and Mary Van Cortlandt, whose ancestors were some of the original Dutch settlers of New York. Peter Jay was widely known and respected as a man of wealth and good character.

Little has been written about John Jay's early years. He was raised in the Protestant religion on his father's comfortable farm in Rye, New York. He was educated at home before leaving at age fourteen to attend King's College (now Columbia University) in New York City.

After graduating from college in 1764, Jay prepared for a career in the law. He did it in the usual colonial way, by serv-

> "[American] power, respectability, and happiness will forever depend on our Union.... Let us keep peace among ourselves, for whenever the members quarrel the whole body must suffer."

Portrait: John Jay.
Reproduced courtesy of the National Archives and Records Administration.

ing as a clerk for an already established lawyer and studying in his free time. In 1768 he opened his own law office in New York City.

In 1769 Jay did legal work for the New York–New Jersey Boundary Commission. In those days, the legal boundaries of the colonies were not clearly defined. Each colony had its own laws, and disputes often arose over which laws had to be obeyed and where. Jay found these issues fascinating, and he learned a lot about how to settle legal squabbles. This early training proved invaluable to him when he later had to settle disputes between the United States and foreign nations.

Jay became well known among his peers for his fine legal mind and his hardworking ways. He was a highly moral young man with a strong religious faith. Those close to him knew Jay as cheerful and possessing a good sense of humor.

Marries into wealth; opposes Revolutionary movement

In John Jay's time, much of the land in the colony of New York was owned by about twenty wealthy and powerful families, whose members were descended from the early Dutch or English settlers. The families were connected by marriage. Jay's mother belonged to one such family. With his marriage to Sarah Livingston in 1774, Jay joined another powerful family: Sarah was the daughter of the governor of New Jersey and had other wealthy connections. Jay and Sarah were devoted to one another. Jay's future seemed bright.

Back in 1686, John Jay's Protestant grandfather, Auguste Jay, had been forced to flee his French homeland because of religious persecution and fear of imprisonment by French Catholics. As a result, the Jay family had no love for either the French or Catholics. Unlike the majority of colonists (who had English backgrounds), Jay's family had no particular affection for England either. Still, when talk of American independence from England began in the 1760s, Jay did not at first support the movement.

As a lawyer, Jay was intimately familiar with the legal issues involved in the dispute between England and the colonies. He believed that many policies adopted by the British between 1765 and 1774 were violations of colonists' rights. Among those policies were British efforts to restrict the power of colonial lawmaking bodies and courts.

Jay saw the struggle between England and America as a fight by the colonists for their rights as Englishmen. He was appalled by colonists who expressed their anger through violence and by persecuting Loyalists (people who remained loyal to England). New York had a great many Loyalists.

Attends First and Second Continental Congresses

In 1774 Great Britain adopted a series of measures called the Intolerable Acts. They were intended to punish the citizens of Boston, Massachusetts, for their violent protests against British taxation. Spurred by sympathy for Boston's sufferings, delegates from twelve of the thirteen colonies met on September 5, 1774, for the First Continental Congress. Jay gave up his law practice and went to Philadelphia, Pennsylvania, as New York's representative in Congress.

At first Jay, like the majority of delegates to the Congress, was not in favor of declaring independence. He feared it would lead to mob rule and chaos. Jay helped prepare several documents sent by Congress to England's King **George III** (see entry). The documents outlined colonial grievances, urged peace, and threatened to end trade with England. Jay's major contribution was an address "to the oppressed inhabitants of Canada" asking Canadians to join the colonists in opposing British policies (they did not). He became known as a skillful writer and a man who favored reasoning and compromise over hasty action.

When King George did not respond to Congress's peace overtures, Jay decided to support the patriots. He worked hard for the adoption of the Declaration of Independence, which was approved by the Second Continental Congress on July 3, 1776.

With the signing of the Declaration, the former colonies were now states. In 1777 Jay was back in New York to help his state write a new constitution. New York's Loyalists were shocked by Jay's support of the Revolution. But this did not stand in the way of his being named chief justice of the New York supreme court. In his short time there, he unhappily presided over many war-crimes trials (including murder, assault, and theft). Jay was

Sally Jay, Toast of Two Continents

Sarah "Sally" Jay, beloved wife of John Jay and mother of his seven children, was beautiful, charming, and lively. She brought to their marriage not only money and family connections but also a pleasing personality. Her husband, whose own personality in public was one of cold formality, was open and loving with his wife; still, she always called him Mr. Jay. In the early days of their marriage, the Jays were often separated as John Jay went about the business of making America an independent nation. While apart, they wrote to each other three times a week. One of John Jay's letters to his wife concluded with these words: "depend upon it, nothing but actual imprisonment will be able to keep me from you."

When John Jay began the diplomatic phase of his career, Sally Jay often traveled with him. By then she was known and liked by many prominent Revolutionary figures. When she accompanied Jay on his failed trip to Spain (1779–82), General George Washington sent her a lock of his hair as a going-away gift. In Madrid, Spain, the Jays suffered the tragedy of the death of their first daughter at the age of four weeks. Their young son had remained at home.

When Jay went to France in 1782 to help negotiate a peace treaty, Sally followed soon after, bringing their newborn daughter, Maria. In 1783, she gave birth to Ann in Paris. Sally was the only wife of an American peace

glad to return to Philadelphia in 1778 to become president of the Continental Congress. He assisted in many of the complicated tasks of running the Revolutionary War.

Sent on mission to Spain

By 1779 it was clear that America needed foreign aid in its struggle with Great Britain. America had very few men who had experience in negotiating with foreign governments. Despite his youth and inexperience, thirty-four-year-old John Jay was appointed America's minister to Spain. He resigned his positions as New York's chief justice and president of the Continental Congress, and in late October 1779, he set sail for Spain to begin his new career in diplomacy.

The voyage to Spain was a rough one, and Jay was terribly seasick. His ship stopped at an island in the Caribbean,

commissioner to be present at the peace talks in Paris. She loved Paris, and Parisians loved her. She was soon involved in the active social life at the court of King **Louis XVI** (see entry). Sally is said to have strongly resembled the king's wife, Marie-Antoinette, and her public appearances caused quite a commotion.

When the Jays returned to the United States in 1783, they built a three-story stone house on Broadway in New York City. Sally was a popular hostess, and invitations to her dinner parties were sought after. The Jays had a second home on over nine hundred acres of farming land in Bedford, New York, then a two-day ride from New York City. Jay retired there in 1801; the next year Sally died. Jay then

occupied himself with "conversation, books, and recollections" until his death. Jay's two sons, Peter Augustus and William, had distinguished careers and carried on the family name. Five generations of the Jay family lived in the home, which is preserved today as the John Jay Homestead.

Historian Richard Morris wrote that Sally Jay brought a "light touch" to her marriage that balanced "Jay's deadly earnestness and strong sense of responsibility." Morris noted that John Jay was a loving parent to his own children and also took care of four siblings who were either mentally or physically handicapped as well as many other members of his large family.

where Jay saw slaves being cruelly treated. He decided that if he ever had the chance, he would do what he could to end slavery in America.

Jay had little luck with the Spanish. Spain did enter the war against Great Britain as an ally of France, but Spain refused to recognize American independence and would not ally itself with the United States. Nor would Spain accept Jay as a representative of an independent nation. Jay was insulted both for himself and his country. He was upset with France, too, for not helping him out in his dealings with the Spanish.

Negotiates Treaty of Paris ending American Revolution

When the war ended in 1781, Jay was still in Spain. **Benjamin Franklin** (see entry) was in France, and he asked Jay to join him in negotiating the Treaty of Paris that would officially end the Revolutionary War. Jay went, but he was still angry with both Spain and France. He was further upset when France tried to push its own agenda in the peace negotiations. He believed that France was trying to win favors for itself from Great Britain, favors that would hurt America. When the complicated negotiating was all over, Jay, Franklin, and **John Adams** (see entry) had gotten very favorable terms for America. American independence was recognized, and America's western borders were extended to the Mississippi River. According to historian Richard B. Morris, "Jay's diplomatic achievements at Paris in 1782 still stand unrivalled in the annals of American diplomacy." Morris called the Treaty of Paris one of "the two most advantageous treaties ever negotiated for the United States."

John Jay returned home to a hero's welcome. While abroad, he had learned enough about the Old World that he wanted to keep America out of its clutches. Upon his arrival, though, he was informed that the Articles of Confederation (the forerunner of the Constitution) had just been adopted, and he was the new U.S. secretary for foreign affairs.

Almost at once Jay realized that he could not carry out his duties under the Articles of Confederation. The articles called for a loose union of all the states. There was no central government with powers to make and enforce treaties with foreign governments. Before Jay could do anything to settle disputes with Great Britain and Spain, he had to get directions from Congress, and the way the government was organized, congressmen could never agree on any directions.

Works to get Constitution ratified; suffers illness, injury

The Constitutional Convention of 1787 drafted a Constitution that proposed the strong central government that Jay favored. He could not attend the convention, but when the document was sent around to the states for ratification (approval), Jay worked hard for its passage in New York. To convince New Yorkers to ratify the Constitution, Jay worked with **James Madison** and **Alexander Hamilton** (see entries) to produce eighty-five newspaper articles that described why the Articles of Confederation were inadequate and explained the proposed Constitution in depth. The papers were later published in book form as *The Federalist*. *The Federalist* is still the best explanation of the U.S. Constitution.

The word "federalist" referred to the belief in a strong central government. The Constitution was opposed by "anti-federalists," men such as **Patrick Henry**, **George Mason**, and **Samuel Adams** (see entries). They had many objections to a strong central government. According to Richard Morris, Jay was "committed to the ideals of a republic in which the people, directed by a virtuous [moral] and educated elite, would govern, and to a national government with power to act."

While the debate over the Constitution was going on, Jay suffered a crippling bout of arthritis (painful joints). Before he had completely recovered, he was struck on the head when members of a mob that had gathered outside the New York City jail began throwing stones. The mob was protesting the then-new concept of doctors performing autopsies (examinations of dead bodies to determine the cause of death). The doctors fled for safety reasons into the jailhouse; Jay was on his way to help rescue them. For a time it was feared that he had suffered permanent brain damage, but he finally recovered.

The Constitution went into effect in 1789. **George Washington** (see entry) was elected the nation's first president and assumed office in New York, then the nation's capital. Washington appointed Jay the first chief justice of the U.S. Supreme Court. When arguments arise, the Supreme Court has the last word on the meaning of all U.S. laws and the Constitution.

Jay used his time on the Supreme Court to stress the importance of the states giving way to the authority of the federal government. He also emphasized the importance of treaties of war, peace, and trade. Jay was still serving as chief justice in 1794 when President Washington asked him to go to England and negotiate a treaty.

At first opposed to independence from England, John Jay was a highly respected lawyer who distinguished himself in several different high state and federal offices, before, during, and after the Revolutionary War (1775–83).

Reproduced by permission of AP/Wide World Photos.

Jay's Treaty

For more than ten years, tensions had been building between the British and America over the terms of the 1783 Treaty of Paris (ending the Revolutionary War). The British complained that America had not honored its end of the bargain—it had not paid pre-war debts to British merchants and had not paid Loyalists for property taken from them during the war. Therefore, the British were refusing to withdraw their soldiers from forts on the American frontier. Then the British Navy seized American ships at sea, and the two countries nearly went to war. Jay was sent to try and restore good relations between the two countries.

In the treaty that bears his name, Jay got the British to agree to withdraw their troops, some trade agreements were made, and more or less friendly relations were restored. But Jay's Treaty was seen at home as favoring the British, and it was not popular. Dummies representing Jay were hanged and burned in his home town and he was widely criticized. Still, he managed to keep the young country out of war until the time came when America was better able to defend itself.

On his return from England in 1795, Jay retired from the position of Supreme Court justice. He then assumed the governorship of New York—in spite of Jay's Treaty, Jay was so popular in New York that he was elected without having to run for office. He served two three-year terms. To his great satisfaction, he helped pass a law that would gradually do away with slavery in New York.

After Jay left the governorship, then-President **John Adams** asked him to return to the Supreme Court, but Jay refused, indicating that he was too tired and in poor health. Jay retired to his estate in Bedford, New York, where he lived quietly until his death in 1829.

In an encyclopedia article about Jay, Mark Boatner quoted historian Samuel Flagg Bemis: "Jay was a very able man but not a genius." In personal character "he was second to none of the [founding] Fathers."

For More Information

Boatner, Mark M. "Jay, John" and "Jay's Treaty" in *Encyclopedia of the American Revolution*. Mechanicsburg, PA: Stackpole Books, 1994, pp. 551–53.

Combs, Jerald A. "Jay, John" in *American National Biography*. John A. Garraty and Mark C. Carnes, eds. New York: Oxford University Press, 1999, vol. 11, pp. 891–94.

Cooper, James Fenimore. *The Spy*. London: J. T. Devison, 1821.

Morris, Richard B. *John Jay, the Nation and the Court*. Boston: Boston University Press, 1967, pp. x, 28–9, 37.

Morris, Richard B. *The Peacemakers*. New York: Harper & Row, 1965, pp. 2–4, 206, 282.

Morris, Richard B. *Witnesses at the Creation: Hamilton, Madison, Jay, and the Constitution*. New York: Holt, Rinehart, and Winston, 1985.

Web Sites

"The Indispensable Mr. Jay." [Online] Available http://www.thehistorynet.com/ (accessed on September 29, 1999).

Thomas Jefferson

Born April 13, 1743
Shadwell, Virginia
Died July 4, 1826
Charlottesville, Virginia

President and vice president of the United States, lawyer, philosopher, writer

"My God! How little do my countrymen know what precious blessings they are in possession of, and which no other people on earth enjoy. I confess I had no idea of it myself."

—Jefferson's comment after observing poverty and inequality while touring in Europe

Portrait: Thomas Jefferson.
Reproduced courtesy of the Library of Congress.

Thomas Jefferson was a brilliant man with broad-ranging interests who greatly influenced the political and intellectual life of America. His gift for language made him the most eloquent leader of the American Revolution. His vision for America helped make him one of its most respected presidents.

Thomas Jefferson was born on April 13, 1743, to Peter Jefferson, a pioneer farmer and surveyor, and his wife, Jane Randolph Jefferson. The family was not wealthy, but Jefferson's mother was from a well-respected Virginia family. As a teenager, Jefferson boarded with the local schoolmaster to learn Latin and Greek. In 1760, at age seventeen, he attended the College of William and Mary in Williamsburg, Virginia. Jefferson was an excellent student who sometimes studied fifteen hours a day.

After graduation in 1762 he studied law in Williamsburg for five years, then began practicing law on his own. He mostly defended small-scale planters in land claims cases. He was well prepared and knowledgeable about the law, but he was not a great speaker.

In 1768 Jefferson began building his beautiful mountaintop home, Monticello, on land he had inherited from his father. He taught himself architecture by reading books. Monticello was a labor of love and he worked on it for the rest of his life.

Becomes active in politics

Jefferson's political career began in 1769 with his election to the Virginia House of Burgesses, the lower house of the legislature (where laws were made). "As a young man Jefferson has been described as tall, loose-jointed, [and] sandy-haired," Mark M. Boatner III wrote. "He was a skillful horseman, an expert violinist, a good singer and dancer and [a lively companion.]" As he got older, the more serious side of Jefferson emerged.

Beliefs about people and government

Jefferson believed that everyone could and should be educated so they could participate intelligently in their government. He believed that the position a person attains in society should depend on his abilities. He believed that everyone had certain rights that could not be denied to them by kings. He opposed the idea that a nation should be governed by people such as kings who inherited their positions or gained them because of wealth.

Jefferson expressed some of those views in his 1774 pamphlet titled *Summary View of the Rights of British America.* At the time the pamphlet was written, some Americans were challenging England's right to tax the colonists (to raise money to pay off British war debts) without their consent. Putting those views in writing went a step further. Jefferson declared that Great Britain had no right at all to exercise authority over the colonists. He said that England's King **George III** (see entry) was merely the "chief officer of the people," not someone chosen specially by God to rule. He also accused King George and his advisers of being responsible for crimes against the colonists. *Summary View* helped establish Jefferson as one of the early leaders of the American Revolution.

Writes Declaration of Independence

In May 1775 Jefferson was elected to the Second Continental Congress in Philadelphia. During this convention the delegates debated whether the colonies should officially go to war against Great Britain (fighting had begun a month earlier, with the battle of Lexington and Concord). Like the citizens of the colonies, the congress was deeply divided on the matter of war, but as hostilities escalated over the next year, war was inevitable.

In June 1776 Jefferson was chosen by Congress to serve on a committee to write the Declaration of Independence, the document that established the United States as a nation. **John Adams** and **Benjamin Franklin** (see entry) made only small changes to Jefferson's draft before the document was sent on for the approval of Congress. For two and one-half days, the delegates in Congress examined and argued it line by line. In the end, the Declaration passed with many changes, but it still largely reflected the style and ideas of Jefferson, including the equality of all human beings, that certain rights belong to all people and cannot be taken away, and that people have the right to govern themselves.

Works for reform of Virginia laws

The Second Continental Congress adjourned in the fall of 1776. Jefferson returned home to Virginia and to his seat in the state legislature. There he was able to get lawmakers to consider passing some far-reaching reforms to Virginia's existing laws. The first, the one he considered most important, did not go into effect until 1786. It was the Virginia Statute for Religious Freedom, which provided for the separation of church and state. Jefferson believed that government must allow its citizens freedom to practice the religion they choose, and must be prevented from favoring any particular religion or establishing a state religion.

Jefferson also got a reform passed making it possible for a child other than a first-born son to inherit his father's estate. But many of Jefferson's reform efforts failed. At that time, Virginia had a list of more than one hundred offenses that could bring the death sentence; most of the listed offenses were minor. Jefferson urged that some criminal offenders be reformed rather than executed. But he was unsuccessful in his attempts to change Virginia's harsh policy for the treatment of criminals.

Slavery was another subject on which Jefferson had strong—though conflicting—views. He spoke of his opposition to slavery, though he himself owned slaves. Still, Jefferson tried to get a plan passed for gradually freeing the slaves.

He was especially disappointed with the failure of his Bill for the More General Diffusion of Knowledge. The bill would have set up a complete system of public education, featuring free elementary schools for all citizens.

Elected governor of Virginia

In 1778 the Revolutionary War shifted to the South. In June 1779 Jefferson succeeded **Patrick Henry** (see entry) as governor of Virginia. The times called for a governor who could make instant decisions, but as Patrick Henry had already discovered, the Virginia governorship was largely a ceremonial position. Furthermore, Jefferson's kind temperament and deliberate way of looking at matters did not well suit him to govern in a time of great immediate danger.

In May 1781 the British invasion of Virginia's capital city, Richmond, forced government officials to flee to Charlottesville, near Jefferson's home. Believing that his term as governor had expired, Jefferson stepped down from the position, despite the fact that a new governor had not been chosen. He sent his family from Monticello to an estate on Virginia's Carter's Mountain, where he soon joined them. The war ended on October 18, 1781, with the surrender of the British at Yorktown, Virginia. Jefferson's political opponents now called him a traitor. They called his move to Carter's Mountain a flight from the British, and they criticized what they called his lack of leadership during the war years. Nothing ever came of their charges, and in the end Virginia legislators expressed their gratitude to Jefferson for his services.

Wife dies; Jefferson joins Congress

The mere suggestion of misconduct wounded Jefferson deeply, and he vowed never again to serve in public office. But then he was beset by a series of personal misfortunes, climaxing with the death of his wife, Martha, in September 1782. Jefferson had married Martha Wales Skelton, an attractive and wealthy young widow, ten years earlier. To his sorrow, three of the couple's six children had died before Martha, and only two survived to adulthood.

With his dream of family life on the plantation no longer a possibility, Jefferson returned to public life. In November 1782 he accepted an appointment by Congress to serve at the peace commission in Paris, France, to work on a treaty to end the Revolutionary War. But the treaty was signed before Jefferson sailed for France.

Congressional activities

In the next stage of his career, Jefferson became a member of the U.S. Congress from Virginia and served on nearly all of the important congressional committees. During the winter of 1783–84, Jefferson helped form American policy in a variety of areas. His proposal for a decimal system (based on the number ten) of American coins was adopted. He drafted a policy for governing America's western region, an area that always fascinated him. His policy suggested a workable method of creating states out of the wilderness.

Serves as Minister to France

Jefferson also had an influence on American foreign policy. By the mid-1780s the U.S. economy was in trouble, in part because of huge war debts. The nation hoped to set up trade relationships with foreign countries, but France was one of the few countries that seemed interested.

In 1784 Jefferson, John Adams, and Benjamin Franklin were appointed to a commission to negotiate commercial (trade) treaties with France and the major European powers. He sailed to Paris, and in 1785 he succeeded Franklin as minister to France. He focused his efforts on improving trade with that country.

Jefferson enjoyed his five years in France, made the most of its cultural offerings, and visited much of Europe. Some of the things he accomplished there had lasting effects on developments in America. For example, the designs he worked out with a French architect for the Capitol of Virginia helped to bring about a revival in America of the architectural styles of ancient Greece and Rome.

Faces challenges as Secretary of State

After his return to America in 1789, the forty-seven-year-old Jefferson became secretary of state under President **George Washington** (see entry). He was mainly responsible for the conduct of the nation's foreign affairs. During the three frustrating years he served in the post, Jefferson's negotiations resulted in few benefits to America. This was partly because he faced opposition from political rivals. Jefferson wanted America to build on its commercial alliance with France and also to have much freer commerce with other European nations. But Secretary of the Treasury **Alexander Hamilton** (see entry) was against the development of free trade with France. He wanted to keep closer economic ties with England, France's longtime enemy.

Jefferson feared that Hamilton's policies would make just a few Americans rich and would also concentrate too much power in the office of the secretary of the treasury. So Jefferson allied himself with those who opposed Hamilton.

Becomes U.S. vice-president

War broke out between France and England in 1793 and threatened American peace. As secretary of state, Jefferson tried to keep America out of the war while maintaining ties with both France and Great Britain. In the case of France, he was unsuccessful, and his plans for a good trade relationship with France came to nothing. He resigned his office at the end of 1793.

After his resignation Jefferson was determined to quit public life once and for all. But in 1796 members of his Republican Party convinced him to run for president against John Adams. Jefferson barely lost the election, but because of the way the election system worked at the time, he became vice-president under Adams.

By 1798 relations between France and the United States were so bad that the two countries nearly went to war. Although war was avoided, Jefferson did not approve of the way President Adams handled the situation and the relationship between the two men—and their Republican and Federalist political parties—was badly strained.

Reacts to Alien and Sedition Acts

One way Adams handled the situation with France was to convince Congress to pass the Alien and Sedition Acts. (Aliens are foreigners; sedition is behavior or language intended to incite others to rebel against the authority of the government.) The Alien Acts were really intended to weaken the Republican Party, which was made up of many recent immigrants who were criticizing Adams's policies. The Alien Acts made it harder to become an American citizen and threatened to force people from "enemy" nations to go back home. The Sedition Acts tried to restrict the public activities of Americans critical of Adams's policies. Jefferson saw the acts as an attempt by Adams to make the federal government far more powerful than the individual states.

In response to the Alien and Sedition Acts, Jefferson secretly wrote the Kentucky Resolutions. They declared the Alien and Sedition Acts illegal and claimed that individual states did not have to abide by such laws. Although Jefferson's planned legislation did not pass, it contributed to the public's demand that Adams stop trying to expand the federal government's power. Jefferson continued to believe that the states should be governed with as little interference from the federal government as possible. Like Adams and Jefferson did, politicians today still argue about the proper role of the federal government.

Serves as U.S. president

In 1800 Jefferson ran for president as a Republican and won. On March 4, 1801, he was inaugurated in the nation's new capital, Washington, D.C. The speech he made that day urged friendship between Republicans and Federalists, the nation's two political parties. "We have called by different names brethren of the same principle," he said. "We are all republicans: we are all federalists."

Jefferson's speech also called for "a wise and [economically sound] government, which shall restrain men from injuring one another, which shall leave them otherwise free to regulate their own pursuits of industry and improvement, and shall not take from the mouth of labor the bread it has earned" by overtaxing. When members of his own Republican Party pressured him to favor them over the Federalists, he tried to remain fair to both parties.

Historians disagree about whether or not Jefferson was a strong and effective president during his two terms of office (1801–09). Some say he did not exercise authority when a strong hand was needed. But others point out that Jefferson enjoyed many successes. He got reforms passed regarding freedom of the press, made it easier for immigrants to become American citizens, and greatly improved the country's financial status. During his two administrations, the national debt was reduced by about 40 percent.

Foreign affairs

Foreign affairs was the area of Jefferson's greatest triumph and greatest defeat. With the 1803 Louisiana Purchase from France, Jefferson gained for the United States an area of 800,000 square miles. For this expansion he paid the remarkably small sum of less than $15 million. He approved the Meriwether Lewis and William Clark expedition (1803–06), which helped to acquaint Americans with their new western lands.

Jefferson was easily reelected in 1804, but he soon found himself involved in yet another quarrel between France and England. It was Jefferson's idea to try and resolve the quarrel by way of an embargo. The embargo prohibited foreign commercial ships from entering or departing American ports. The embargo was unpopular at home and had little effect on the behavior of France and Great Britain. Congress finally brought an end to the embargo in 1809 during the last days of Jefferson's presidency.

Life in retirement

After his retirement from politics, Jefferson seldom ventured farther than a few miles from Monticello. He enjoyed a long and active retirement. He corresponded with many people, maintained an interest in the latest happenings in a variety of fields, and welcomed visitors to his home from all over America and Europe. Although he still had political enemies, he was enormously popular among the American people.

Jefferson's efforts to revive plans for public education in his home state resulted in the founding of the University of Virginia in 1819. Jefferson was involved in all aspects of the project, from planning the grounds and buildings to choosing the teachers and classes.

During his later years Jefferson's health began to fail and he suffered a number of financial losses. At the time of his marriage, Jefferson had inherited both property and debts from his wife's family. His involvement in national affairs meant that sometimes he failed to pay close enough attention to his own personal finances on the plantation. Money difficulties became part of his life. In 1815 he had to sell his ten-thousand-volume library to the federal government to help relieve his financial difficulties. His books served as the core of the collection of the Library of Congress, the large public library he had helped establish in Washington, D.C., in 1800. The library was inspired by Jefferson's belief that in order to do its job, a democratic legislature needed information of all kinds.

Death of America's hero

Thomas Jefferson died at his home on July 4, 1826, the fiftieth anniversary of American independence. His colleague, John Adams, passed away on the same day. Jefferson was buried next to his wife on a little hill at Monticello.

As he had done in life, Jefferson carefully controlled aspects of his death. He had designed his own tombstone and wrote the words he wished to appear on it: "Here was buried / Thomas Jefferson / author of the Declaration of American Independence / [and] of the Statute of Virginia for religious freedom / And Father of the University of Virginia."

Biographer Willard Sterne Randall pointed out how curious it was that in composing the words for his stone, Jefferson "did not think it important enough to mention that he had been twice elected and served as the president of the United States."

For More Information

Allison, Robert J. "Thomas Jefferson" in *American Eras: The Revolutionary Era, 1754–1783*. Detroit: Gale, 1998, pp. 222-23.

Boatner, Mark M., III. "Jefferson, Thomas" in *Encyclopedia of the American Revolution*. Mechanicsburg, PA: Stackpole Books, 1994, pp. 553-58.

Bourgoin, Suzanne M., and Paula K. Byers. "Jefferson, Thomas" in *Encyclopedia of World Biography,* Vol. 8. Detroit: Gale, 1998, pp. 238-41.

Ellis, Joseph J. *American Sphinx: The Character of Thomas Jefferson.* New York: Vintage Books, 1998.

Malone, Dumas. *Jefferson, the Virginian,* Vol. 1. Boston, MA: Little, Brown, 1948, p. 204.

Peterson, Merrill D. "Jefferson, Thomas" in *American National Biography,* Vol. 11. Edited by John A. Garraty and Mark C. Carnes. New York: Oxford University Press, 1999, pp. 909-18.

Randall, Willard Sterne. *Thomas Jefferson: A Life.* New York: Henry Holt and Co., 1993.

Index

Boldface type indicates entries and their page numbers.

Illustrations are marked by (ill.).

Intolerable Acts *1:* 12, 75, 202,
203, 221, 239; *2:* 368, 504

J

J. C. B. *2:* 334
Jacobins *2:* 270
Jacobites *2:* 295, 298
Jamaica *1:* 153
Jamaica Plains, Massachusetts
2: 395
James II, King *1:* 142 (ill.); *2:* 295
Jay, John *1:* 15, 191, 237 (ill.),
237–45, 243 (ill.); *2:* 304, 351
Jay, Sally *1:* 240
Jay, Sarah *1:* 238
Jay's Treaty *1:* 244
Jefferson, Jane Randolph *1:* 246
Jefferson, Martha Wales Skelton
1: 250
Jefferson, Peter *1:* 246
Jefferson, Thomas *1:* 14, 16, 18,
29, 101, 112, 121, 160, 192,
194, 220, 224–226, 246 (ill.),
248 (ill.), **246–55**; *2:* 262,
268, 271, 278, 306, 307, 316,
319, 358, 405, 428, 431, 432
Johnson, Chrisfield *2:* 334
Johnson, Samuel *1:* 83
Johnson, William *1:* 64, 65, 68
Jones, David *2:* 329
Journal of Events *1:* 24
*Journal of the Reign of George III
from 1771 to 1783* *2:* 465
Jusserand, J. J. *2:* 280

K

Kemble, Margaret *1:* 140
Kentucky Resolutions *1:* 253
Kettle Creek, Georgia *1:* 211
Kilbride, Scotland *2:* 297
Kilmuir, Scotland *2:* 301
King, Hannah Waterman *1:* 38
King's Chapel *2:* 397
Kingsburgh, Scotland *2:* 301
Kite, Elizabeth S. *2:* 281
Knowlton, Thomas *1:* 181
Knowlton's Rangers *1:* 181
Knox, Henry *2:* 487
Kosciuszko, Thaddeus *2:* 257
(ill.), **257–63**

L

Lafayette, Adrienne de *2:* 271
Lafayette, Anastasie de *2:* 271
Lafayette, George Washington de
2: 271
Lafayette, Henriette de *2:* 271
Lafayette, Marquis de *2:* 264
(ill.), **264–74**, 267 (ill.),
374, 445
Lafayette, Virginie de *2:* 271
Lagrange, France *2:* 271
Lambert, Mary *2:* 354
Lamington, New Jersey *2:* 328
Lane, Anna Maria *1:* 93
Lane, John *1:* 93
LaNotre, André *2:* 275
Laurens, Henry *2:* 381
Lauterbach Castle *2:* 406, 407
Lavien, John *1:* 187
Lavien, Rachel Fawcitt *1:* 187
Lee, Charles Henry *2:* 259
Lee, Henry *1:* 193
Lee, Richard Henry *1:* 220, 223,
224, 226; *2:* 429
L'Enfant, Pierre Charles *2:* 275
(ill.), **275–83**, 278 (ill.)
Letter to George Washington *2:* 358
*Letters and Memoirs Relating
to the War of American
Independence* *2:* 407
Letters, and Sketches of Sermons
2: 343
*Letters from a Farmer in
Pennsylvania* *1:* 107
*Letters from an American
Farmer* *1:* 99
Lewis, Meriwether *2:* 431
Lewis and Clark expedition
1: 254; *2:* 431
Lexington, Massachusetts *1:* 28,
204; *2:* 394, 395, 444
Liberty affair *1:* 3, 5–8, 200
Liberty Bowl *2:* 393
Liberty Tree *1:* 200
Library of Congress *1:* 254
Lincoln, Benjamin *2:* 405, 449
Litchfield, Connecticut *1:* 31
Little Egg Harbor, New Jersey
2: 375
Livingston, Robert *1:* 14
Livingston, William *1:* 110
Logan, James *1:* 169

Monticello *1:* 246, 247, 255
Montpelier estate *2:* 311
Montreal, Quebec, Canada
    1: 34, 40
Moore's Creek Bridge, North
    Carolina *2:* 299, 300
Morris, Robert *1:* 110; *2:* 279, 418,
    420 (ill.)
Morris, William *1:* 196
Morristown, New Jersey *1:* 110
Morse, Jedidiah *2:* 341
Moses Kill, New York *2:* 333
Mount Olivet Cemetery *2:* 280
Mount Vernon, Virginia *2:* 479,
    481 (ill.), 488
Mum Bett , see **Freeman,
    Elizabeth**
Mumbet, see **Freeman,
    Elizabeth**
Munich, Germany *1:* 103
Murray, John *2:* 339, 343
Murray, Judith Sargent *2:* 338
    (ill.), **338–44**

N

Nagle, Patrick *1:* 81
*Narrative of Colonel Ethan Allen's
    Captivity 1:* 35
Natchez, Mississippi *2:* 338
National Assembly *2:* 287, 291
National Republican Party *1:* 17
Native Americans *1:* 54–61,
    63–69, 118, 151-52, 164–171;
    2: 330, 331, 334, 335
Nevis, British West Indies *1:* 187
New Hampshire Grants *1:* 32
New Haven, Connecticut *1:* 39
New Jersey Medical Society *2:* 346
New Jersey Plan *2:* 305
New Jersey Provincial Congress
    2: 347
New London, Connecticut *1:* 43
New Orleans, Louisiana
    1: 150, 151
New Providence, Nassau,
    Bahamas *1:* 153
New Rochelle, New York *2:* 357
New Spain *1:* 148
New York City Common Council
    1: 196
New-York Gazetteer 2: 408,
    410, 411

New York, New York *1:* 34, 99,
    102, 180, 187, 188, 190, 195,
    232; *2:* 277, 347, 350, 359,
    394, 405, 413, 415, 486
Newark, New Jersey *2:* 340, 345
Newport, Rhode Island *1:* 206;
    2: 396
Newspapers *2:* 410–415
Newspapers in Colonial America
    1: 174; *2:* 408, 410, 411–415
Noailles, Adrienne de *2:* 265
North, Sir Frederick *1:* 159, 161
Norwich, Connecticut *1:* 38

O

"Objections to the Proposed Fed-
    eral Constitution" *2:* 318
Odell, Jonathan *2:* **345–52**
Odell, Mary *2:* 347
Odell, William Franklin
    2: 347, 352
Ohio Company *2:* 313, 314
Old Granary Burying Ground
    1: 29
Old Mill Prison *2:* 422
Old North Church *2:* 395
Olive Branch Petition 1: 35, 109
Ollive, Elizabeth *2:* 355
On American Taxation 1: 84
On the Equality of the Sexes 2: 340
Onion River Land Company
    1: 32, 35
Otis, James *1:* 188; *2:* 393

P

Pain, Frances Cocke *2:* 353
Pain, Joseph *2:* 353
Paine, Thomas *1:* 87, 88;
    2: 351, 353 (ill.), **353–60,**
    358 (ill.), 428
Palace of Versailles *2:* 266,
    269, 275
Panther *2:* 331
Paris, France *1:* 250; *2:* 265, 270,
    275, 427
Parish, Elijah *2:* 341
Parks Commission of
    Washington, D.C. *2:* 280
Parliament *1:* 74, 76, 106, 118,
    120, 156, 200; *2:* 366